Archaeological Curatorship

Leicester Museum Studies Series
General editor: Susan M. Pearce

Archaeological Curatorship

Susan M. Pearce

Leicester University Press
(a division of Pinter Publishers)
London and New York

© Leicester University Press 1990

First published in Great Britain in 1990 by Leicester University Press
(a division of Pinter Publishers Ltd)

Editorial offices
Fielding Johnson Building, University of Leicester,
University Road, Leicester, LE1 7RH

Trade and other enquiries
25 Floral Street, London, WC2E 9DS

British Library Cataloguing in Publication Data
A CIP cataloguing record for this book is available
from the British Library
ISBN 0-7185-1298-7

Library of Congress Cataloging-in-Publication Data
Pearce, Susan M.
 Archaeological curatorship / by Susan M. Pearce.
  p.   cm.—(Leicester Museum studies series)
 Includes bibliographical references..
 ISBN 0-7185-1298-7
 1. Museums—Administration.   2. Archaeological museums and
collections—Administration.   3. Archaeology—Sources—Exhibitions—
Handbooks, manuals, etc.   4. Museum techniques.   I. Title.
II. Series.
 AM7.P43   1990
 069.5—dc20   89-13441
                                                        CIP

Typeset by Acorn Bookwork, Salisbury, Wiltshire
Printed and bound in Great Britain by Billings and Son Ltd, Worcester

Contents

General preface to series

Museums are an international growth area. The number of museums in the world is now very large, embracing some 13,500 in Europe, of which 2,300 are in the United Kingdom; some 7,000 in North America; 2,800 in Australasia and Asia; and perhaps 2,000 in the rest of the world. The range of museum orientation is correspondingly varied, and covers all aspects of the natural and the human heritage. Paralleling the growth in numbers comes a major development in the opportunities open to museums to play an important part in shaping cultural perceptions within their communities, as people everywhere become more aware of themselves and their surroundings.

Accordingly, museums are now reviewing and rethinking their role as the storehouses of knowledge and as the presenters to people of their relationship to their own environment and past, and to those of others. Traditional concepts of what a museum is, and how it should operate, are confronted by contemporary intellectual, social and political concerns which deal with questions like the validity of value judgments, bias in collecting and display, the de-mystifying of specialized knowledge, the protection of the environment, and the nature of our place in history.

These are all large and important areas, and the debate is an international one. The series *Leicester Museum Studies* is designed to make a significant contribution to the development of new theory and practice across the broad range of the museum operation. Individual volumes in the series will consider in depth particular museum areas, defined either by disciplinary field or by function. Many strands of opinion will be represented, but the series as a whole will present a body of discussion and ideas which should help to redress both the present poverty of theory and the absence of a reference collection of substantial published material, which curators everywhere currently see as a fundamental lack. The community, quite rightly, is now asking more of its museums. More must be given, and to achieve this, new directions and new perspectives must be generated. In this project, *Leicester Museum Studies* is designed to play its part.

SUSAN M. PEARCE
Department of Museum Studies
University of Leicester

List of plates

List of figures

Acknowledgments

A book of this kind is a long time in the making, and owes a great deal to a great many people. I should like to thank those with whom I have worked in Liverpool and Exeter, especially Elaine Tankard, Stephen Locke, and members of Devon Archaeological Society. I am grateful to my students for many fruitful discussions and contributions over the years, and to my colleagues in the Department. I owe much to fellow curators throughout the museum world, and I am particularly grateful to those who completed my questionnaire *Survey of Archaeological Museums in Britain* (see Appendix).

Particular thanks go to those who gave help with specific parts of this book, to Simon Timms, Dr. Gary Lock, Dr. Paul Robinson, Dr Henry Cleere, Dr. Harold Mytum, Dr. David Prince, Bernadette Higgins-McLoughlin, Dr. Myna Trustram, the Society of Professional Archaeologists (USA), Dr. Mike Parker-Pearson, Michael Corfield, Mark Hall, Helen Grundy, Neil Curtis, Kevin Gosling, Linda Greene and David Pearson. I am grateful for assistance with illustrations to Richard Doughty, Dr. Eilean Hooper-Greenhill, Elizabeth Hartley, Roger Peers, the Jorvik Viking Centre, Kevin Leahy, Bob Rutland, John Allen, Dr. Hugh Chapman, British Museum, National Museums and Galleries on Merseyside, Alan Baxter and West Stow Anglo-Saxon Village Trust, Pauline Beswick, Archaeology Media Unit at Southampton City Museums, and the National Museum of Scotland. I also acknowledge that some may find the use of language in this book sexist, but I assure them that this is for reasons of convenience only.

I offer my warmest thanks to Jacky Smith for typing the manuscript, and for the care which she took with it. Finally, as always, my grateful thanks go to my husband.

SUSAN PEARCE
Department of Museum Studies
University of Leicester
March 1989

List of abbreviations

This list includes both organizations, and volumes and journals.

AMC	Area Museums Council
AMSEE	Area Museum Council for South-East England
Antiq	*Antiquity*
Arch Comp News	*Archaeological Computing Newsletter*
Arch 'Obj' in Interp	*Archaeological 'Objectivity' in Interpretation* (papers from world Archaeological Congress, Southampton, 1986)
Arch Rev Cantab	*Archaeological Review from Cambridge*
BAA	British Archaeological Association
CBA	Council for British Archaeology
Cur Arch	*Current Archaeology*
DES	Department of Education and Science
DoE	Department of the Environment
DUA	Department of Urban Archaeology, Museum of London
Dust to Dust	*Dust to Dust: Field Archaeology and Museums*, 1986. Society of Museum Archaeologists Conference Proceedings, Vol. II.
GCSE	General Certificate of Secondary Education
GLC	Greater London Council
HBMC(E)	Historic Buildings and Monuments Commission for England
HBMC(S)	Historic Buildings and Monuments Commission for Scotland
HMSO	Her Majesty's Stationery Office
ICOM	International Council of Museums
ICCROM	International Centre for the Study of the Preservation and Restoration of Cultural Property
IFA	Institute of Field Archaeologists
ILEA	Inner London Education Authority
IRGMA	Information Retrieval Group of the Museums Association
LA	Local Authority
LEAG	London and East Anglian Group for GCSE Examinations
MDA	Museum Documentation Association
MET	Metropolitan (County or District)
MGC	Museums and Galleries Commission
Mus Arch	*The Museum Archaeologist*
Mus Bull	*Museum Bulletin*
Mus J	*Museums Journal*
OAL	Office of Arts and Libraries
RCHM(E)	Royal Commission for Historic Monuments (England)

Res News	Rescue News
SMA	Society of Museum Archaeologists
TAG	Theoretical Archaeology Group
UKIC	United Kingdom Institute for Conservation
UNESCO	United Nations Educational, Scientific and Cultural Organization

Introduction: people, archaeology and museums

The past is closer to us than we sometimes think. If we reckon the usual three generations to a century, we see that the building of the Tower of London is only 27 forefathers behind us; the final occupation of the important late Roman fort at Richborough in Kent is 45 generations behind; and even the erection of the great trilithons at Stonehenge in the Early Bronze Age is not much more than 100 forefathers away. Equally, the people who made and used these places, in spite of enormous differences in their social organization, were, in all the most important respects, human beings like ourselves. It is this potent combination of the strange and the familiar which makes the past so fascinating to us all.

Today the study of the past is, rightly, regarded as one among several cultural spheres supported (almost entirely) by public funds, and therefore one from which the public has legitimate expectations. Recent work (see chapter 9) has revealed what many archaeologists suspected, that there is a huge reservoir of public interest in the past, demonstrated by the number of visits to famous monuments like Stonehenge and the Tower, by museum visits (73 million visits to museums overall in 1985–6, Myerscough *et al.* 1988), and by the steady appeal of television programmes like *Chronicle*. For most people this is a casual interest, focused on aspects like the bizarre and the financially valuable, or, alternatively, on the very personal and local, which do not chime in with the concerns of the professional archaeologists.

More fundamentally, all kinds of people are now questioning the validity of professional judgment and the kind of value assessment which appears to be implicit in it. We are now sharply aware of the ethical, political and legal issues which arise through our presentation of the past, and through our approach to our common inheritance of the past. Thinking of this kind produces questions like: Whose past is it? How should archaeology, its product, be conducted? Who should decide? These are much easier, and much more exciting, to ask than they are to answer, and they arise, one way or another, throughout this book.

Archaeologists, generally, have responded by making genuine, and often successful, efforts to make their work more accessible to people. Archaeological curators have a particular responsibility here, because an important part

1

of our role is to act as a bridge between people in general and the professional archaeological community. Museums, together with interpreted open-air sites with which curators are much involved, are the principal means through which an experience of the past, and, especially, of the genuine objects made in the past, can be mediated to people. It is here that the immediacy of past people and their belongings, referred to earlier, can strike such a chord.

Balancing equally the claims of public interpretation and presentation, comes the responsibility which the curator holds towards the archaeological archive, both artefactual and documentary, in his care. Museums hold the stored material culture of the past (which as a matter of practicality is reckoned to be in the archaeologists' sphere up to about AD 1700, after this it belongs to the social and industrial historians), and the associated documentation which makes it intelligible.

The museums and their collections have come into being piecemeal over the past two centuries (in the main), and the institutions show a correspondingly wide diversity. Archaeology curators operate within a wide range of museum types, which differ considerably in terms of the constituencies to whom they speak, the staff they maintain, the collections they are responsible for (including those of industrial archaeology, enthnography and exotic archaeology, which are outside the scope of this book), and the level of physical resource within which they work. Equally, museums are changing, in their approaches to finance and to management structure, and in the ways in which they see their relationships to their communities. The implications of these changes arise throughout the book, and they are pursued in the final chapter. All this makes discussion in general terms difficult; nevertheless, underlying the obvious differences it is clear that the fundamental concerns of all archaeological curators are very similar. There are probably similarities of temperament and training across the curatorial group. There is certainly a fundamental commitment to the archive of the past, and to what it can tell us.

Accordingly, this book is concerned with the philosophies, intentions and approaches of those museums that address themselves to the conservation, better recording, and interpretation of the stored material archive of the past, including its associated documentation. It is written against the background of broad archaeological developments in Britain, which go back over two centuries and which have resulted in a strong and complex structure that runs across national life, from the Civil Service to local amateur groups. These developments embrace academic archaeology as a major intellectual tradition; philosophical and analytical developments here have transformed this tradition over recent decades and much of the new thinking has centred upon artefact study, with implications which have yet to be fully assimilated by museum archaeology. In parallel with this runs a greatly increased interest in the heritage of the past, and a recognition that it is part of the proper concerns of local communities.

The book is divided into three main parts. The first discusses the historical processes, distant and recent, which have brought contemporary archaeological museums into existence, and places this beside the state of the law and tone of current ethical and political feeling, all of which together make up the context within which archaeological curators operate. The second is concerned with the issues which surround the curation of the archaeological archive, and the formation of the archive (although much important detail about collections care has not been repeated, since it has been thoroughly published elsewhere in literature referred to in this part). The third addresses the interpretative function of the archaeological museum, and looks at the interest of the public, and the nature of exhibitions, at managed open-air sites, and at a range of interpretative projects. The final chapter tries to pull the threads together, and to offer a personal view of future prospects.

This book is conceived not as a manual of archaeological curatorial practice (and still less as a manual of broad museum practice). Rather, it sets out to concentrate on the issues and concerns, in theory and practice, which are now in the forefront of curator's minds, to see how these have developed, and to draw together the variously coloured threads. Such a book is inevitably selective, and much interesting material has had to be omitted. In particular, the author has deliberately chosen to centre most of her discussion upon those archaeological museums which have at least one professional member of staff (but taking a broad view of how this difficult word may be defined). She makes no apology for generally omitting discussion of the problems of very small museums, although a broad review of them is included in Chapter 1, because she believes such museums should be encouraged to transfer their archaeological collections to larger museums nearby, while retaining, of course, an appropriate exhibition facility.

The book is offered to practising and prospective archaeologists and curators, and to those with an involvement in the ways in which museums operate. Beyond these, it should be of interest to those who are concerned with cultural studies of all kinds, especially those which involve the interpretation of the past, and to those who play a role in the management of the historic heritage. In a changing world, all our pasts are set to become more, not less, significant.

Part one. The contemporary context

1. Origins: museums and collections to 1960

The past in the present

The cultural tradition of Europe, especially of Northern Europe, is significantly different to that of other parts of the world and one of the ways in which this manifests itself is a very different, and a much greater, concern for the past than that which is expressed, for example, in the native traditions of India or China. This qualitatively different interest in the past has, with various vicissitudes, been centred upon the effort to produce a credible narrative of 'what really happened' across the fabric of society during its progress through time; and this, in turn, has generated both a wide-ranging series of techniques by which documents, objects and sites may be assessed and compared so that they yield 'accurate' information, and an intellectual tradition which wrestles with the problems of historical reality.

This European interest is relatively new. Although some of its roots go back into the Renaissance, which was, of course, interested in the writings of the Greek and Roman historians, it is broadly true that the uniquely European endeavour to produce substantial, critical narratives of the native past did not begin until the later seventeenth century, and that it is largely a creation of the last two hundred years. The reasons why northern Europeans developed this specialized interest are many and various. Any discussion of its origin is likely to centre around the Protestant ethic, which stresses the importance of the individual and of his personal moral history (the discussion of which in economic terms by Tawney, 1938, is still the best), and indeed around the whole Christian tradition which, unlike many others, sets supernatural events firmly in a specific time and place. Linked with this is the growth of commercial wealth, which supported a large dividend-collecting and professional middle class with leisure and education to devote to intellectual interests socially endorsed as a genteel pursuit, and the Romantic movement, which had begun to stir by the 1740s and which has made every generation since lovesick for the past.

Finally, perhaps, and underlying all this, Europe has a structure of kinship and family which is more competitive and less monolithic than those of most other societies (see Goody 1983), and which therefore encourages interest in men's careers because it encourages the careers themselves. Somewhere in this nexus of kinship, feeling, and commercial success lies the reason why we see around us today the writing of history, both academic and popular,

7

raised to the level of a small industry, the very considerable effort put into the practice of archaeology, the development and range of museums which are concerned with the past, and the creation of heritage sites and of the whole 'heritage' concept.

The history of archaeology in museums has been as little studied as has the history of museums in general, and apart from accounts of the great national collections (e.g. Miller 1973; Bell 1981; Hunter 1983; Ovenell 1986; Simcock 1985) and of the princely sixteenth and seventeenth century cabinets (Impey and MacGregor 1985), and with some honourable exceptions (e.g. Thomas J. 1986; Rumsby 1981; Hebditch 1985; Rutland 1984–5), such information as is available is often scattered through (rather ephemeral) museum catalogues and the like, and the pages of local journals and newspapers. The dearth of information is accompanied by a corresponding lack of interpretative thinking, of what would now be called a critical historiography of museum archaeology (Fahnestock 1984), and yet the history of a field is not a dilettante side-line but part of the ever-developing philosophy of knowledge, and it is probably true, as the effort to write the history of science has shown, that areas of study only come of age when they can start to consider their own past.

During the last twenty years or so, all of the fields of study concerned with human affairs have changed fundamentally, and in archaeology we are accustomed to call this change 'the New Archaeology and its successors', the impact of which will be touched upon in Chapter 2. What is important for the present purpose is the corresponding shift in the way in which we view knowledge, and its accumulation and change (see, especially, Kuhn 1970). Instead of identifying a linear chain of progression which cuts out all that is seen as irrelevant, the contemporary view sees knowledge as essentially *social in character*, performing a particular role which is not more or less 'correct' but which is congruent with its own specific time and place, its historical context. So, the older view saw William Stukely's (1687–1765) ideas about Stonehenge and the Druids as a regrettable deviation, while the new would seek to appreciate their own kind of validity as part of contemporary early Romanticism and the struggle to define a contemporarily acceptable view of religion; our own struggles with history and prehistory may perhaps look equally peculiar two centuries hence.

There are obvious difficulties in this approach, in so far as it seeks to undermine the value of 'objective' or 'scientific' facts, but its virtue is to remind us that all 'objective facts' are themselves culturally relative. Similarly, changes in the way in which information is known and organized tend to be not as a result of impeccable logical inference, but to come from quirky jumps and starts in unexpected places, and they are part and parcel of broader social change. Recent work would identify the units of development as *the research community*, individuals who know each other and who share general research interests, and the *speciality*, a particular research problem which some of the community are working on, and which may eventually develop into a separate discipline of its own. In this instance the community are those (as yet relatively few) archaeologists who are concerned with the history of their subject and its historiographical problems, and the speciality is the particular problem of archaeological collection and museum history; both are beginning to grow and how they will develop remains to be seen.

The number of museums which hold some archaeological material in Britain today is well known to be very large. The best available source of information at this broadest level is that contained in the Museums Association's Data-Base Project (Prince and Higgens-McLoughlin 1987; see Appendix). This data survey discovered that 522 museums considered themselves to have archaeological collections. They were asked to class their collections as of local, regional, national and international importance, and it is important to note that this classification was made by the museums themselves. It is clearly an uneasy area, which is open to various kinds of interpretation, and may have been a naive question to ask, at least as far as archaeology is concerned. The museums were also asked about their archaeological conservation facilities, what proportion of their archaeological material was on show during the last complete year for which a record is available, and the nature of the museums' governing body (among other questions less relevant to this study). They were not asked about the nature, history or extent of their archaeological collections, or any details of archaeological staffing, responsibility, documentation, storage and exhibition facilities, or collecting policies.

Two hundred and fifty-four museums said that their collections were of local importance. As figure 1.1 shows these are largely small local society museums, trusts and heritage centres, together with collections held by bodies like local authority library services which lack museum provision. Of

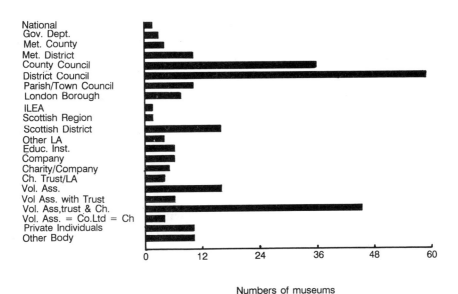

Numbers of museums

Figure 1.1 Governing authorities of museums with 'local' archaeological material (after Museums Database Project)

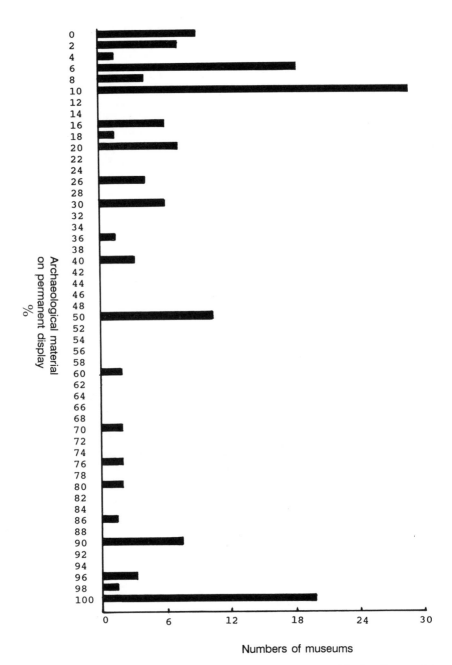

Figure 1.2 Proportion of material on display in museums with 'local' material
(after Museums Database Project)

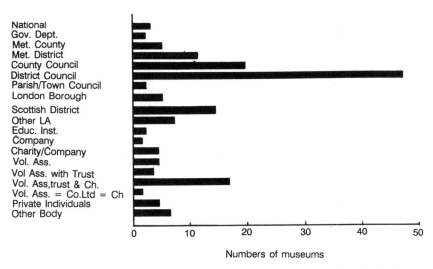

National
Gov. Dept.
Met. County
Met. District
County Council
District Council
Parish/Town Council
London Borough

Scottish District
Other LA
Educ. Inst.
Company
Charity/Company
Vol. Ass.

Vol Ass. with Trust
Vol. Ass,trust & Ch.
Vol. Ass. = Co.Ltd = Ch
Private Individuals
Other Body

0   10   20   30   40   50

Numbers of museums

Figure 1.3   Governing authorities of museums with 'regional' archaeological material (after Museums Database Project)

the 16 museums who replied to the question, 6 said that they had conservation laboratories which covered archaeology, but no further details are available. The 144 museums who gave an estimate of the proportion of archaeology on display show a considerable variation (figure 1.2).

One hundred and fifty-five museums state that their collections are of regional importance. This group represents the heartland of museum archaeology across Britain and includes most of the substantial museum services maintained by local authorities in England and Scotland, together with a surprisingly large group of 16 who are volunteer association based. Most of these are important site museums, like Fishbourne, whose governing body is the Sussex Archaeological Society (figure 1.3). Of the 19 museums who replied, 13 said that they had archaeological conservation facilities, but the silent majority is probably accounted for by a variety of conservation agency arrangements. There is a clear tendency in these museums for material not to be on display, which undoubtedly reflects the large excavation collections which most of them hold (figure 1.4).

Sixty-one museums considered themselves to have nationally important collections, but most of these do not differ from the museums who, more modestly, classed themselves as 'regional', and the exceptions are chiefly the national museums and the university museums who put themselves into this group (figure 1.5). Thirteen museums said that they had conservation facilities, but again many other arrangements will be in operation. The tendency for material to be in store is again clear (figure 1.6).

Fifty-two museums stated that they hold collections of international significance. Some of the entries here are so absurd that one must suppose either genuine confusion or megalomania on the part of the curators who

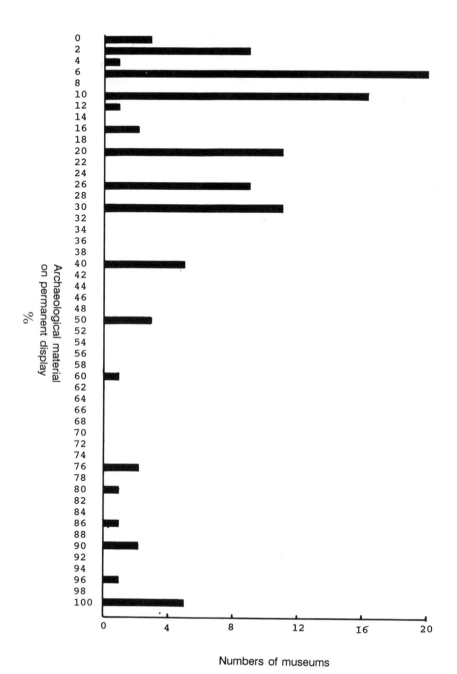

Figure 1.4   Proportion of material on display in museums with 'regional' archaeological material (after Museums Database Project)

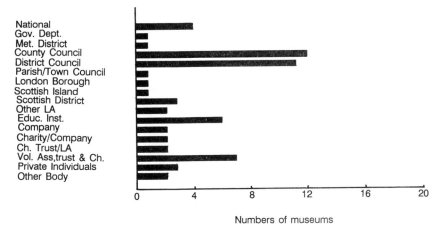

National
Gov. Dept.
Met. District
County Council
District Council
Parish/Town Council
London Borough
Scottish Island
Scottish District
Other LA
Educ. Inst.
Company
Charity/Company
Ch. Trust/LA
Vol. Ass,trust & Ch.
Private Individuals
Other Body

0   4   8   12   16   20

Numbers of museums

Figure 1.5   Governing authorities of museums with 'national' archaeological material (after Museums Database Project)

responded. The listed museums which would generally be accorded an international archaeological significance are the big national and university museums, comparable local authority museums like Glasgow, and small museums which hold genuinely international material relating, for example, to the Early Bronze Age: a total, perhaps, of some 25 museums. Of the 52 museums the majority are national, educational institution and district council based (figure 1.7). Of these 17 admitted to conservation facilities. The returns showed that there is a much greater range in the proportion of material on display than there was in the regional/national categories (figure 1.8).

The Museums Association survey was intended to work with a broad brush, rather than to produce specifics relating to individual museum disciplines. At this level, what it chiefly demonstrates is the considerable number and variety of institutions who hold archaeological collections of some kind, although many of these are small and poor in documentation. This is not new information, but its organized format and the museum lists are valuable. It is evident, also, that most people must have an archaeology display of some kind close enough for them to visit easily, although the differences between the displays will be very considerable. The historical processes which brought about this diversity are themselves very complex, and it is to these that we must now turn.

The development of archaeology in museums to 1960

The earliest public collections of archaeology were those in the possession of the Ashmolean Museum, Oxford, founded 1683, of the British Museum, founded in 1759, of the Museum of the Society of Antiquaries of Scotland,

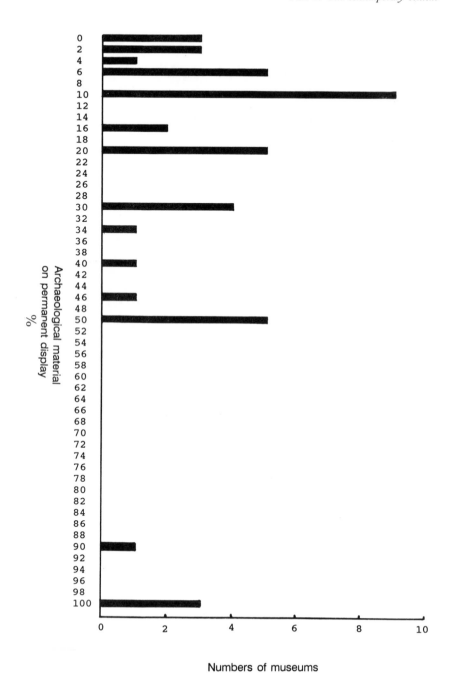

Figure 1.6   Proportion of material on display in museums with 'national' archaeological material (after Museums Database Project)

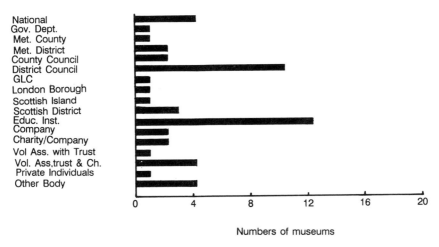

National
Gov. Dept.
Met. County
Met. District
County Council
District Council
GLC
London Borough
Scottish Island
Scottish District
Educ. Inst.
Company
Charity/Company
Vol Ass. with Trust
Vol. Ass.trust & Ch.
Private Individuals
Other Body

Numbers of museums

Figure 1.7   Governing authorities of museums with 'international' archaeological material (after Museums Database Project)

founded 1780 (now part of the Royal Museums of Scotland), and of the Hunterian Museum, Glasgow, founded in 1804. These were all university or national (or national society) museums, reflecting the interests of the small national learned establishments, and the British archaeological material among the collections of the English museums seems to have been limited to a few pieces, included rather incidentally. The trustees of the British Museum, for example, long maintained a disdainful attitude to ancient British material as barbarous and unworthy of a scholar's attention. It was not until 1848 that some Romano–British monuments were put on display, and not until two years later that the (rather reluctant) acquisition of the Iron Age bronzes from Stanwick prompted a display on Smaller British Antiquities (Francis 1971: 261).

In the country at large, the first fully public archaeology museums came as a result of the Museums Act of 1845 (although a number of the museums involved trace their origins beyond this). This Act, as figure 1.9 shows, stimulated a substantial number of local authorities, like Leicester, Stoke-on-Trent, Colchester and Maidstone, to pick out just a few, to found museums which had British archaeological materials among their original collections (for a discussion of the data expressed in this and similar succeeding figures, see Appendix).

The Museums Act authorized local authorities with a population of over 10,000 to spend up to ½d rate on museums to promote 'the instruction and amusement' of the public. It forms a part of that great constellation of Acts between 1828 and 1848 which threw public life open to men of all Christian persuasions (1829), began the process of electoral reform (1832) and of local government reform (1835), and made some progress in the protection of factory workers (1833, 1844), all measures which stand, in their different ways, at the beginning of the modern welfare state. These Acts were

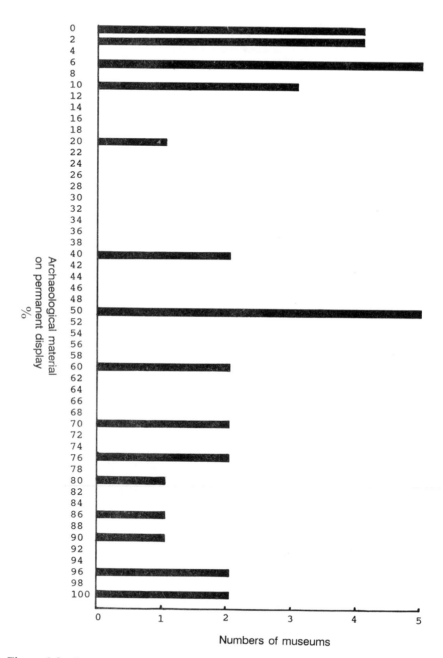

Figure 1.8 Proportion of material on display in museums with 'international' archaeological material (after Museums Database Project)

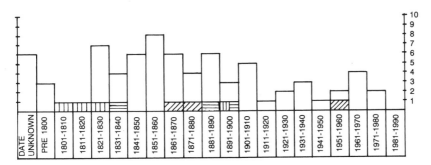

Figure 1.9   Dates at which archaeological collections were started

genuinely enlightened, but they were inspired equally by the dread that the revolutions currently sweeping Europe might spread to England, and they were intended both to reform and to make possible different kinds of control. It is undoubtedly true that museums were seen as playing their part in the transformation of the unruly into the kind of sober, responsible and sufficiently informed citizen which Victorian society needed and approved. As late as the end of the century, Pitt Rivers saw an ideological purpose in his museum demonstration that Nature worked by slow evolution rather than by swift revolution.

Conspicuously absent in the roll-call is any Education Act, with which we might have expected the Museums Act, with its intention to promote instruction, to be linked. The reason, of course, lies in the sectarian bitterness of the different Christian organizations who ran the elementary schools, which meant that Britain had to wait until 1870 for a state education system. By the 1870s the first great wave of museum foundation, stimulated by the Act and by the Great Exhibition of 1851, had gathered its own separate momentum and new interests had moved elsewhere, so, to the great loss of both, no formal links were established between museums and schools.

Much of the archaeological material had come to the new public museums from the older established county and city learned societies of the 'Literary and Philosophical' kind, which had begun to be founded early in the nineteenth century, and with whom the new institutions had important relationships which were, however, often complex, and differed from place to place. At Canterbury the members of the Literary and Philosophical Society started forming an archaeological collection in 1825 and this went to the

Canterbury City Museum when it opened in 1846. Weston Park Museum, part of Sheffield City Museum, opened in 1875 with the collections of the Sheffield Society, while the Leicester Society started collecting antiquities soon after 1835, but handed its material over to the City Museum when this was founded in 1849.

Probably some or all of these society collections had been on semi-public display from time to time, but sometimes the societies had founded formal museums. The Yorkshire Museum was opened in York by the Yorkshire Philosophical Society in 1822. The Devon and Exeter Institution established a museum in the Cathedral Close, Exeter, the formation of which had been one of the aims of the Institution from its founding in 1813. The Royal Institution of Cornwall premises opened in Truro in 1818, and the Scarborough Museum was opened by the Scarborough Philosophical Society in 1829. Some of these museums have enjoyed an unbroken existence to the present day and in some of them the societies still retain important collections, although much funding is now provided by the local authorities, and the museums services function in broadly the same ways as do the wholly local government institutions.

In 1843 the growing interest in British archaeology, stimulated in part by the philosophical societies, led to the formation of the British Archaeological Association for the Encouragement and Prosecution of Researches into the Arts and Monuments of the Early and Middle Ages, to give its full title, which clearly signifies the contemporary view of archaeology as consisting primarily of artistic objects and upstanding monuments, usually barrows or standing stones, and demonstrates the vagueness of chronological perceptions. In 1844 the BAA held at Canterbury what seems to have been the first residential archaeological conference, an idea so revolutionary that it led more or less directly to the famous split which resulted in the creation in 1845 of the rival Archaeological Institute. These events concentrated the growing interest in local archaeology throughout the country and stimulated the foundation of the county archaeological societies, first the Norfolk Archaeological Society in 1845, followed in 1846 by the Cambrian and Sussex societies, the Surrey society in 1854 and the Kentish one in 1857. By about 1870 most of the country had been covered, and the societies were actively exploring and publishing: most continue to flourish to this day (Piggott 1976).

Interestingly, these new departures in the organization of archaeology coincided with the Museums Act of 1845 and in many of the cities and county towns the same men must have been active in both the new archaeological societies and the new institutions. Sometimes the two came together and the societies themselves created very important archaeological museums, particularly that in Dorchester founded by the newly-formed Dorset Archaeological and Natural History Society in 1846, and that in Devizes founded by the new Wiltshire Archaeological and Natural History Society in 1853 (and how delightfully the names roll off the tongues of those many of us who have had the pleasure of working with the societies and among their archives). In these museums, also, and in others of their kind like those at Taunton (Somerset County Museum Service) and Torquay (Museum of the Torquay Natural History Society) the founding societies still retain important rights, especially over the collections, although again most now receive local authority funding and operate accordingly. Elsewhere, as at Exeter (1868), where no legal link existed, the relationship between local museums and societies has been, usually, cordial, and the museums have been the normal repositories of the archaeological material which the societies have generated.

The impetus provided by the 1845 Act continued to produce new civic museums through the 1850s, 1860s and 1870s. A late burst in the period 1900–1910 filled what must have seemed to contemporaries to be shameful gaps, but by 1910 virtually all the substantial public archaeological collections had been started (figure 1.9) and they have continued to collect to the present time.

The history of archaeological museums to 1960, then, seems to fall into four main phases. The earliest phase, running from about 1683 to about 1800 covers the early national and university museums, but in England these showed relatively little interest in native archaeology. There followed the growth period of the literary and philosophical societies, who were collecting privately from roughly 1800 to 1850 or rather later. Then came the development of the county archaeological societies from around 1845, and the foundation of many local authority museums around the same time. The long period from about 1860 to the Second World War and its aftermath was one of consolidation. By the 1860s much of the societies' collections, and many privately formed collections also, were housed in formal museums, either public museums or private society museums which would, eventually, take on most of the characteristics of the public museums. From the 1850s all these museums have been adding actively to their collections, from private donations and from the collecting and excavating activities of the county societies, of forceful individuals, and of a growing range of organizations.

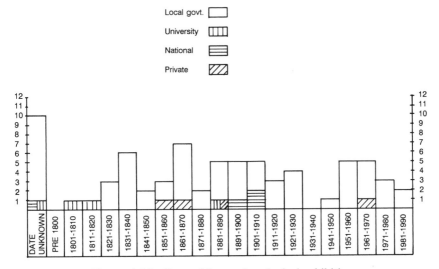

Figure 1.10 Date of first archaeological exhibition

During the same period, too, some new museums were founded which were similar in character to those which were already in existence. The opportunity to display material was often one of the main reasons why a museum was founded, and so, through the nineteenth and into the twentieth century, the pattern of first archaeological exhibitions broadly mirrors that of museum foundation (figure 1.10).

The nature of archaeological collections

Bearing this developmental framework in mind, we must now turn to the nature of the archaeological collections involved, and the reasons why they were made. The process of collecting in England has been a complicated one, partly because the archaeologists themselves have often had complex personalities and motives, and partly because old attitudes have persisted alongside newer views, sometimes for many decades and sometimes resulting in the accumulation of very significant material.

Interest focuses first upon the early collectors, men like Elias Ashmole and the Tradescants whose material went to the new Ashmolean Museum in 1683, and Sir Hans Sloane, Sir Robert Cotton and the Earl of Oxford whose collections were housed in the new British Museum in 1759. Sir Ashton Lever's museum could be viewed in London from 1774 to about ten years later, and William Bullock showed his museum first in Sheffield in 1795, then in Liverpool in 1801 and finally in London from 1801 to 1819 when it was sold up. The Liverpool merchant, Joseph Meyer, formed his broadly similar collection during the first half of the nineteenth century and this eventually went to the Liverpool City Museum in 1867 (Nicholson and Warhurst 1984; Gibson and Wright 1988).

These men are the well-known and better-documented members of what by the late eighteenth century was clearly a large fraternity, and collecting had become something of a mania among the county gentry, clergymen and army and naval officers always prominent in antiquarian pursuits. Their collections were of the 'cabinet of natural and artificial curiosities' kind, where natural history specimens from Britain and abroad were mixed with artefacts, often also from abroad. British material found a place in these early collections more or less by accident. Joseph Meyer's collection contained some famous pieces of Iron Age metalwork, like the Meyer Mirror and the Trawsfyndd tankard, and collections like that of Bronze Age pottery from the Whitby area purchased from Samuel Anderson in 1854, or the Faussett Collection (see below) bought in 1854, but these took their place beside Egyptian antiquities, European archaeological material and gems and ivories.

The pieces in all these collections were valued for their intrinsic rarity, for the romantic echoes of the far-away and strange with which they tantalized the imagination, and, sometimes, for their aesthetic virtue and workmanship, and these qualities were sufficiently highly regarded to give at least some of the artefacts a substantial monetary value. During the Renaissance and perhaps up to the end of the seventeenth century, specimens for such cabinets seem to have been collected according to an intellectual rationale which saw the collection as a microcosm of the real world organized to demonstrate 'the ancient hierarchies of the world and the resemblances which drew the things of the world together' (Hooper-Greenhill 1989:64). By the 1750s the philosophies of the Enlightenment had discarded such mystical ideas in favour of the new rationalism. This could be applied much more successfully to collections of natural history specimens than to collections of material culture, but these disadvantages did not inhibit the collectors of objects.

Their material was, of course, only idiosyncratically listed or recorded, and the collections were arranged to what seemed to be their best advantage by their owner; often, indeed, they seem to have grown up around him as an extension of his person, as the picture of Joseph Meyer in his study shows (Plate 1). This notion touches the heart of the matter. Although outwardly collections were maintained because they were the proper ornament of a gentleman's library, and many half-hearted glass cases no doubt did this and no more, the great collections were formed by men whose imaginations identified with the objects which they desired to gather. Their relationship to their collections may be described as fetishistic (see Stewart 1984; Gathercole 1989) in that powerful emotions were aroused by the artefacts which the artefacts seemed to return, stimulating a need to gather more and more of the same broad kind.

This nervous tone, strong in many collectors, gave us, in the generations after about 1850, the parody of the mad collector who crops up regularly in publications like *Punch*, and a modified version of this view, which condescends to the collector's lack of intellect, has been the general verdict since that time. This brings us back to the problems surrounding the progressive and judgmental view of history discussed earlier. In their own day the collectors inherited something of the Renaissance prestige, if not its worldview. They were admired as men of discernment and wide-ranging interest, which in an age before specialization was considered a hallmark of cultivation. At a more practical level, our museum collections today would be infinitely the poorer without their contributions. This kind of collecting continued well into the present century, and continues, like the Montague Collection which came to Exeter City Museum in 1942, or the collection of Dr Fawcett of Essex which was acquired by the Bristol City Museum by 1985, to arrive in museums.

Alongside this collecting spirit ran another with a rather different emphasis. The great prestige of the material remains of Greece and Rome had, in the earlier seventeenth century, inspired the Earl of Arundel, the Duke of Buckingham and Charles I himself to accumulate collections of classical antiquities. The great period of the classical collectors began with the travels of James Stuart and Nicholas Revett in Greece in 1751–3, and continued with the collecting activities of Sir William Hamilton in the late eighteenth century and of Lord Elgin in the early nineteenth century.

These grand designs were beyond the reach of most, but, it came to be realized, Roman remains could be collected much closer to home. The building of the Georgian bathhouse suites at Bath, which began in 1727,

Plate 1 Joseph Meyer in his house at 20 Clarence Terrace, Everton Road, Liverpool, where he lived from 1839–42. He is shown considering a Wedgewood urn, while light falls on classical marbles, and Greek and Etruscan antiquities on the table. Painted about 1840 by William Daniels. Liverpool Museum (WAG 7355), reproduced by courtesy National Museums and Galleries, Merseyside.

yielded a range of impressive sculptured stone from the preceding Roman bath and temple complex, which came into the possession of the Bath Roman, Literary, and Scientific Institution in the mid-nineteenth century (and finally passed formally into the possession of the Bath City Museum in 1940). This material seems to have been open to inspection by interested parties from the 1720s.

The early collections in the Yorkshire Museum seem to have included similar material from Roman York, while those collected from 1835 at Shrewsbury had material from Wroxeter, and those held by the Canterbury Literary and Philosophical Society from 1825 seem to have included material from Roman Canterbury. At Lincoln the collection of the Dean and Chapter was started in the eighteenth century, and finally arrived in the City Museum in 1908. In London, Charles Roach Smith, a friend of Meyer's, started to collect and record Roman (and also medieval) antiquities which were appearing during the rebuilding, dredging and sewer-digging which began about 1835. By 1840 he had a growing private collection on display in his house in Liverpool Street, and his privately published journal *Collectanea Antiqua* first appeared in 1843, while in the same year, with Thomas Wright, he founded the British Archaeological Association. His collection was finally purchased by the British Museum in 1856 (Kidd 1977).

It seems likely that most of the public museums founded after 1845 in towns and cities with a Roman past had local Roman material among their earliest archaeological accessions. The records are vague but there are signs that the early societies had often formed this kind of collection, no doubt because Roman remains were more literary and more philosophical than barbarities from home and abroad. Roman material was prestigious, it could be taken seriously as high art, and, most importantly, at a time when chronological concepts had nothing to offer for pre-Roman times, dateable local finds like the occasional inscriptions and the relatively common coins could be fitted into an accepted historical framework derived from the Roman authors and from historians like Gibbon, although this was not, of course, extended into the dating of associated finds and structures.

By the middle of the century a considerable quantity of archaeological material had also been accumulated by excavation, principally from barrows. Digging into barrows from antiquarian motives seems to have begun in the early decades of the eighteenth century, but the first man to do this on a large scale was the Rev. Brian Faussett (1720–76) who began in 1757 to open barrows in his native Kent, and finally clocked up some 777 excavated burial mounds, the illustrated record of which was finally published eighty years after his death through the efforts of Joseph Meyer and Charles Roach Smith. The excavation technique was, naturally, according to the standards of the day, and Faussett could only refer to the burials as of 'Britons Romanized' or 'Romans Britonized' since he lacked any dating reference. The barrows were in fact Anglo-Saxon, and they yielded a superb collection of metalwork including some 400 jewelled pieces. The collection stayed at Faussett's home at Heppington, Kent, apparently attracting virtually no attention, until the Canterbury Conference of 1844. In 1853 the British Museum refused to purchase the collection, and finally it went to Meyer's own collection, and so eventually to Liverpool City Museum (now part of the National Museums on Merseyside).

In the generation which flourished around 1800 there were probably as many gentlemen interested in barrow opening as there were those interested in forming collections by purchase and exchange. Excavation seems to have been regarded as simply another method of acquiring material, linked, however, to the 'county interest' which characterized the rural English upper middle class, and regarded as an acceptable form of field sport for those of a romantic turn of mind. Among these Sir Richard Colt Hoare (1758–1838) and his colleague William Cunnington (1754–1810) stand out as the forerunners of what was to become the new nineteenth-century scientific realism. Cunnington described himself digging barrows on Salisbury Plain in 1803 'in the hopes of meeting something which might supersede conjecture', and Colt Hoare was later to declare 'we speak from facts not theory' (Marsden 1984: 15–20). Their work included the opening of some 450 barrows in Wiltshire, which were classified into long barrows and four types of round barrow, and records of settlement site, and earthworks.

All this went into Colt Hoare's *Ancient Wiltshire* which appeared in parts between 1810 and 1821. The volumes inspired the activities of men like the Rev. John Skinner (1772–1839), Rector of Camerton, Somerset, whose barrow material went to Bristol City Museum, and William Miles who published his excavation of the famous Deverel Barrow near Dorchester in 1826, the material from which also went to Bristol. William Williamson published his *Description of the Tumulus opened at Gristhorpe near Scarborough* in 1834; this described the skeleton, the lidded oak coffin and the grave goods from the barrow. The finds went to Scarborough Museum soon after as part of the early material assembled by the Scarborough Society. The most energetic excavator inspired by Colt Hoare was Thomas Bateman (1821–61) who began his work among the barrows of the Derbyshire Peak in 1843, and in 1848 published his results in *Vestiges of the Antiquities of Derbyshire*. The finds were kept in his own house, which became a virtual archaeological museum. Like Faussett, all these early workers lacked any chronological scheme, and could only describe their prehistoric material as 'Celtic' or 'British'.

While the smaller and more manageable collections like those of Skinner and Williamson soon found permanent homes in the Society and other early museums, the history of the larger and more important collections was more chequered, and shines an interesting light on the views of the day. As we have seen, the Faussett collection lay neglected for over sixty years and its final home had no connections with Kent. The Bateman collection was placed on loan with Sheffield City Museum in 1876, and not purchased by the Museum until 1893 when the death of Bateman's improvident son meant that his father's library and collection had to be sold up (Plate 2). The material excavated by Cunnington and Colt Hoare was preserved at Colt Hoare's home at Stourland, Wiltshire, until 1878, when it was placed on loan in the Museum of the Wiltshire Archaeological Society in Devizes. A contemporary local newspaper regarded this as 'a degree of antiquarian eccentricity which few persons will be able to appreciate' and dismissed the collection as 'more like the refuse of a marine store than anything else' (Marsden 1984: 19). It would be pleasant, but incorrect, to regard this as an attitude long since dead.

The great early excavations and publications in Britain may have helped the development of archaeological practice in the field, but the resulting collections themselves were not studied for what they could contribute to our understanding of past times. They were treated as negotiable family prop-

Plate 2   The Bateman Gallery at Weston Park Museum, Sheffield, in February 1921. Reproduced by courtesy Sheffield City Museum (City of Sheffield Metropolitan District).

erty, and as treasure or as art objects where this was feasible; they stimulated no intellectual interest in material culture and its potential for knowledge and, monetary value aside, they were chiefly regarded in the antiquarian way as merely the relics of ancient men, and as the souvenirs of excavating activities now over and done with, attitudes which were to prove very stubborn.

The mid-nineteenth-century intellectual revolution

When the first provincial public museums began to be founded from 1845 to about 1860, then, their earliest archaeological material derived from the accumulations of the early collectors, the haphazardly salvaged groups of local Roman material and some of the fruits of early barrow digging, but only the Roman material could be fitted into any conceptual system. The intellectual revolution of the mid-century, of which the Museums Act and the founding of the British Archaeological Association were themselves parts, was to work a fundamental transformation.

The change in attitudes among the educated classes was very slow. Charles Lyell published his theory of the natural formation of successive layers of deposits in his *Principles of Geology* which appeared from 1830 to 1833, but it was not until the 1860s that William Pengelly's application of this theory to the stratified cave deposits in Kent's Cavern, Torquay, and at Brixham, was generally accepted as demonstrating that the antiquity of man went well back before any Biblical flood, and as showing the principle that associated remains are of the same date and can be used to date each other. The theory of evolution was first fully stated by Darwin in his *Origin of Species* (1859), and precipitated a battle which did not die away until the late 1860s, by which time Thomas Huxley's book, *Man's Place in Nature* (1863), had extended Darwin's idea of a universal biological mechanism which produced changes of form stimulated by changing circumstances and competition to man himself. All this was, of course, scientifically 'more correct' than what had gone before, but it was also part of the new aggression which character-izes all walks of national life in the 1850s and 1860s; a theory of the survival of the fittest suited the new men who were making good livings by their competitiveness.

Meanwhile, in Denmark, prehistoric material was for the first time being approached in ways which could make it intelligible, from the point of view both of chronology and of function (see Graslund 1987). The classification of artefacts by material, particularly by stone, bronze and iron, and the conceptual leap which turned this distinction into the chronological scheme of the Three Age System can be traced back to the earliest phases of the Danish National Museum, between 1807 and 1836, by which time the galleries had been arranged by Thomsen according to this principle. However, the idea did not reach a wider world until the publication of the National Museum guide book, for which Thomsen wrote the sections on the early monuments and antiquities of the north in 1836, followed by Worsaae's most important book in 1849.

The ideas of Thomsen and Worsaae did not reach the English public until a translation of the guide book appeared in 1848 entitled *A Guide to Northern Antiquities*, and that of Worsaae's work in 1849 under the title of *The Primeval Antiquities of Denmark*. The Three Ages System gained ground slowly in Britain. When Vaux, assistant in the Department of Antiquities at the British Museum, published his *Handbook to the Antiquities in the British Museum* in 1851, subtitled 'A Description of the remains of Greek, Assyrian, Egyptian and Etruscan Art preserved there', he explained in his preface that the collections 'known by the names of British or Anglo-Roman antiquities' were deliberately omitted, 'being as yet too insufficiently arranged to admit of classification and description'. By 1866 Franks had been appointed the first Keeper of the newly created Department of British and Medieval Anti-quities, and he reorganized his collections, abandoning an arrangment based upon the archaeology of art which put sculptures or terracottas together regardless of their origins, and instead setting out the pre-Roman antiquities in forty-two cases and according to the tripartite system. He himself, however, viewed this arrangement with less than complete conviction. In the *Guide to the Exhibition Rooms of the Departments of Natural History and Antiquities*, published in 1871, he wrote 'The remains of the inhabitants of the British Island, previous to the Roman invasion, embrace the *Stone, Bronze*, and a portion of the *Iron* period of Northern Antiquaries. They have, for conveni-ence, been classed according to their materials, in the order corresponding to that of the supposed introduction of such materials into this country' (Daniel 1950 : 82).

By the late 1860s those with a serious interest in the past could draw upon a concept of the antiquity of man and of a chronological scheme based upon easily recognized materials which made this antiquity intelligible. Such people had access to the idea of the principles of stratification, and the beginnings of a theory of material culture interpretation; and linked with all this was a keen sense, aroused by the bitter controversies scarcely yet concluded, that to interest oneself in the remote past was to be in the intellectual vanguard of the day. The impact upon collecting and museum collections was very considerable. One of the easiest ways in which to participate in the interest of the time was to join an archaeological society and collect flint implements, a pastime which could be carried on in virtually every part of the country. Such collections started to be made from the 1870s, although often they did not arrive in museums until donated by the collector in old age (or by his widow).

Typical of their day are the flint collections made on the Pennines and donated to Rochdale Museum by Horsfall (1902), by the Rochdale Field Naturalists (1902) and by Sutcliffe and Parker (1903), or the palaeolithic material, especially that from Swanscombe, which the Horniman Museum had acquired by 1907. All the collections of this type contain much material, but the recording was usually poor and the choice highly selective, with waste, cores, and 'poor specimens', generally left behind, and the appreciation of prehistoric artefacts was dominated by the ideas of the 'fine example'. Such collectors still exist, as every curator knows.

General Pitt Rivers and material culture theory

Meanwhile, rather apart from the world of local collectors and county archaeological societies , a new personality was coming onto the scene, and this was Augustus Henry Pitt Rivers (as he is usually called, although he did not adopt the Pitt Rivers surname until 1880 when he came into his Cranborne Chase inheritance). He began collecting, first firearms and then more generally, in 1851, stimulated by the Great Exhibition, and by 1866 the collection could be described by E. B. Tylor as extending from the basement to the attic of his home, with labelled objects displayed on walls and cabinets in all the principal rooms (Chapman 1985 : 29). The collections included a certain amount of archaeology in the strict sense, and also some groups of what would now be called social history material, but the bulk of it was composed of ethnographic specimens which Pitt Rivers either purchased or had given to him by widely-travelling friends. After a number of false starts, the collection was finally given a permanent home at Oxford University in 1883, on condition that the original arrangement of the collection would be retained.

By the 1880s Pitt Rivers was installed on his new estate and beginning the series of excavations which were to be published as *Excavations in Cranborne Chase* (1881–98). In 1883 he began to assemble new acquisitions, including the local archaeological material, folk life material and fine art objects, in a new museum at Farnham, in four rooms of an abandoned schoolhouse on his estate. The museum, together with its wildlife park, Sunday concerts and visitors' pavilions was 'calculated to draw the interest of a purely rural population ten miles distant from any town or railway station', and by 1890 there were some 15,000 visitors annually. The Farnham Museum remained a private venture, and by the 1970s it was running into financial difficulties. Eventually, after a good deal of public anxiety, the archaeological material was acquired by the Salisbury and South Wiltshire Museum in 1975.

The mainspring of Pitt Rivers' collecting drive was a philosophy of man and of material culture, which he believed revealed man's essential nature and development and extended our understanding of it. His model was that of Darwin's, by whom he was much influenced: artefact types developed one from another by a process of selection which modified their forms according to natural laws. These were essentially deterministic and did not depend upon human choice. Artefact sequences, in guns or clubs or lances, exhibit a progression from a simple original to more complex later forms, designed to function in more specialized ways. These sequences can be reconstructed, as his diagram of, for example, the development of Pacific material culture demonstrated. The sequences can then show the different levels of culture attained by different human groups, the historical process by which forms were diffused from one group to another, and the nature of human progress itself, because they showed 'the sequence of ideas by which mankind has advanced from the condition of the lower animals'.

His views were presented in three lectures on 'Primitive Warfare' at the United Service Institution in 1867, 1868 and 1869, and culminated in his general statement *The Evolution of Culture* published in 1875. His final museum ideal embraced a rotunda building, arranged in concentric circles which would show the major phases of evolutionary development with the innermost circle for the Palaeolithic, the next for the Neolithic, and so on, culminating in the outer ring for 'specimens of such modern arts as could be placed in continuity with those of antiquity'. The rotunda would also place art into wedges so that 'separate angles of the circle might be appropriated to geographic areas' and allied civilizations would 'occupy adjacent angles within the same concentric ring' (Chapman 1985:41). The material in both his collections was arranged in typological series designed to demonstrate his ideas, and hence his anxiety that Oxford should preserve his arrangement.

Even this brief summary serves to show how powerful Pitt Rivers' views were, and how they constituted the most compelling statement of the first substantial British attempt to give the interpretation of material culture an intellectual framework. His collection contrasted sharply with the fetish-like accumulations of earlier generations, in that it operated not by the accumulation of samples but by the arrangement of examples intended to demonstrate principles. Objects were acquired in order 'to fill a gap in the collections', that phrase still so common upon curators' lips, and in this structural sense it was one of the first of the true collections. His ideas were very influential in many areas. Museum exhibitions of human history material continued to be displayed along evolutionist lines until well after the Second World War, and the notion that changing forms give typological sequences which represent both cultural development and passage through time remained the basic organizing principle for archaeological finds to the end of the 1950s, and is still extremely important.

Two fundamental objections can be made to Pitt Rivers' views. The first revolves around his neglect of specific context. Most of the Oxford material, at least, came from inadequately recorded contexts, and the sequences were built up using artefacts from differing dates. This gave the whole concept a formal and artificial rigidity, where theories were rather brutally imposed upon the artefacts, and in the universal grand design the particular nature of individual cultural contexts was ignored. The evolutionary principle might have generated a research community, to repeat the phrase used at the beginning of this chapter, with individual specialists plotting particular typological sequences in relation to particular human groups, and fitting these into an all-embracing evolutionary structure showing the diffusion of ideas across the globe. This is what Pitt Rivers hoped would happen at Oxford, but it did not because anthropological imaginations were turning rather to topics like religion, subsistence and kinship. In the years after Pitt Rivers' death in 1900 research into a whole culture, looked at in the first instance for its own sake, seemed more fruitful in both anthropology and archaeology, and this is one major reason why material culture, tied, it seemed, to variants of Pitt Rivers' views, became unfashionable as a study in its own right and, consequently, why museums themselves dropped in academic esteem.

The second objection is essentially one of taste and outlook. Pitt Rivers, like most of his contemporaries, saw every reason to welcome a theory which seemed to validate the view that contemporary white civilization stood at the peak of the evolutionary process, with all other societies ranged beneath. This line was linked by contemporaries with activities like the measuring of skulls, designed to distinguish the 'races of mankind' on a 'scientific' basis. Such ideas embody unashamed and overt racialism, and now appear both distasteful and theoretically unacceptable.

Trends up to c.1960

The typological principle, shorn of its more far-reaching evolutionary and diffusionist theories, was taken up by Sir John Evans (father of the excavator of Knossos) who between 1863 and 1881 produced three outstanding volumes of systematic artefact studies: *Coins of the Ancient Britons* (1863), *The Ancient Stone Implements, Weapons and Ornaments of Great Britain* (1872) and *The Ancient Bronze Implements of Great Britain* (1881). These established the sequence of type forms, and classified them into a sensible chronological structure. Evans continued the spirit of the Scandinavian archaeologists, his work established a basis for bronze and lithic studies, and it remains valuable to this day. He was able to write as he did because he had a sound knowledge of museum collections, public and private, one of the first people in Britain to work in this way, and his own collection came into the possession of the

Ashmolean Museum. Evans' approach was taken up in an increasing number of ancient artefact studies in the period from about 1900 to about 1960, as the volumes of the archaeological journals show.

The period was also characterized by increased excavation, some of it to a high standard, and, in the phase between the wars, by major excavation campaigns like that at Maiden Castle, Dorset, by Mortimer Wheeler, or at Hembury, Devon, by Dorothy Liddell. This meant that a steady flow of excavated finds began to reach museums, sometimes involving very large collections indeed. The staffing levels and the storage facilities were grossly inadequate in most places, and to these problems must be added the disruption caused by two world wars in which museum buildings were bombed or requisitioned and collections scattered (the present writer well remembers reassembling the Devon collections, as late as 1967, from a range of wartime storage which included disused RSPCA kennels). There is no doubt that problems which were to appear in an acute form after 1960 had begun to develop some decades before.

A number of significant trends, then, can be identified at work in the period up to about 1960. By then, most substantial museums with archaeological material were into their second century, and in many cases they had been the earliest publicly funded cultural institution in their area. The museums had an intimate and intricate relationship with their local communities and their local learned bodies and, in the way of British provincial life, the same leading figures, drawn from the professional and landed classes, tended to be influential in all these related areas. The archaeological collections were equally old, and by 1960 most of these museums had accumulated collections which belong within all the broad traditions described here. The impact of change in the years after 1960 must now be assessed.

2. Developments between 1960 and 1990

The climate of opinion

The years around 1960 were a major watershed, so much so that it is probably true to say that those who spent their formative years before the early 1960s and those who spent them after 1960 are in many ways quite different kinds of people, with fundamentally contrasting assumptions about the moral nature of authority, the reasonable expectations of the individual, the structure of society and of personal relationships, and the validity of value judgments.

The new initiatives were not immediately accompanied by any substantial reformation in the public museum services, either national or local, but indirectly their effect upon museums, and upon archaeology, has been enormous. This has come about principally through the growth of the heritage movement, very much a child of the times, and the particular aspect of that movement known as Rescue Archaeology. Running parallel to the broader public issues, but stemming from the same philosophical climate, was the development of fresh theoretical approaches to the study of the past, which began with 'the New Archaeology' and continues with its successors.

Theoretical archaeology

Archaeological theory has generated a substantial literature of its own, and some of its main directions may be followed in the writings of Binford (1983), Hodder (1986, 1987, 1988) and Schiffer (1976), and in the useful critical review published by Shennan (1986). Much of this critical thinking has been directed towards the better interpretation of material culture. Theoreticians have always recognized the obvious fact that archaeology is, above all things, the discipline which depends upon our understanding of material culture in the broad sense, and that much of this material takes the form of artefacts secured in museum collections. For this reason those responsible for important theoretical developments in the subject have often, like Childe and Hawkes in the earlier generation, and Clarke, Rowlands and Hodder in the new, been more concerned with the study of material culture than they have with the conduct of excavations.

Up to the 1950s archaeologists had tended to work as historians who lacked documents and who had, therefore, to use material culture as a kind of non-literary historical evidence which could provide information about technology and material goods and, up to a point, economics. It could show through the construction of typological sequences how groups possessed of the various forms, regarded as indicating cultures or social and ethnic groupings, came and went across the face of Europe.

By about 1960, it was clear that this approach left unaddressed many conceptual problems about the study of the past. It offered only the most naïve explanations of cultural change, it had no theory about the nature of objects in relation to society, and it could not grapple with the workings of power and politics in the past. At much the same time, archaeologists were recognizing a broad range of analytical techniques relating to dating, characterization, location, and measuring, many of which were already employed in other social sciences, and notions about hierarchy, community typing (bands, chiefdoms, and so on) and modes of exchange. The marriage of the two resulted in the 'new archaeology' which, in its various forms, attempted to build quasi-scientific generalizing models to show the regularities of processes working across historical and cultural contexts.

As the 1980s dawned, the 'new archaeology' itself began to seem flawed because its application of positivist ideas about process to individual ancient (or modern) societies robbed them of, and was dislocated by, their historical particularity, their unique and characteristic flavour, the appreciation of which is, after all, one of the principal pleasures of study in the humanities. At the present time, archaeologists like Hodder (1987) are developing ideas of contextual analysis which encapsulate the environmental context, the structured 'text' and the particular situation, with the intention of giving full weight to specific circumstances while retaining the analytical insights provided by previous studies.

It emerges from all this that there are three fruitful ways in which the interpretation of objects may be approached. They may be seen as artefacts, that is as raw material worked upon by technology to produce goods which operate functionally and synchronically across the social body. Analysis here will involve most of the techniques developed in the 1960s and 1970s. They may be seen as a mode of communication and structure which can create symbolic categories through which the social positioning of groups and individuals may be ordered; and they may be seen diachronically or historically as embodying the past experience of the group and so carrying ideological values or moral judgments into the present (Pearce 1986a; 1986b). All objects carry all these kinds of content, to varying extents, and so all these approaches must always be borne in mind, and a range of techniques, which include systems analysis diagrams and structuralist plots have been devised to express what the student perceives (for further discussion see Hodder 1982, 1986).

Underlying all this, however, is the post-structuralist insight developed by Shanks and Tilley (1987a, 1987b) that meanings in society, and the nature of material culture as part of that meaning, are constantly in a state of negotiation and renegotiation through social practice created by the actions of the individual: objects are a form of narrative or discourse and the story is constantly changing. The three analytical approaches to objects already discussed remain valuable, provided the archaeologist remembers that they deal, as it were, only with moments, each occurring with highly selective content at irregular intervals in time and space across the social flux; and the extent to which archaeological investigation can offer a closer mesh than this remains debatable.

It follows from this that archaeological study itself is a part of present social negotiation. Archaeology is an active project of persuasion, a rhetoric aimed at an audience, which necessarily has a political or ideological character, intended either to disrupt or (and more probably) to preserve the present. Archaeology in museums constantly negotiates, or structures and restructures, the past, and this happens in three distinguishable forms of activity. Firstly, there is the formation of collections, accumulated in all the modes described in this book, all of which, of course, embody the narratives of their day and contribute their mite to intellectual and so to social change. Linked into this is the selection of material for non-collection or disposal. Secondly, there is the curatorial process of care, study and publication, which lavishes much more resource on some material than it does on some other. Finally, there is the process of exhibition, which, however it is approached, involves a further project of selection (see Chapter 10).

All this has an enormous bearing on the curation of the archive, on a better understanding of the nature of collections, and upon the artefact-based research projects and the exhibitions (in the broadest sense) with which curators should be concerned. It is fair to say that the potential of artefact and collection studies, and their implications, is only now beginning to be developed, and it is to be hoped that curators will play a major role in the work.

Heritage and rescue

From its beginnings around 1960 or a little earlier, the Heritage Movement has established itself as one of the few things which genuinely runs all through national life, from debates in Parliament to arguments over the design of a local bus shelter. It may be defined as a concern to identify and protect the natural and historical environment in order to conserve and interpret the traditional identity of every part of the United Kingdom, so that citizens may better understand their origins, enjoy an enhanced quality of life in their own time, and pass a good environment on to their children. The threat to the heritage is identified as the post-war industrial, housing and road-building boom, and modern methods of farming and forestry, all of which are destroying traditional environments at a horrifying rate. The emotional appeal of heritage conservation can be very strong. It embraces the intellectual and social climate already described, it offers roots to people who must live increasingly in anonymous suburbs, and its fundamental concept of an inheritance which is owned by all of us and can be passed to all our children draws strength from the belief that democratic rights override proprietorial ownerships.

It is unquestionably true that the heritage movement as a whole has been a considerable success in the popular and commercial sense. If, as has often been said, in the twenty-first century, North America will provide the world's management, Asia will provide the manufacture, and Europe will offer the cultural cabaret, then the British heritage is well positioned to play its part. Figures issued by the English Tourist Board for 1986 show that in that year 14 million tourists visited this country, spending £10.5 billion, which amounts to an industry larger than British agriculture, oil, or car construction.

Of these tourists about a third visited a museum, and although the visits are currently concentrated upon the British Museum and the other London national museums, there are signs that the numbers overall are rising, and that museum visits are diversifying more. The Tourist Board estimates that the tourist figures generally will have doubled by the 1990s. The heritage is now an industry in its own right, and in the new competitive climate of the 1980s it has proved its worth (Hewison 1986). In his report prepared from the Policy Studies Institute, John Myerscough (1988) stresses the economic importance of the arts, including museums, for Britain, and shows how artistic and economic considerations are inextricably intermingled, with a potential together to create jobs, boost overseas earnings and encourage urban renewal. The impact of all this on the conservation of the archaeological heritage, however, is likely to be highly problematic (see also Chapter 11).

Paralleling the history of the broad heritage movement has been that aspect of it known as rescue archaeology. The history of rescue archaeology is now acquiring its own literature (Jones 1984; Barker 1986; Sheldon 1986; Rahtz 1974), wherein is described the concern felt in the later 1960s at the rate of the destruction of archaeological sites without investigation, and the lack of any national policy in Britain around which excavation could be organized. The pressure did not produce a comprehensive structure, but did generate a wide range of excavating bodies across the country. Most influential archaeologists at times felt that these should be kept separate from the museum services, which were regarded as incapable of rising to the challenge (Fowler 1970a; 1970b).

The resulting huge increase in the quantity of excavation was clearly going to create responsibilities. As early as 1973 the Museums Association had adopted at its Annual General Meeting a policy statement on Museums and Field Archaeology which stressed the need to recognize that 'the recovery element in rescue excavation represents a short intensive financial commitment only to be followed by long-term care, storage and usage of the finds recovered', and recommended the need for storage and conservation grants (Davies 1986:2). These conclusions were shared by the findings of the Wright Report (1973) which had surveyed 46 provincial museums with archaeological collections.

By 1975 the general recognition that the financial burden of publication had become intolerable was unavoidable, but most archaeologists were unwilling to abandon the principle that work should be completed to full publication standard. The result of this was the Frere Report (October 1975) which aimed to limit traditional-style publication, but on condition that 'all the original records of the excavation, properly organized and curated, are housed in readily accessible form in a permanent archive', that this archive should include the whole excavation and post-excavation record, and that it should be produced to a very high standard. In October 1975 the Society of Museum Archaeologists held its inaugural meeting, and defined among its objectives the encouragement of museum involvement in field archaeology and in the proper curation of the excavation archive.

In 1978 the general principles for archive curation set out in the Frere Report were defined in greater detail in the final chapter of the Dimbleby Report (1978). This stated that:

1 It must be recognized that the creation, housing and use of an archive is a single continuous process.
2 All archives should be housed in a museum or a museum controlled building.
3 Ideally, no excavation should take place until arrangements for the adequate future storage, conservation and maintenance have been made.

The firm use of the word 'museum' was, in its own way, a major break-through, and the crucial concept of the complete excavation archive had been established.

After two decades of rescue activity, three points emerge as of fundamental importance. The archaeology network may still be thin, but it is better than it was before. Archaeologists now realize that the public pays for what they do, and therefore that they must give visible value for money, and that public opinion and politics, in the broad sense, are indivisible. Finally, the rate of destruction increases rather than decreases, and something like 50,000 acres per year are probably lost by development (Fowler 1986). Preservation rather than excavation is now the preferred solution, but in a heritage-conscious world political questions of choice and resource are as urgent as ever. In practice the work of archaeology has settled down in three broad areas: the gathering of data and their input into the planning process; excavation and field work; and the curation of the archive. We must investigate how museums have been involved in these areas and what responsibilities they are carrying, but this is part of the wider question of the response museums have made to the archaeological heritage movement as a whole, and trends here must be examined first.

Archaeology in museums, 1960–1990

The impact of the heritage movement brought into being a number of independent museums, like Jorvik, opened in 1984, Fishbourne (1968), and Mary Rose (1983). These have been associated with some of the most prominent patrons and archaeologists in the country because they focus on sites which have a very particular historical and dramatic appeal. They have been in the vanguard of developments in exhibition and preservation, and all these things have made it possible for them to maintain themselves, and the research functions associated with them, by entrance fees and grant raising. Enterprises like Jorvik are often greeted in influential circles as the desirable shape of things to come, combining, as they do, genuine archaeology and entrepreneurial thrust, but this is to miss the point. The market can possibly sustain a dozen or so Jorviks distributed across the country but not more; and the presumption that dramatic sites, linked preferably with substantial surviving remains, always tell us most about the past is quite untrue.

In the public sector, including local authority, national and university museums, the impact of the heritage movement has not resulted generally in the formation of fresh institutions. The exception is the Oxfordshire City and County Museum created in 1965, and to this might be added the Edinburgh City Museums created in 1976 by amalgamating existing museums and collections, and the Museum of London, created in 1975 by the amalgamation of the old Guildhall Museum and London Museum (see figure 1.9). These were all rather special cases, because all three of their cities already had ancient and famous museums whose commitment, however, was to a national and international role, not to a local one, and the newly organized museum services were created to fill the gap which the growth of heritage concern had made obvious. From the beginning all three museums were intended to concentrate primarily on local history and archaeology.

The existing local authority museums, however, have undergone a range of reorganizations, particularly in 1974 when the three-tier structure of metropolitan counties, shire counties and districts was created, and again in 1986, when the metropolitan counties were abolished. Both schemes were intended to reflect the idea of the caring democracy, as it was seen by the government of the day, but neither showed any particular interest in museums, or archaeology, apart, perhaps, from the special arrangement made for politically explosive Liverpool in 1986, by which the old City Museum became a national museum.

In 1974 some 24 museums, like Leicester and Lincoln, were made into shire county services, but only about 19 of these have archaeological staff. The vast majority of the 100 or so local authority museums with archaeological staff are operated by district councils, like Bristol or Stoke-on-Trent. This has had far-reaching effects on the management of archaeology, partly because central government thinking has tended to centre upon a county structure which for museums has never come into being, and partly because the extremely uneven spread of museums throughout the districts of England has meant that in practice staff of a district museum have taken a degree of curatorial responsibility for archaeology in neighbouring districts which lack museum staff, a practice which may be highly desirable on academic and heritage grounds, but which is politically vulnerable.

The 1974 reorganization had a further important implication: at district level there was to be a Leisure Officer and his department. This development has been implemented in a number of ways (or not implemented at all) but in many areas, especially those with a strong tourist industry, the amalgamation of the museum into a leisure service seemed an obvious move. This has meant that the museum director is no longer a Chief Officer, and that curatorial activity, especially in the broad history field, may well be judged by the extent to which it is geared to popular consumption, a trend which the development of the privatization philosophy will presumably encourage.

Within all this, a very significant development has been the great increase of archaeological staff in the local authority museums. In 1950 the numbers of trained archaeologists were negligible. The 1950s saw a thin but steady recruitment, so that by 1962 the 55 museums consulted in a survey carried out in 1972 had 51 archaeologists on their staff, or roughly one each. By 1967 this had risen to 73, a 43 per cent increase, and by 1972 it had risen to 88, a further 21 per cent increase (Pearce 1974). This limited sample gives a clear idea of the trend, which has continued strongly in the last eighteen years, so that the 100 or so local authority museums with substantial archaeological responsibilities now employ about 280 archaeologists in fully established posts, and to these can be added a further 50 or so in national, university and independent museums. Comparative figures are difficult, but this body must constitute a considerable proportion of the working archaeologists in the country.

The figures do, however, conceal a rather mixed picture. They include the whole range of archaeological expertise, but as figure 2.1 shows, there is a very uneven distribution. About half the sampled museums have only one curator, and very few have more than four. Similarly, less than a quarter have specialized excavation and conservation staff, and very few have other staff with directly archaeological responsibilities. In fact, one, or at the most two, curators is the norm, and the additional staff, curatorial and other, are concentrated in those museums like Southampton, Museum of London and Leicestershire which manage large field operations. Moreover, the single curators are usually responsible in their museum services for a range of collections, which as figure 2.2 shows, extend well beyond the scope of British archaeology, and some of these additional collections are large and important.

To these established staff must, of course, be added those who have been employed on a temporary basis under one or another of the central government job creation schemes. It is generally accepted that, whatever the rights and wrongs may be, the employment of personnel under the schemes operated since 1974 by the Manpower Services Commission have played a crucial role in the maintenance of an archaeology service in Britain. As far as excavation is concerned, there were a total of 1,394 places in March 1984, 1,759 in March 1986, and 1,790 in September 1986 (Crump 1987). The number of places for archaeological work in museums has been considerably less. Figure 2.3 shows the number of schemes which the museum services have employed, but the numbers of staff on these schemes differ considerably and not all of them were employed on archaeological work. Some scheme members have worked on specifically archaeological projects, like those who made up the Southampton Museum Archaeological Media Project, and many other individuals have taken part in general museum schemes where they have worked with an archaeology curator. A significant proportion of

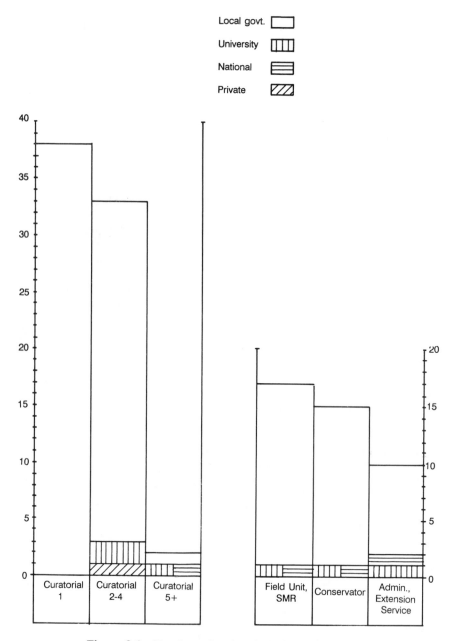

Figure 2.1   Numbers of archaeological museum staff

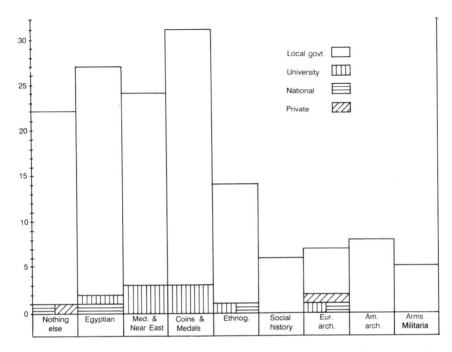

Figure 2.2 Collections for which curators of British archaeology are also responsible

the museums had no schemes at all, either as a result of union embargoes or because they were felt to be inappropriate.

The nature of the schemes has changed regularly, and in recent years the stress has been on part-time employment, and, of course, there have been limitations on the area from which unemployed people might be recruited on to a scheme, and on those who were eligible (Drake and Fahy 1987). In some parts of the country these limitations raised considerable problems, which have resulted in the recruitment of poorly motivated and educationally ill-equipped people, but elsewhere the schemes have been successful from the museums' point of view because the team members have been drawn from the pool of young volunteers. Frequently, a person has started on a project as a volunteer, continued with it as a team member, and then stayed on to finish the job after the scheme has ended. Since experience as a volunteer/team member is now a recognized asset in the search for more permanent employment, this system has often worked to the advantage of the young graduate in what is, inevitably, a very difficult employment situation. Where the schemes have worked well, they have interacted with the volunteers, the museum service and the general public to the benefit of all. In September 1988 the MSC activities ceased, to be replaced by Employment Training. At the time of writing it is not clear how this will work out, but the signs are that museums may find it difficult to benefit from the new arrangements.

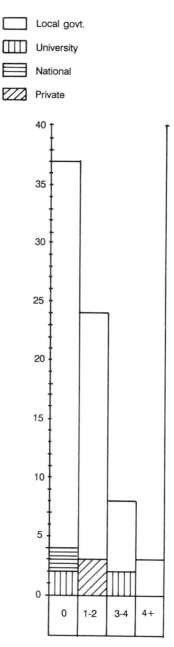

Figure 2.3   Numbers of Manpower Commission Schemes, 1985–7

The new museum appointments of the 1960s were made as a general response to early pressures of the heritage movement, but the greater and more recent increase in staff has been as a specific response to the needs of rescue archaeology, and it is to these developments that we must now turn. The discussion earlier in this chapter identified three areas of activity which crystallized from the whole rescue movement: the organization of excavation and field work, the gathering of data and their application to planning procedures, and the curation of the archive. The actual structures which have emerged to carry out these tasks are extremely diverse, but it is possible to identify trends, and to assess the role of museums within these.

At the moment (1989) there are in England about 67 bodies receiving public funds to carry out excavations, although the numbers tend to fluctuate as a result of local marriage and divorce. To these should be added the Central Excavation Unit, a section of HBMC(E), which receives direct central funding. Of the 67, 9 are based in universities, 15 are in local authority departments, chiefly county planning departments where there is no county museum service, and 23 are in museums (figure 2.4), 3 in national museums (Manx, Guernsey and Jersey), one in a private museum (Fishbourne), 9 in county museum services, and the rest broadly in district services. The remaining 20 are independent trusts with areas of responsibility ranging from a large region, like that of the Wessex Archaeological Trust which covers Wiltshire, Hampshire and Dorset, to smaller areas like those in Kent (Davies 1986 and information from Survey).

Wales is covered by four regional units, all of which are independent trusts, and Scotland has seen excavations in Perth, Dunfermline, Dunbar, Falkirk and elsewhere, and the establishment in 1977 of a Central Excavation Unit for Scotland, but no broad network has emerged. All these units operate on a mixed funding basis, which includes a local government staff establishment where this exists and central staff funding from HBMC where it does not; excavation project money, and some field survey project money from HBMC; various grants from public and private sources; and, of course, in the past, a substantial central government input through the Manpower Services Commission.

It is immediately obvious that in England museums are now directly responsible for roughly a third of the excavation units, in spite of early desires to keep museums and units separate, although this probably amounts to rather less than a third of the excavation activity because some of the regional units work on a large scale. The figures, however, cover a very wide range of local arrangements. At one end of the scale is the Museum of London, with its Department of Urban Archaeology (DUA) and its Department of Greater London Archaeology. The DUA was founded in September 1973, the last major local unit to be created supported by the then DOE Inspectorate of Ancient Monuments, in what was then the Guildhall Museum, and it is responsible for the square mile of the City of London. The necessary complement of permanent professional staff was originally thought to be only five, but within a few years the demands of excavation and post-excavation work on some 10 or 12 sites a year showed that a core team of over

60 staff was required, and it was clear that substantial funding would be needed from the developers (Hobley 1987b).

The work of the DUA has been to a very high standard, and many of the recording and archival techniques developed there have set new goals and standards across the country. In 1983 the very uneven coverage of the London boroughs was rationalized by the creation of the Museum's department of Greater London Archaeology which, in conjunction with the Passmore Edwards Museum's Archaeology and Social History Section, is responsible for excavation in London outside the City. The two excavation units of the Museum of London have a permanent staff of about 20–30, while the Passmore Edwards has about 8, and between them the three units have over 200 contracted staff employed more or less permanently (Richardson 1988).

Next come the county museum services which operate county-wide archaeological units. In Leicestershire, for example, there are two separate museum departments, of archaeology headed by a Keeper, and of the archaeological unit headed by a Senior Field Archaeologist, with an assistant, four field officers, a Roman pottery assistant, and a fluctuating force of short contract people and volunteers. In Sheffield, following the abolition of the metropolitan counties, the South Yorkshire Archaeological Unit has been run by Sheffield Museum Service.

About ten district museums, many of which might be called the 'old city' museums since they are in authorities which lost their 'city and county' status in 1974, operate excavation teams with responsibility primarily for their own cities. The Exeter Archaeological Field Unit, which operates as a department of the City Museum, has a permanent staff of three. Similar operations are undertaken by Bristol City Museum, where the field team is part of the Archaeology Department, or, rather more loosely, at Cirencester where the Curator of the Corinium Museum is the Hon. Secretary of the Cirencester Excavation Committee. At the smallest end of the scale are the museums where the one or two archaeological staff are expected to undertake both curatorial and excavation duties, which they do often very successfully, but with a considerable sense of strain. In all these museums, the resulting archive becomes a curatorial responsibility.

Those museum services which do not operate units (of whatever size) of their own normally have a close relationship with the local field unit. As figure 2.4 shows, this unit may belong with a neighbouring local authority or museum, it may be with a university, or it may be an independent body. A few museums, also, have worked with the Central Excavation Units in England and Scotland, and with the Welsh units. Sometimes a single museum may work with a range of excavating bodies, as local circumstances dictate. Normally, the museum concerned will eventually receive the archive which the unit generates, and the haphazard arrangements of the past are gradually being improved.

In most places, again, whether or not they are actively involved in running a field operation, the museum staff have a place on the local rescue archaeological committee (figure 2.4), often on more than one such committee. These committees are sometimes concerned with a city area, and

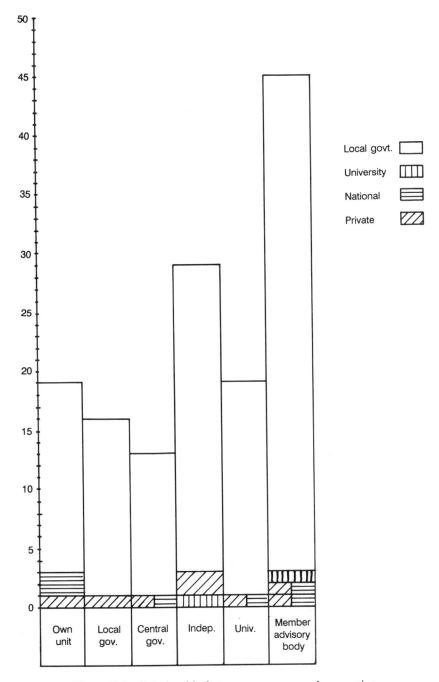

Figure 2.4 Relationship between museums and excavation

sometimes with a county or a national park (as Exmoor, for example), or a number of counties, and they are intended to bring together representatives of all the various interests involved. Their formal function is usually purely advisory, but they do provide a forum within which issues can be raised and projects monitored through their various stages. There is no denying that in their early days these committees were characterized by some bitter exchanges and personal differences, but time has softened some of these and now many of them do manage to provide a meeting-place where strategies can be co-ordinated, although this is never easy.

A surprisingly large proportion of the sampled museums are organizing field work (figure 2.5), often on the basis of local amateur field walking groups (see Chapter 12). This work frequently leads to the identification of new sites, often sites at risk, and so complements the role of the excavation units. It also helps to provide better information about the density and range of activity through the past, information which is usually fed into the Sites and Monuments Register.

In some museum services, conspicuously the big county services like Leicester, Oxfordshire, or Lincoln, the museum runs the Register for the whole county. More usually, the County Register is housed and run within a county planning department as in Devon, Dorset and Chester, although there are some aberrations, as in Wiltshire where it is held by the county library and museum service or Cornwall where it is still (1989) operated by an independent rescue archaeology committee. In addition to this, some twenty non-county museums are running Registers which relate to their own districts or areas. These sometimes form part of a physically fragmented county cover and more usually run in parallel to the county service. These arrangements have grown as a result of past history, and, in any case, it is extremely useful for a museum to have easy access to its local records. In the islands of Man, Guernsey and Jersey the records are run by the museum services. Relationships between museums and Registers seem in general to be very good and close, with the museums giving in data originating from field work, public enquiries and collection work, and receiving helpful information in return (figure 2.6).

This broad involvement in fieldwork and in the operation of data Registers means that a large proportion of the museum services have some input into planning procedures (figure 2.7). This normally takes the form of supplying information to a planning department when an application for local development has been received, but curators are sometimes drawn into full-scale planning enquiries, with all that this implies.

The curation of the archive, the third major area to emerge from the rescue process, is now, following the Frere and Dimbleby Reports, universally regarded as the responsibility of museum services, and the principle of the need for appropriate provision has been accepted. This has been of the very first importance, and much thinking has and is being devoted to developing all aspects of archive curation, including the political and other skills required in managing collection policies, documentation, and conservation and storage, topics which are considered in Chapters 5–8. The important point to stress here is the intimate relationship which the archive bears to

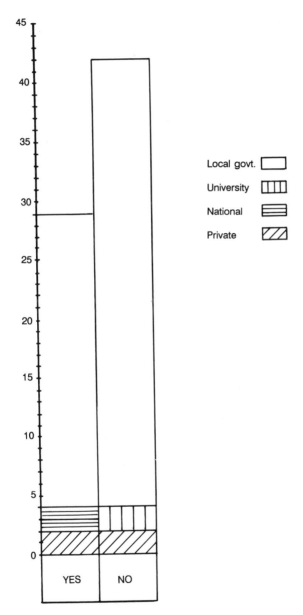

Figure 2.5 Relationship between museums and fieldwork: Do you organize field-work?

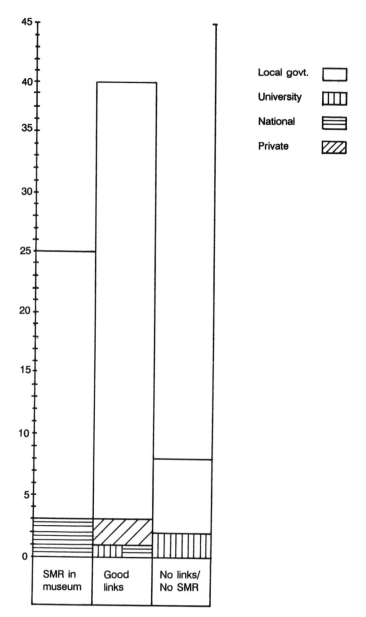

Figure 2.6 Relationship between museums and Sites and Monuments Registers

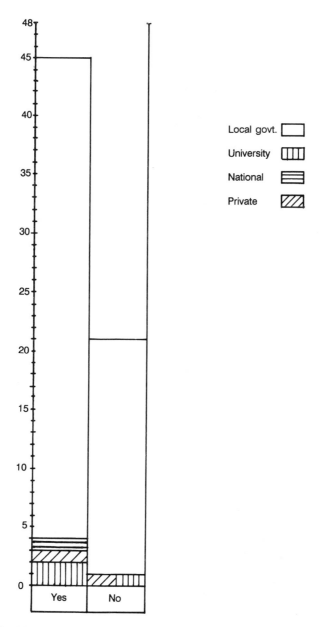

Figure 2.7   Museum involvement in planning procedures: are you involved in planning procedures?

strategic archaeological planning in each area, and the consequent need to integrate museum and other aspects of the work as comprehensively as possible in broad terms and from the beginning in each individual project. In many places, this integration is still no more than an ideal, but it remains the sensible and desirable course.

In spite of past confusions and present diversity, then, a picture of museum involvement in field archaeology does emerge. Museums care for the archive; they have a good mutual relationship with Register data-banks; and they operate about a third of the grant-receiving excavation units. In addition to this, although more difficult to quantify, they play a leading part in organizing amateur groups, under various umbrellas, in fieldworking and survey projects. All of this now probably adds up to a greater input into rescue archaeology than any other single kind of organization, although this is not said with any intent to belittle the operations of other branches of local government, of the independent unit sector, or of universities. Equally, it is not said with any complacency, but in full recognition of the difficulties some museums and their staffs face in their particular circumstances.

Nicholas Thomas (1986) reflecting upon the tangled history of recent years, voiced the feelings of many curators when he said that the 'decision taken a decade or so ago to house units outside museums . . . was a mistake'. Nor has the breach between 'archaeologists' and 'museum archaeologists' entirely been healed, even though the two groups are now considerably closer. The development towards a broadly-based archaeological service might have been simpler and less wasteful, and would certainly have been less acrimonious, if the potential of museums, perhaps in conjunction with planning departments, had been recognized earlier. Nevertheless, many sensible local arrangements have been worked out, and the present climate of ruthless realism will encourage others, so that much good work is being done.

In terms of the broader heritage movement, museums now have more archaeological staff, and these are better equipped academically and professionally. They, and their governing bodies, have a greater sense of their responsibilities, both to archaeology and to their public, which may be expressed through collecting policies, exhibitions and presentations of all kinds, through education in the more formal sense, and through the development of community archaeology. Facile optimism would be out of place, and undoubtedly difficult negotiations and decisions lie ahead, particularly in areas like the relationship between multiple funding and privatization, and the maintenance of quality services, but archaeologists in museums are now making good their role in their own communities, to a greater degree than has ever been achieved before.

3. Archaeology, museums and the law

Background

The legislation concerned with the historic heritage is extremely complex, both in its legal forms and in the ways in which these are put into practice. These problems are by no means limited to Britain, but for various historical reasons they are often particularly acute here, not least in the fact that the various arrangements are organized slightly differently in England and Wales, Scotland, and Northern Ireland (for a major international study of all aspects of the law protecting the cultural heritage see O'Keefe and Prott 1984 and the further volumes planned in that series, and also Cleere 1984).

Three important points must be stressed at the outset. Firstly, archaeology does not command the public concern which alone could make it become a matter of serious political calculation, and therefore, like all similar areas, the law and practice governing archaeology is geared to a mixture of broad political commitments and archaeological needs, in which, on the whole, archaeology always takes second place. Secondly, law and practice has grown up piecemeal, usually in response to specific pressures, so that the various elements are not in step, and, like all law, tend to represent opinion as it was, rather than as it is. Thirdly, in general at present, the law in England and Wales does not concern itself specifically with archaeological artefacts or historical material; these are simply subject to the normal laws governing movable property. Rather better legal arrangements apply in the other parts of the United Kingdom.

This is not the place to discuss in detail the legal and administrative arrangements for archaeology in the United Kingdom (see Baker 1983). The National Heritage Act of 1983 created the Historic Buildings and Monuments Commission (HBMC) usually known as English Heritage, which is intended to implement all the previous protective legislation regarding scheduled monuments, guardianship sites and historic buildings; it also operates the central government rescue archaeology budget and has an important presentation role. In Scotland these responsibilities are taken by the HBMC(S) and in Wales by Cadw. 'Scheduling' means that the site is recognized as nationally important, and that any alteration or damage to it constitutes an offence at law, unless 'scheduled monument consent' has been gained. The Ancient Monuments and Archaeological Areas Act of 1979 added to this concept that of 'areas of archaeological importance' for the purposes of rescue investigation in advance of development. The same 1979 Act also prohibited the use of metal detectors on scheduled sites or areas of archaeological importance, without permission.

The Royal Commission on the Historical Monuments of England is responsible for record-making and maintains holdings of archaeological data, architectural records and air photographs, an archive of unique value. Its sister body performs a similar role in Scotland. This whole framework is intended to gather information and to protect archaeological sites. It has a number of weaknesses, which are touched upon later in this chapter. Meanwhile, we must turn to the law regarding ancient artefacts, which has a significant bearing on museum operation.

Portable antiquities

As has already been said, the present English law does not, in general, pay any particular attention to historic artefacts, usually known as portable antiquities, but there are some exceptions and the most important of these is the legislation relating to Treasure Trove in England and Wales, with its equivalents elsewhere, and Wreck, together with some measures which relate to church property. (British antiquities only are considered here. Exotic objects now in British museums are discussed in Chapter 5.)

In English law the ownership of objects found on a property belong to the owner of the land or of the building in which they were found, unless the property was a scheduled ancient monument, or a designated Area of Archaeological importance. There is, however, one exception to this rule, and this is the concept of Treasure Trove (from the Old French *trouver*, 'to find'), which is concerned with objects of gold and silver. The whole proceeding, with its medieval origins, its concern with exciting artefacts, and its romantic associations with treasure is highly picturesque and can be relied upon to attract the attention of the local media. It is unlikely to arise often in a curator's working life, but most curators do have to deal with it at one time or another. The concept of treasure trove says that objects of gold and silver deliberately concealed by an untraceable owner with intent to recover are the property of the Crown: such objects are said to be treasure trove. Objects which are considered to have been either lost or deliberately abandoned become the property of the finder. In any case, no award is made to the owner of the land.

The responsibility for deciding whether or not finds are trove in this sense rests with the local coroner, and generally hoards of coins, silver or gold plate, or later prehistoric gold work are held to be trove, while metalwork buried with the dead is considered to have been abandoned without intent to recover, and single pieces are considered to have been lost. Objects which have been found to be trove may be acquired by the British Museum for the national collection if this is thought desirable, and in this case, since 1929, the finder has been paid an *ex gratia* payment of the market value of the material. If the objects are not wanted for the national collection, they may be acquired by a provincial museum who must make a similar *ex gratia* payment. If no museum wishes to have them, or the necessary payment cannot be raised, the objects revert to the finder, who may then sell them on the open market.

The finder of the gold or silver objects is legally obliged to report his find to an appropriate authority, so it often happens that the curator is the first person in an official position to be approached by somebody who has found such archaeological material, and it is essential that he takes an attitude which is both tactful and correct. The finder is often on the defensive, anxious and confused about his rights and yet worried about putting himself on the wrong side of the law, and frequently with a highly inflated idea of the value of his coin hoard or other find. He, quite rightly, looks to a curator to provide accurate information about what he should do, and trusts him to act as an honest broker (otherwise he will not have come to the museum in the first place).

The curator must explain the law and its procedures as clearly and calmly as possible and give cautious advice about the likely outcome in the particular case. He must make it clear that he will ensure that the police are informed of the find, and that the police will wish to have custody of the objects (or object) until the inquest has reached its verdict. If the objects are declared to be trove and they are required for the national collection, then the responsibility passes to the British Museum. If, however, they are granted to the finder, or the British Museum does not want them, the curator who originally saw them is likely to be involved in negotiations concerning their future. Discussions of this kind are often delicate, and an atmosphere of goodwill developed from the beginning is extremely helpful.

The law operates in rather different ways in particular areas of the United Kingdom. Franchises to profit from the process have been granted by the Crown to the Duchies of Cornwall and Lancaster and the Cities of London and Bristol, although these have not been fully defined. In Scotland all ownerless objects, *bona vacantia*, belong to the Crown, and so the principle of public ownership can be extended to include articles in materials other than gold or silver. This means that there are mechanisms by which all kinds of archaeological material may be acquired by museums, but otherwise the process is similar to that in England and Wales. In Manx law, any person who discovers an archaeological object is required to report it to the police within fourteen days. In Northern Ireland the Historic Monuments Act (Northern Ireland) 1971 requires the finder of any archaeological object to report the find within fourteen days to the Ulster Museum or to the police.

The English system produces many difficulties, and has been much criticized. The system means that the finder of the gold or silver objects ends up (normally) with their market value no matter how the procedure has gone, which makes a nonsense of its complexities. The payment is intended to act as an encouragement to the public to come forward with finds, although it also, of course, encourages metal-detector-using treasure-hunters. The present procedure does not make archaeological sense at any level. We have no idea in many cases what the original intentions were—a hoard of late Bronze Age gold armrings may have been a votive deposit regarded as wholly lost by its original owners, while a single Iron Age torc could have been buried with intent to recover, and in any case this kind of distinction has no archaeological value. The law only applies to gold and silver, so objects of base metal or pottery, for example, found with the treasure are treated quite separately and may end up in different places, while such objects found alone have no protection at all. In sum, at a basic legal level, the English law fails to provide a means by which all important ancient objects may (not necessarily will) find their way into publicly-owned collections, or by which they should be reported and recorded, so leaving a fundamental aspect of the national heritage unprotected.

An effort to improve the law in these general directions was embodied in the Antiquities Bill of 1983, but this aroused great hostility from the treasure-hunting lobby, and for this, and other political reasons, it was dropped. However, in January 1987 the government announced that it would undertake a review of the present arrangements for reporting important archaeological finds so that a proper record can be made of them. This resulted in the *Consultation Paper on Portable Antiquities* issued early in 1988, which was circulated to archaeological bodies for comment, with the stated objective of finding a solution which reconciles as far as possible the various conflicting interests, including those of metal detectors, and which commands general support, for the good of the heritage.

The *Consultation Paper* takes the form of a series of questions. These ask respondents to estimate the extent of the problem, to judge the adequacy of existing laws and controls and to suggest solutions. Respondents are further asked to define which finds should be reported and what form any reporting or acquisition should take, to comment on a system of rewards or fines, and to suggest how reporting arrangements might work. The paper acknowledges that new legislation will present problems of enforcement and policing. It also accepts that any new arrangements will have resource and workload implications for the 'receiving bodies', expected to be principally museums and the police. It is important to note that the paper is addressed essentially to the reporting and recording of finds: the ownership of newly-discovered ancient objects is not discussed.

Parallel to this government initiative runs that of the Law Commission who in late 1987 published a short document entitled *Treasure Trove: Law Reform Issues* (Robertson 1987a). This paper recognizes the problems presented by treasure hunting and by the escalating value of antiquities, and suggests the reform of antiquities legislation is different from, and should precede, any revision of Treasure Trove arrangements. It accepts that fundamental questions of public policy are involved, with important potential implications for the law relating to personal property, and perhaps for the criminal law also, and it recognizes that the availability of resources to enforce any new arrangements is a crucial factor. It suggests that the debate should be broadened so that, 'various specially concerned groups, including museums ... and (if an appropriate body can be identified) consumers of museum services' (p. 7, section 14) should be involved in the discussion. At a more specific level, legal authorities like Matthews are questioning whether the coroner's courts, where the bulk of the work concerns enquiry into human deaths, should have any part in the administration of Treasure Trove (Matthews 1988).

All this is adding up to a considerable pressure for reform, although when and in what form this reform will come is not clear, and past experience does not encourage optimism. In some quarters (Selkirk 1988b) the trend of the new demands for the reporting of discoveries is seen as harmful to the real purposes of archaeology because it will be extremely difficult to encourage the public to report only objects of archaeological significance rather than miscellaneous material like Victorian pennies, it will drive treasure hunters underground, make farmers and others less likely to admit to finds, and in general, create much adverse publicity. Most museum archaeologists probably sympathize with efforts to require at least the reporting of finds, but are worried about the problems of policing and of increased workloads. The way in which resources could be made available from central government to museums for the extra work which such legislation would bring has scarcely yet begun to be discussed.

Historic wrecks

The legal protection of historic wrecks and their fittings and contents is comparatively recent, and arose as a result of pressure following the great increase in sub-aqua diving and wreck hunting as a profitable sport. The Protection of Wrecks Act of 1973 enabled the Secretary of State for Trade and Industry to designate restricted areas around the sites of wrecks of more than a century old and which are in British territorial waters, on account of their historical, archaeological or artistic importance (Baker 1983:120). There is an advisory committee to review possible designations, and by 1982 twenty-seven sites had been designated, including the *Mary Rose* at Spithead, the *Colossus* off Scilly, and two Bronze Age sites, off Dover and off Moor Sands, Devon. A licence is required to work within the designated area, which is issued to named individuals who must operate under the overall direction of an archaeologist, and the finds have to receive expert conservation. Essentially, the Act controls the recovery of the material and its ownership and disposal are not affected, and although licences have sometimes been issued to *bona fide* archaeological groups, it is accepted that in some cases the material will be sold on the open market to recover diving costs and yield a profit. Needless to say, the great majority of historic wrecks do not enjoy even this limited protection.

Wrecks are also mentioned in the 1979 Act (Part III, Section 53) which states that 'a monument situated in, on or under the sea bed within ... territorial waters ... may be included within the Schedule', or, in other words, may be designated as a scheduled monument with all that this implies (*Ancient Monuments and Archaeological Areas Act*, 1979, 48–9). At present the two Acts continue in force together. In March 1984 the Department of Transport issued a consultative document *Proposals for Legislation on Marine Wrecks* which, among other proposals, suggested that museums should be given title to unclaimed wreck, which would include most material over a century old, but that they should be responsible for making appropriate payment to the salvor (that is, the divers) and that they must be able to show that they can conserve the artefacts 'in the public interest'. All this would place a heavy financial burden upon museum services around the coasts, and the document did not suggest the provision of financial assistance. In May 1989 further proposals were published by the National Maritime Museum, which draw attention to the problems museums face in accepting material from underwater sites.

Ecclesiastical property

The only other artefacts of historical importance for which special provisions exist are those which are church property. For these, as for all ecclesiastical matters, separate and highly complex provisions are in force, and a useful overview of all archaeological problems relating to churches has been published by Rodwell (1981). If a curator becomes involved in affairs concerned with church artefacts, his best course is to approach the Council for British Archaeology who maintain a network of Diocesan Archaeological Consultants, and these will be able to give advice.

Implications

Two crucial areas of concern are apparent in all this: the protection of ancient monuments and landscapes, and the protection of ancient artefacts, both of which are valued partly for their intrinsic interest and beauty, and partly for the contribution which they can all make towards our understanding of our past. In the United Kingdom generally, the existing law is weak in the protection which it offers to field monuments because it depends upon the scheduling process which is very selective, and it is weakly applied in the courts with, usually, trifling penalties for transgression. The Royal Commission's national archaeological archive, and other registers, contains a huge body of information, but it has proved difficult to co-ordinate this with the mechanisms of law and practice. In practical terms, the national system is grossly under-funded and under-staffed, and the way in which the various elements are split between several organizations makes sensible, concerted planning more difficult.

There are few statutory links between the archaeological legislation and the local authorities, and if curators are brought into matters involving scheduling or site damage (other than the removal of objects), this is normally in an advisory role only. The county planning departments, who have the great advantage of good local knowledge, are empowered to manage and interpret monuments, carry out excavation and recording through planning conditions and agreements, and to run Sites and Monuments Registers. The members of the Association of County Archaeological Officers are likely to be a good source of information and advice for museum staff. It may be that the way forward in monument protection which offers the best chance of success is as much through development of the existing county authority role as it is through new archaeological legislation.

English law does not recognize any particular significance in ancient artefacts, other than those of precious metal, and providing treasure hunters are not operating on a site protected under the 1979 Act and that they have gained permission from the owner of the land where this is appropriate, there is no legal reason why they should not dig artefacts up and either retain them or sell them, without any obligation to report the find. The same, of course, applies to those who discover objects in the course of their normal daily activities. Elsewhere in the United Kingdom there is a clearer obligation to make a report, but even in these areas the mechanisms for reporting are fragile.

Several separate issues are involved. Firstly, there is the danger of damage to an ancient site. The procedures discussed above are intended to prevent site damage, but, as we have seen, they are woefully inadequate. Secondly, there is the loss of information which results from separating object and context, whether this has happened deliberately by treasure hunting or accidentally in the course of development or deep ploughing, and thirdly, there is the potential loss to archaeology of any knowledge of the object itself. The obligation to report finds would help to minimize the information loss, and it would, of course, enable the object itself to be properly recorded. At the heart of the problem lies the tension between, on the one hand, the desirability of creating a proper record and, on the other, the huge problems posed in enabling and enforcing such a procedure, and the hostility which it would arouse.

Museums, who hold the comparable material and who already, usually, operate some form of enquiry service are the obvious organizations to take responsibility for making the records, but any such system would require new resources and would again highlight the uneven distribution of museums capable of even contemplating such an addition to their responsibilities. None the less, an obligation to report finds either to a museum or to the police who would then themselves contact a museum, would be an important move in the process which is, very gradually, bringing archaeological museums into a national network of obligation and provision, and this, on balance, must be a good thing.

Finally, there is the issue of ownership. The acquisition of material by museums is further discussed in Chapter 5, and suffice to say there that the problem presented by newly found portable antiquities can be solved only by either new law which makes all such finds public property, which is very unlikely because it would infringe the cherished principle of private ownership and drive much activity underground, or by making available to museums considerable funds earmarked for such purchases.

Progress in this whole exceptionally difficult area is likely to be made not by a single sweep, legal or otherwise, but through a combination of carefully considered efforts. This kind of approach stands a better chance of furthering archaeological knowledge than pressure on the part of the archaeological community for a flat condemnation of metal-detecting activities (for which see further Chapter 9). An improved national policy, whether legal or through agreed guidelines, embodied in a code of practice and a system of rewards, would help to create a better framework, within which individual curators could work with local organizations and individuals. Perfection will not come about; but improvement may.

4. Ethics and politics

Contemporary attitudes

The ethical basis of archaeological operation, in general and in the museum, is a large and complex subject, and provokes a number of initial thoughts which are to be regarded not as a hierarchy, but rather as a network. A fundamental point revolves around the proposition that ethics and politics are, today more than ever, seen as essentially the same thing: ethics can be regarded as the set of favoured philosophical principles, and politics as the working-out of these principles in social life and daily action. The whole process can be described as ideological, a word to which we shall return. It is, of course, true that the ethical principles and political actions working in archaeology today have developed as a result of the history of the past century or so, the museum and collecting aspects of which have been traced in the first two chapters. Archaeology has been studied, and collections formed, almost exclusively by the upper and middle classes who were educated in the English tradition of Christian liberal humanism, heavily tempered by a strong and conservative attachment to parish, county and country, and who were characterized by a complete confidence in the rightness of their views and actions.

Post-war thinking has tried to stand back from received tradition, and has come to two concepts which are important here, and which have already arisen in discussion of historical research and theoretical archaeology. The first is that no study in the humanities (and probably in the sciences also) is objectively pure and free from bias or subjective distortion; archaeological work, like all other, arises from its past, and is not divorced from the realm of political, social relationships (Pratap and Rao 1986; Trigger and Glover 1981). It follows that all archaeological projects, whether they are collecting and archiving policies or exhibition and other interpretative work, have ethical and political content, whether we like it or not, and whether we intend it or not.

The second turns on the conviction that the range of social systems which the world has produced, with all the emotional and economic networks that these involve, are equally valid and legitimate in their own terms. To discriminate between them by making 'value judgments' which, for example, exalt the Western tradition above others, is untenable, because no system can be *shown* to be superior, and because such an approach discredits fundamental beliefs about human equality. This conviction, unfortunately, is simplistic and presents dangerous flaws and superficialities, which begin with the spectre of Nazi Germany and continue with that of some contemporary states as measured against the self-same Western humanist tradition; but in general terms, the principle of equal legitimacy today commands considerable respect and support. This has far-reaching consequences for the collecting and interpreting of all historical material, from the British Isles and beyond.

There are probably as many definitions of 'ideology' and of what constitutes an 'ideological stance' as there are people who use these words. 'Ideology' may be described as a way of looking at societies, past and present, and seeing a pattern in which the relationships between facts are more important than the facts themselves, and of recognizing values in these relationships which reflect their perceived role in the exercise and maintenance of power and subjection. For archaeology (and related subjects like social history and ethnography) in museums, therefore, this approach involves a recognition that those parts of the past pattern of relationships, which have remained obscure because they were not seen as a significant part of the history of a dominant group, should be a focus of attention in their own right. It requires an acceptance of the responsibility that the production of knowledge about the past is very important for the present and the future because it helps to legitimize roles and create change. These ideas link up with points made previously about contradictions inherent in the attribution of absolute value to all human communities, and the subjective nature of all historical interpretation, our own as well as that of our predecessors.

Issues like these are very much with us in archaeology today. Many of them crystallized out around the protracted and contentious history of the World Archaeology Congress held at Southampton in 1986 (Ucko 1987, and The World Archaeological Congress, *Archaeological 'Objectivity' in Interpretation*, Vols I–III, 1986). They have been the subject of two issues of *World Archaeology* (No. 13, parts 2 and 3) and one of *Archaeological Review from Cambridge* (Spring 1986), and they were the topic for the 1984 Young Archaeologists Conference, some of the papers from which were published by York University (Dobinson and Gilchrist 1986). They were canvassed again at the Durham meeting (1982) of the Theoretical Archaeology Group, and *Bias in Museums* was chosen by the Museum Professionals Group for their 1986 Annual Study Weekend (Carruthers 1987). A transatlantic view, which concentrates upon ethics and values in archaeology from an essentially professional standpoint is provided by the papers gathered together by Green (1984). The effect of all this has been a marked degree of consciousness raising. Museum curators have come to recognize that, particularly in terms of their own local community, they are at the sharp end of many of these issues, because the conservation, communication and interpretation of the past to a wider world is a major part of the curator's role.

Multi-culturalism, ethnicity and elites

We may now identify some specific themes and areas. A large theme revolves around multi-culturalism and ethnicity, that is an understanding of what conceptions, and misconceptions, have gone into ideas about being 'English' or 'British', or 'Polish' or 'Nigerian', and how the various cultural traditions can be perceived. Behind the powerful feelings which questions of personal identities arouse, stand ancient confusions which cluster around words like 'culture', 'ethnicity', and 'a people', and the relationship of these to cultural manifestations like language and religion.

In the early part of this century Gordon Childe defined a culture as 'a constantly recurring assemblage of artefacts' which could be recognized in the archaeological record, and he usually wrote as if the humans who used these artefacts thereby constituted 'a people', an ethnic group. Today an ethnic group would mean a group of people who recognize themselves as distinct, who have their own name for themselves, and who can point to a particular complex of artefacts, customs and language—that is culture—as the precious mark of their distinctiveness. It is important to note that this has nothing to do with 'race', in whatever quasi-biological fashion this may be conceived, and nor does it necessarily relate to political organization, although it may do so. Similarly, the same language and the same religion may be shared by people who do not regard themselves as the same. Moreover, ethnicity may be a matter of degree, because some groups or individuals may 'belong' more positively than others (Renfrew 1987: 214–18).

The difficult legacy of the past, for museums as for the community in general, has been the extent to which those ethnic groups which have produced 'high culture' often associated with political power, have been privileged over those which apparently have not. Ethnography curators at Birmingham, Bradford, Leicester and elsewhere are giving much attention to the redressing of these balances, especially to those involving relationships between the Western World and the Third and Fourth Worlds. Throughout North and South America, and in Australia and other parts of the Pacific, archaeologists have had to reassess their relationships with the local indigenous peoples, particularly in areas like access to land, the survey and excavation of sacred sites, and the curation and study of collected material, old and new, whether obviously 'sacred' or not. Burial grounds and human remains are often the flashpoint from which a range of issues arise (see, for examples drawn from a now extensive literature, Ucko 1986; Cheek and Keel 1984; Zimmerman 1986; Ferguson 1984; Adams 1984).

Most British archaeological material belongs too far back in the past to arouse similar political passions, although after the experience of the 'Mary Rose' excavation, where the human bodies were relatively recent and exceptionally well documented, curators would think more carefully now than once about the curation and display of human skeletons. Among museum archaeologists in Britain these issues arise in their most acute form in the question of the repatriation of archaeological finds, especially those like the Parthenon Marbles, which are part of 'high culture' seen as the self-identity of their people of origin. The fallacies surrounding superficial and prejudiced views about what constitutes ethnicity can, however, be transferred back into the past. Merriman (1987) has shown how the typical view of 'the Celts' as heroic and dynamic derives from a classical view of 'barbarians' and a modern romantic view of 'noble savages' and that we need a more self-critical view of Celtic values and motives.

Further pressures, acute sometimes in North America, which arise from strongly-held anti-scientific views about the theory of evolution, the origins of mankind, or the nature of the earth and of the cosmos, and which often include racialist elements, can create problems for curators who are anxious to transmit in their displays the received scientific truths of the day; but mercifully these kinds of difficulties do not seem very likely, at the moment, to develop in the United Kingdom. Much more serious here is the large area of concern which revolves around the interpretation and presentation of the nature of the class system in history, the past of working people, the development and maintenance of social elites, and the operation of warfare, questions which are linked with issues like ethnicity and multi-culturalism because ethnic ideas have often been used to justify and bolster the position of white middle-class elites, and have provided routes through which working-class people may aspire to join them.

As Durrans (1986) has pointed out, modern archaeology is a product of the capitalist system, and its interpretative modes tend to reflect these origins, creating all kinds of problematic biases in our views about the nature of work and the relationship of different groups in the past, particularly the pre-industrial past. Archaeology exhibitions certainly do give greater prominance to past elites, chiefly, of course, because elites leave more in the way of eye-catching material culture, and they do tend to glorify the pursuit of war by highlighting weapons of all periods. More insidiously, perhaps, they also tend to offer a progressive view of the past, with the suggestion that Roman Britain was 'better' than prehistory, with more space given to villas than to slaves, and that the high Middle Ages were 'preferable' to the Dark Ages. Every interpretation is arguable, and the important point is that curators are now aware that they are participants in the debate.

Gender bias

Gender bias or 'sexism' is another large and difficult area which is attracting a steady flow of discussion and publication (see for example Conkey and Spector 1984, and the whole issue of *Archaeological Review from Cambridge*, 1988, 1, which is devoted to the subject, and references there). In archaeology, it tends to revolve around the study of women in the past and the problems of finding an acceptable methodology through which past women can be studied, and the effort to break down automatic assumptions about roles and about the interpretation of evidence. This is coupled with an all-pervading conviction that the value attributed to women's lives and so to these studies is the central core of the problem.

In 1972 Edwin Ardener was able to write, 'The problem of women has not been solved by social anthropologists. ... At the level of "observation" the behaviour of women has been exhaustively plotted ... when we come to the second or 'meta' level of debate ... there is a real imbalance. We are, for practical purposes, in a male world. The study of women is on a level little higher than the study of the ducks and fowls they commonly own—a mere bird-watching indeed' (1972: 134–5). He concludes that this is because in a fundamental sense women do not fit into the male-generated models of society with which anthropologists, sociologists and archaeologists are accustomed to work. The problem of the 'anthropology of knowledge' and its application to hunter-gatherer societies, especially those of the Palaeolithic, was returned to by Slocum (1975), and both writers note that the work produced by (professionally successful) women archaeologists and anthropologists is little different from that produced by their male colleagues, although Gimbutas' (1982) analysis of 'Old Europe' in the fifth millennium BC and Moore's (1986) work on space, text and gender are interesting exceptions.

The problem from a specifically museum point of view has recently been thoroughly discussed by Jones and Pay (1986) who, in a paper entitled 'The legacy of Eve' consider the interpretation of women's past experience with reference to current research practice and the presentation of the past to the public. They argue that, 'current archaeological theory and methodology and museum practice reflects contemporary values and notions relating to gender which prevent an understanding of women's roles in past societies', and they try to suggest alternative strategies towards a fuller exploration of the representation of women in the archaeological record. They suggest a number of areas in which archaeologists should interest themselves, and these include the value given to certain tasks, the division of labour, the study of symbols in which women can be seen as active in the production of cultural forms, funerary evidence, and the appropriation of power through social relations.

They agree that museums faithfully reflect the androcentric bias within society as a whole, and quote Horne's recent survey of European museums (1984) with its conclusion that, 'with exceptions such as the Virgin Mary, or Joan of Arc, women are simply not there' and that the museums on the tourist itinerary serve only to reinforce the dominant values in public culture, notably, 'the continuing legitimization of male authority'. This is well shown in the concept of the family in the past, especially in displays like those in Jewry Wall Museum, Leicester, with its sequence of nuclear family tableaux from the mesolithic to Anglo-Saxon, 'in which each adult male clutches his symbol of power and authority and each adult female anxiously watches over a small child' (Jones and Pay 1986). These displays are retained primarily because the families reflect our own, and are therefore easy to understand and so comfortable and unchallenging to the visitor. The same kinds of criticism can be applied to the representation of women at Jorvik, and, of course, the same objections arise in the male-based language used in labels and guide-books.

If stating the theory and framing the methodology is difficult, how much more difficult it is to put these ideas into practice in actual research or display is shown by recent attempts. Shennan's analysis of social organization in the Branc cemetery (1975) raised a range of questions about the meaning of wealthy female burials and Pierpoint's discussion of the Yorkshire barrows (1981) produced similar problems. Hodder (1982) has suggested that decorative styles can symbolize women's independence and the notion of 'contextual archaeology' (Barrett 1987) may, when it is more completely worked out, provide a fuller and more legitimate frame of reference, which in turn would affect the way in which the past is presented and displayed.

Jones and Pay (1986) suggest that women's work could be tackled in displays, and at Southampton they have highlighted medieval business-women in the exhibition, and experimented with graphics showing prehis-toric women knapping flints (debatable though this idea may be). Gail Durbin at Norwich has, in conjunction with the Open University, produced *Womens' Work and Leisure: A guide to the Stranger's Hall and Bridewell Museum* (1983) which gives a perspective of female domestic experience from the sixteenth century onwards, and at the British Museum Vanags has used educational work sheets centring on images shown in black and red figure wares to explore the roles of women in Greek society. The founding of *Women, Heritage and Museums* (WHAM) in 1984 and of a Women's Group with *Archaeologists Communicate, Transform* (ACT) provide a forum for the inter-change of ideas.

Political pressures

Curatorial awareness of all these essentially interlinked issues has, ironically, developed at a time when related pressures may have the effect of limiting curatorial choice of interpretation. Museums, like all cultural enterprises, are now being encouraged to seek sponsorship from the business world, for exhibitions and excavations. At the material level, as in the Lloyds Bank sponsorship of the *Age of Chivalry* exhibition at the Royal Academy in 1987–8, this approach can be very successful, although its translation to smaller ventures is more problematic. In any case, there is no reason to suppose that it will necessarily pose any major moral or ethical problems, provided that the chosen topics are fully and realistically discussed, and that commercial sponsorship remains only one source of funding, although the profession will naturally bear the potential difficulties in mind.

More serious are the views which are beginning to be expressed by some governing bodies, especially local authorities. Edinburgh District Council took the decision to mount two controversial exhibitions, *Not Just Tea and Sandwiches* and *No Easy Walk to Freedom*, which raised questions about the political bias, or political pressure, exercised by Edinburgh's then Labour administration. The then Chair of the Recreation Committee responsible for Museums, Mark Lazarowicz, when invited to speak at a Museum Professio-nals Group meeting, quoted the leader of Walsall Metropolitan Borough Council who said, 'The council will *not* tolerate any action by any officer designed to hinder or frustrate any of its policies. We expect to be advised not led, we expect to be supported not hindered, we expect above all loyalty to the political will of the council'. He stated that this statement encapsulated his view of the fundamental relationship between a local authority and any of its staff, including museum staff (1987: 16). He added that legal responsibil-ity and governing power for a local authority museum is vested in the Council and, 'if the Council decides that an exhibition will be organized to show the contribution trades unions have made to a particular area, . . . then that is what should be done'. Similarly, operating principles based upon a code of practice are only valid if that local authority . . . has chosen to accept such a code' (1987: 16–17).

In Lazarowicz's view, once this right relationship between council and curators is accepted, the museum will reap many public and political benefits. Many curators will find this line of argument distasteful, but, providing always that the information presented is factually accurate, it probably represents the legal position fairly enough. The danger lies in the possibility of undue or improper political pressure in the area of interpretation of facts, and, with a militant council, this might be difficult to withstand. Such difficulties arise not only over exhibitions and publications, but also over issues like planning enquiries, often here with quite moderate councils, where the moral dilemmas can be very painful.

Codes of practice

Lazarowicz referred in his paper to codes of practice, and it is to these that the final part of this discussion must turn. The definition and general acceptance by practitioners of a code of ethics and practice is one of the hallmarks of a profession, in that, among other things, it plays a considerable role in defining a corporate body and corporate views, and helps to create a kind of professional solidarity which is intended to protect both the profession and its public. It comes as no surprise, therefore, to realize that there is not in Britain any code which is intended to be applicable to all archaeologists, nor is there a code intended specifically for museum archaeologists. There is the Museum Association Code of Ethics (Thompson *et al.* 1984: 530–40) which is intended for all museum staff, and there is the relatively recent Institute of Field Archaeologists *Code of Conduct* which is intended for that Institute's members, who are chiefly excavators. The Society for Museum Archaeologists issued a statement describing its aims, objectives and activities, but this is not conceived as a formal code.

The situation in the United States is very different, perhaps because free-market professionals of all kinds are more common there, and because there the ethical strains already discussed have a longer and more acute history. The Society for American Archaeology, which includes amateurs and professionals, and is a little like the Council for British Archaeology, issued its *Four Statements for Archaeology* covering the scope of archaeology, its methods, its ethics and recommended training in 1961 (Champe 1961: 137–8). The ethics statement says that collections and data inside and outside museums should be available to *bona fide* students, that buying and selling is censured because it leads to loss of data, and that wilful destruction, distortion or concealment of data is also censured. In very general terms, this broad line has been followed by a number of state archaeological societies, including those of California and Texas.

In 1976 the Society of Professional Archaeologists (SOPA) was formed and in the same year it issued a Code of Ethics, and Standards of Research

Performance and Disciplinary Procedures (Davies H. 1984). This valuable statement is not as well known in Britain as it deserves to be. The thrust of SOPA's thinking is to define archaeological ethics in terms of a three-fold responsibility, to the public, to fellow professionals and to employers or clients. It offers guidelines in most of the areas which have been discussed here and a range of others, and probably would be regarded as a broadly sensible position statement by most professional archaeologists working in Great Britain today. The Institute of Field Archaeologists drew on it when designing their own Code, but it is a pity that that Institute was so narrowly conceived in the first instance, and does not, like the American organization, embrace all professional archaeologists.

The Society of Museum Archaeologists is organized rather as a pressure group intended to improve standards generally in the light of current professional practices, and its objective is 'to promote active museum involvement in all aspects of archaeology and to emphasize the essential role of museums within the archaeological discipline'. This role is extremely important, but it is not, of course, incompatible with the framing of a Code of Ethics and Practice, and this is perhaps an activity to which the Society may turn.

Ethical codes are fallible creations which need to be kept up-to-date, and they do not, needless to say, solve the difficult problems which come up in the course of daily work and which are beginning to be documented in a body of case literature (for example Green 1984). They do, however, produce guidelines which try to bridge the gap between broad ethical positions and professional realities and needs in a political world, and they can give support to a professional faced with a particular problem. Their potential, in a world where cultural values are supported primarily by moral pressure and with increasing difficulty, should not be underrated.

Part two.   Curating the archive

5. The formation of the museum archive

Introduction

The title of Part two, *Curating the archive*, represents the two crucial aspects of collection management, and collection management itself is at the heart of the museum operation, because without collections there would be no broader issues of context and interpretation. The archive and its curation are the twin faces of what is essentially a continuous process, and it is the nature and the operation of this process which these four chapters try to explore.

'The archive' was a term brought into prominence by its use in the Frere Report (*Principles of Publication in Rescue Archaeology*, 1975) where it meant the whole product of excavation organized in an accessible form, which rendered it capable of critical re-examination. The archive was seen as the prime information source, and the form of final publication correspondingly less significant. The background to the archive concept lay in the enormous increase in excavation which the Rescue movement had stimulated, linked with a general refining of recording systems which by the early 1970s could produce a much more detailed and precise record of the excavated site, and the development in information yield from environmental sampling procedures. With this ran an acute awareness that excavation is essentially a destructive exercise, so that a former site now exists only in its preserved archive.

The archive concept can be usefully extended to cover the entirety of archaeological collections, whether or not these originated from recent excavations carried out to a full archival level. The museum archive then embraces the whole product of archaeological activity over the past decades and centuries, to the extent that this survives physically in museum collections, and it includes both the material remains and the associated documentary record. It is in this sense of the inherited, historic archive that the term is used here.

The implications of this archive for curatorship are obviously enormous, but the curatorial role is an active, not a passive, one, and the curator's relationship with his archive is a steady process of interaction in which the existing and incoming collections, the management of museum policies, and the exercise of judgment, are woven together in the explicit actions and decisions which make up every working day. The structure which gives coherence to the relationship between curator and collected archive is the collection management policy, and this is why the framing of collection

67

management policies is today seen as the hallmark of a professional museum service and is a requirement of museum registration (*Guidelines for a Registration Scheme* 1988: 4, 7–9; see also Ware 1988 which relates specifically to the private sector, and National Audit Office 1988, which relates to the national museums).

Collection management policies are often expressed in a range of written statements of various standing, and although it would be better to bring these together into one coherent document, this is not always achieved. The archaeological collections policy, like all others, should embrace a description of the existing archive, a written acquisition policy, and its dark twin, a policy on the disposal of material. It should relate these to policies on documentation and research, storage management and conservation practice, and also to general matters like inventory control and stock-taking, and security against fire, theft and vandalism. Each collection management policy must take into account the history and character of the archive and the broader legal, ethical and political issues discussed in previous chapters. It must be individually designed for its own museum and the circumstances within which that museum operates, and it must also perform the difficult feat of being practical without too great a sacrifice of principle.

The rest of this chapter is concerned with the nature of the museum archaeological archive and with acquisition and disposal policies, and their implications. The next three chapters carry the review of archive management through its other main areas.

Nature of the archive

The archive was defined in the introduction as the complete archaeological holding of a museum service. This will involve a very wide range of material, much of it collected more or less at random, or by what is usually called 'passive collecting', over, often, a very long period. A mythical but typical museum accumulation might include material dug out of Bronze Age barrows in the nineteenth century, substantial local surface collections of worked flint, boxes of 'eoliths', Palaeolithic hand axes loosely attributed to the Thames Valley, regional finds of Bronze Age and Iron Age metalwork, the product of a wide range of excavations carried out over the years in local prehistoric, Roman and Medieval sites, material from Roman London, boxes of finds from 'the Swiss lake dwellings' and, arriving at a steady rate, the material from recent and on-going excavation and field-walking projects. Some of this material will be only a part of its find, because the group was split between several museums.

Associated with all this will be a considerable volume of written, printed and pictorial record, including early manuscript letters and note books, annotated maps, offprints from journals, water colours and photographs, and assorted excavation records, all of which will vary considerably in size, format, and storage needs. To this must be added old packaging, boxing and labelling, which sometimes survives to give crucial links between objects and provenances. In 1904 the Egyptologist Petrie could say, 'our museums are houses of murdered evidence' (Petrie 1904: 48) and his picturesque words give a fair idea of the nature of at least parts of our collection legacy and of its problems. The picture is a daunting one.

The nature of this archive can be analysed from a number of angles, and of these the four most helpful are its archaeological nature, its nature from what may be called an historical point of view (Watkins 1986), its museological nature, and an overview of the variety of physical materials which it includes. Archaeologically speaking, all the ancient material in the archive, and its record, relates to a particular past time and place. It is this, of course, which gives it its unique value, and justifies all the resource expended on its care. Historically speaking, several elements are involved and these may be summarized as:

1. Single pieces or small groups found as chance finds, often with very limited records attached. The majority of these in any given museum collection are likely to be local finds.
2. Large groups formed as private collections, sometimes with substantial records attached. These may be from anywhere in Britain or abroad, but may well include local material. They were mostly acquired before *c.* 1950.
3. Material from museum-based excavations. These will be local, with, of course, excellent records and admirable mutual consultation between all involved at all points. The material is likely to be of relatively recent accession.
4. Material from excavations conducted by other bodies, including that from all old excavations, and from new excavations where consultation is a possibility.
5. Material from fieldworking projects. This is likely to be of recent and ongoing accession, and the museum should have links with the organization.
6. To this list must be added material which has been discovered through the use of a metal detector. Here a judgment has to be formed about the value of associated information.

Both the archaeological and the historical aspects of the archive have an important bearing on the ways in which storage may be organized (see Chapter 6).

In terms of museum practice, all of the material will have arrived in the museum by donation (including bequest), by loan, by purchase or by exchange, and any of it may have arrived by any of these means. In fact, it is not uncommon for a large collection to have arrived in several lots, perhaps during the course of a lifetime and after a death (or a widow's death), and by several of these acquisition routes. Associated with the material may be a range of constraints, such as an obligation to display in whole or part, or a requirement to keep a personal collection together in one room, which usually holds display cases with storage cupboards below. Such collections also frequently include personal belongings like books, portraits and scientific instruments.

Finally, we come to the range of physical material which the archive embraces. The material types run across all the other categories which have been discussed, all of which will include a selection from the range, and recent and on-going excavation collections are likely to include most of the types. The material can be divided into three broad areas—artefacts, environmental evidence, and documentary record. The artefacts include organic and inorganic materials, and both small finds and structural fragments. The environmental evidence includes bones, both human and animal, and a large range of samples. The documentary record will be on paper, film and tape. The nature of this material and its needs will be further pursued in the following two chapters.

The important point here is that the nature of the archive as a whole, both existing and potential, is not simple, but embraces a cross-cutting range of identities, depending upon whether it is seen from a physical, a museological, an archaeological, or an historical view. It is a recognition of these complexities, and an ability to organize and effect strategies that take all the interplays into account, which make up successful collection management.

Acquisition

An acquisitions policy for the present and the future must be framed in relationship to the nature of the existing collection, but it must also take into account the needs of modern museums and of professional curatorship. It will encourage staff to think more clearly about the functions of the museum, and it will serve as a reference document to protect the service against personal whims. It makes it easier to reject material and to maintain the relevance of the collections, it encourages public confidence, and it helps to make the best use of limited resources. It should be noted that, legally, curators only acquire material under delegated powers from the governing body, and that all final decisions lie with that body. The written archaeological acquisitions policy is likely to be part of a more general document, which will take into account legal needs and any specific terms of reference which the museum may have. It will reflect the nature of the governing body, the character of the museum itself, which may range from a university research institute to a small general museum, and it should take notice of any relevant visitor research, and the policies of neighbouring museum services.

The specifically archaeological acquisitions policy should take a further range of questions into account, and not all of these can be adequately expressed in the written document, so that such a document serves chiefly as a guideline for curatorial judgment rather than as a rule book, and it should be drawn up with this in mind. These questions will be concerned partly with archaeological matters, and partly with curatorial concerns, although the two intermingle to a considerable extent. Decisions need to be taken about the type of archaeological material which is accepted, and whether there are to be any constraints placed upon character or period: a museum like Fishbourne, for example, would not collect prehistoric material, while one like Bristol would, other things being equal, take collections of any date or type. These decisions will be taken in the light of existing collections and the general character of the service. Equally, there needs to be a decision about the geographical area from which material is normally accepted. This presents a number of difficulties and is discussed in a separate section (below p. 80–83.

The curatorial concerns fall into two groups: those involved with the nature of acquisition, and those linked with the management of documentation, conservation and storage. As in the past, so still, material is acquired by donation, by loan, by exchange or transfer, and by purchase. Donations can originate as museum enquiries, as straightforward gifts, and as bequests, whether or not these have been discussed beforehand. It is true to say that the vast bulk of British archaeological material has arrived by donation from the general public over the years, with all the moral obligations which this implies. The chief curatorial difficulty with donations is that they are sometimes of mixed material, involving some objects which the museum is extremely anxious to acquire and others which it does not want. The curious nature of much past acquisition is to be explained in these terms, and it does not cease to be a problem because collecting strategies are now carefully considered policies. As so often, the curator must make the best judgment he can in terms of the individual circumstances.

Most curators dislike material deposited on loan, whether or not the loan carries strings like the obligation to display, and their reasons revolve around the insecurity of tenure which such arrangements involve, and the feeling that the museum's resources are sometimes being wrongly exploited. Important loan collections can be, and sometimes are, withdrawn, and personal acrimony can result, especially if the material is then offered to the museum for purchase. Nevertheless, most museums have loan material, usually deposited according to the peculiar (and legally baseless) formula of 'permanent loan', and curators sometimes still cannot avoid acquiring such material. It is, of course, crucial that such deposits (as all others) are thoroughly documented, and where difficulties do arise, they usually result from poor earlier documentation and bad storage. 'Short-term loans' present a lesser problem, because they are usually made for a defined period and project, normally research or display. Museums may be involved in this kind of archaeological loan as either lender or borrower, and again the overall documentation and security of the objects must be paramount. Extracting the material from a borrower at the end of the loan period can be dishearteningly difficult. The exchange of collections between institutions, or the transfer of material from one museum to another, is today used as a satisfactory method of collection rationalization, which can result in both the acquisition and the disposal of material (see further p. 77).

Acquisition by purchase is a more delicate area. The market for British antiquities is as yet fairly small, but 'important' pieces fetch very large sums, and smaller pieces, like a Middle Bronze axe, will sell at auction in London for anything up to £50.00 at current prices. The problem is greatly compounded by the activities of treasure hunters and by the dealers to whom they sell their finds, and it may only be a matter of time before more landowners become aware of the potential value of some of the material excavated from their property. Landowners in England and Wales have a legitimate interest in the financial value of antiquities while the present law

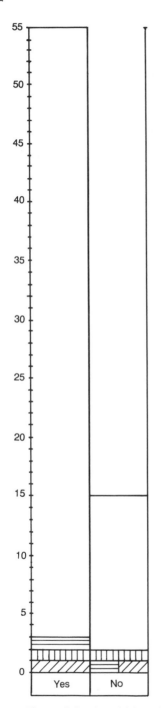

Figure 5.1   Acquisition of British archaeological material by purchase

stands, and treasure hunters a much more dubious interest, but museums, and archaeology as a discipline, are best served by a very small British antiquites market in which values remain generally low. In comparison with the traffic in foreign antiquities, this market is still low, in part because the museums who might otherwise be among the chief purchasers have only very small funds at their disposal, but there are some signs that it may develop in a disturbing fashion.

Faced with these difficulties, an individual museum should develop an antiquities purchasing policy at several levels. Figure 5.1 shows that a considerable proportion of museums have purchased material, but most appear to have done so on an *ad hoc* basis, depending upon the antiquities offered and the funds currently available. Those museums who have made no purchases generally state that this is due to lack of resources. The occasional spectacular piece, like an Iron Age mirror or a hoard of Bronze Age gold armings which the British Museum does not want, command a legitimately high price, which is likely to be arrived at by consultation between a number of specialists. The appropriate museum will naturally try to raise the purchase price, probably by a mixture of grant aid (probably through the Museums and Galleries Commission's *Purchase Grant Fund for the Regions*), existing budget monies and possibly a special vote or a fund-raising programme.

Smaller finds, often arising as enquiries, present a genuine problem. Implements of stone or metal do have a financial value, which can be deduced by keeping an eye on the records of the London sales, especially the catalogues and price lists published by Sotheby's and Christie's (and if a museum is operating a policy of collection insurance, or if a short-term loan piece has to be insured, these sales are one of the best sources for valuations). Although the value of a small find may mean a good deal to the owner, regular purchases of this kind will place a strain on the museum's resources. It will also focus attention on the true ownership of the piece, which will probably not lie with the finder. For these reasons, museums are often reluctant to discuss the question of purchase in relation to enquiry objects, which they would in any case often like to acquire by donation, but this potentially unprofessional stance is badly in need of review. Finally, there remains the question of metal-detected material, which is discussed in detail in Chapter 9; sufficient to say here that an acquisitions and purchasing policy must take this material into account.

The question of legal title to material found in Great Britain has arisen several times in the course of this discussion. The general legal provisions have been described in detail (Lewis 1988) and need not be reviewed here, and some of the specifically archaeological applications have been discussed in Chapter 3. The curator is under a clear obligation to take all reasonable steps to ensure that all material which is acquired comes from its legal possessor. Treasure-hunted material raises particular problems and so does any material coming from abroad. In the case of chance finds or family property, the establishment of ownership can often in practice be difficult, and it can be equally difficult sometimes to make donors understand that donation means a genuine transfer of ownership for good, however carefully the curator has fulfilled his professional obligation to explain clearly and to back this up by letter. Family quarrels and the much publicized prices of some antiquities often feature here. Clear and correct documentation is the key, and, fortified by this, a curator should resist pressure to return donated material.

Linked with an acquisitions policy must be a policy for refusing material which is offered, but which it is judged improper to add to the collections. The simplest area here is where the museum guidelines of type, period and, perhaps most importantly, geographical location, can be applied. Material which falls outside these lines will normally be refused, and the owner may be offered advice about suitable museums to approach. Legal title, as we have seen, can present problems. An equally difficult area of a different kind is that which centres upon poor material, which will usually involve collections that were badly documented originally and perhaps badly cared for subsequently: there is still a very considerable quantity of excavated material of this kind which remains in private hands, but which, sooner or later, is likely to be offered to its local museum. A decision has to be made on the basis of just how poor the whole archive is, and how significant is the information which the material still embodies.

The most difficult problems involved in refusing material, however, are those linked with resource levels, in the areas of documentation and, particularly, storage and conservation. There is a strong body of opinion which believes, in the words of the *Code of Conduct for Museum Curators*,

> It is clearly improper to expand an acquisitions policy unless the institution is able to provide high standards of curatorial care ... many instances of neglect have resulted from uncontrollable collecting and many museum stores contain unclassified residues that are the legacy of passive collecting (Thompson *et al.* 1984: 530–1).

This implies that inadequate care provision should be grounds for refusing material, even though in other respects it falls within the museum's acquisition policy. The application of this policy might (but might not) mean that the quality of existing care can be improved and that, at any rate, additional problems will not be created. It might also mean that important material has to be refused. Solutions lie in better discussion and organization, and perhaps skilful use of political levers, at the earliest possible stage, but the most careful management will sometimes be faced by the unpredictable.

The disposal of archaeological material

Hand in hand with an acquisitions policy must go a policy for the selection and disposal of archaeological material already in the collection. The *Code of Conduct* (Thompson *et al.* 1984: 531) states:

> there must always be a strong presumption against the disposal of specimens to which a museum has assumed formal title. Any form of disposal, whether by donation, exchange, sale or destruction requires the exercise of a high order of curatorial judgement and should be recommended to a curator's governing body only after full expert and legal advice has been taken.

The following *Guideline* draws attention to the same principle in the *Code of Practice for Museum Authorities*. Again, it should be noted that technically it is always the governing body, not the curator, who takes the decision to dispose of collections.

This rule embodies the concept that what museums hold they will continue to hold as a matter of principle, maintaining collections in trust for future generations, and keeping faith with past and potential donors, who present material to museums so that it may be held in perpetuity for the general good. It reflects the instincts of curators, who by character and training are framed to curate, to care and to conserve, and to take a long-term view of their responsibilities. At the end of the day, it makes the fundamental value judgment that collections are precious, and any museum worker who feels otherwise has clearly chosen the wrong profession. Once this has been recognized, and most strongly stressed, it must be said that the difficulties surrounding the selection and disposal of archaeological material mean that the application of the principle is not a simple matter.

In broad terms, the problem has three important facets, involving the public, the law, and the operation of the curatorial principle in real museum situations. It is clear that the general public has difficulty in appreciating why museums should hold very bulky archaeological reserve collections which will never be displayed, and this gap in understanding shows up particularly vividly when it is mundane fragments of pot, stone and bone which are being lovingly stored. The difficulty usually appears in acute form when it is uttered by members of the governing body. It is usual to say at this point that the fault lies with the curators, who have failed to make clear the research potential of the material, but unhappily experience shows that the problem is not simply one of communication failure, but rather sometimes of a fundamental difference in values and perceptions. Curators must take the stand that an institution without its reserve collections ceases to be a museum and dwindles into an exhibition centre, and in many cases the matter is allowed to rest on this professional judgment, backed by a genuine willingness to explain and to demonstrate what the stored material can tell us. There is no doubt, however, that this is one of the most difficult problems now facing museum archaeologists.

The law governing the disposal of museum collections by sale appears to be in a state of some confusion (Loynd 1987). The inference seems to be that if the governing bodies of many museums made a determined effort to sell, or destroy, collections, they would be successful. The way to protect collections is therefore likely to be administrative rather than legal, with stress laid upon the Museum Association *Codes*, on the nature of professional curation, including of course the framing and implementation of appropriate collection management policies, and on the proper public standing of the institution concerned. All this should help to preclude clandestine arrangements which put curators in a false position.

In practice, the vast bulk of British archaeological material does not (at least as yet) have a marketable value of any significance, and where elements in a regional collection, like coins, metal objects, or particularly fine stone and ceramic artefacts, would command a price, local patriotism usually ensures that the question does not arise. The case is very different with non-

British material, and sometimes with non-local British material if this is of intrinsic value, not to mention the collections of general numismatics, arms and armour and ethnography for which a curator of archaeology often finds himself responsible, all of which are of monetary worth, often very considerable worth. Curators should resist the temptation to sell such objects in order to house local material more satisfactorily.

Once the principle of collection integrity has been established, and all parties concerned understand and agree that reserve archaeological collections are not to be disposed of simply because they are seldom seen, or because they present practical maintenance problems, or because the proceeds of sale could be used for other (often very laudable) purposes, then the selection of archaeological material for retention and disposal in any particular collection becomes a matter for curatorial judgment. The distinction is genuine, but it needs to be carefully and clearly made.

There are a number of areas in which this judgment must be exercised, and one of the most important concerns material from excavation, whether from an old excavation which has been a formal part of the collection for some years, or from an on-going or recently concluded excavation, the material from which is in the process of transfer to the museum. Similar problems can also arise in the case of old and very poorly documented collections, as, for example, worked flints provenanced only to 'the Sussex Downs'. The problem revolves around the often very considerable quantities of samples taken for environmental evidence, animal remains including bulk samples of bones and shells, residues from industrial production like slags, bulk artefactual material like body sherds and lithic debitage, bulk building materials, and quantities of large timbers where these occur. Human remains come in a distinct category. In practice, varying procedures are applied to the study and disposal of human bone, and there is need for a consensus to be developed among the archaeology and palaeopathology (or biological anthropology) community, which might take the form of a Code of Practice issued by a body like CBA.

The British Museum Working Party Report on the selection and retention of material from excavation (British Museum 1982) considered all the interrelated problems which arise with excavated material, and concluded that 'the ability to re-interrogate the primary data is in our opinion crucial', so far as the retention of the archive is concerned, and that, 'sampling procedures . . . in the main are not applicable to archaeological material', so that the problem cannot be resolved by the adoption of different excavation and research procedures (1982: 3; see also Longworth 1986). The steady development of research techniques means that, potentially, virtually all excavated material can be made to yield fresh information, and to satisfy this theoretical basis it should be retained in its entirety. It follows that any rejection should be very modest in scope, and should be undertaken only after very careful consideration between excavator, specialist and curator.

This position is undeniable in philosophical and research terms, but it represents an ideal which must be modified in the light of the present situation. The level of recent excavation activity has meant an enormous accumulation of finds, so that in Wiltshire, for example, the material from the

Littlecote Villa runs to some 100 cubic metres and that from Potterne to some 5,000 standard boxes (Robinson pers. comm.), while in London the work of the units and societies has generated some 1,000 cubic metres of finds, with the same quantity again expected in the next twenty years (Richardson 1988). Most museums could describe similar experiences, and it is obvious that the proper storage and care of such huge collections would absorb an absurd level of resource. The difficulty is not simply a practical one, although the practical problems it poses need no stressing. For all kinds of cogent reasons, archaeologists must try to live in harmony with their fellow men, and the community in general is entitled to ask archaeology to order its priorities so that its demands are not perceived as luxuriously excessive.

All this means that the curatorial balancing act is a very difficult feat, and that operational decisions must be taken afresh, as a consensus of all concerned, in every new case. Drastic disposal of bulk finds is professionally unacceptable, but a cull of undecorated bulk building materials, for example, may well be possible. A certain amount of surplus artefactual material can be absorbed into educational projects, even to the point of giving it away, and the recycling of such material into 'new finds' is probably not so acute as is sometimes feared, provided a record is kept of what material was distributed (Robertson 1987b). Bulk materials of little educational use can be buried, perhaps on known archaeological sites earmarked for dumping, and again proper records should cut down any possibility of future mistakes. It is helpful if material from recently concluded excavations can be culled before it is formally received into the museum, because this helps to maintain the standing of the final archive. If material from an old excavation already in the collection has to be culled, this is best done with the minimum of drama. In either case, it may be useful to refer to the process as 'discard' rather than as 'disposal', because the two words have different associations of value, which match the curatorial distinctions that have been made.

The rationalization of collections by exchange or transfer is another important area of curatorial judgment. In the past, such transactions were sometimes disconcertingly idiosyncratic (to use a polite term), leaving an odd legacy for contemporary curators, but this can sometimes be eased by fresh arrangements. Generally speaking, it is often sensible for non-local British material to be transferred to the properly-constituted museum whose collecting policy covers the area from which the material comes, whether or not other material can be received in exchange, and considerations of financial value, or of 'important pieces', should not be allowed to affect the issue. Perhaps the chief difficulty which can arise here is the conflicting desire to preserve intact one single collection made perhaps by a significant individual, which comes from a range of localities. Needless to say, any such transactions should be properly documented by both museums, and any necessary permissions or approvals formally obtained.

The restitution of non-British material to a museum in its country of origin is a very different and a very difficult matter. At present in Britain the pressure to repatriate material is moral rather than legal, in spite of UNESCO resolutions which relate to the return of cultural property (Lewis G. 1979). So far, the political problem, as far as archaeological material is concerned, has revolved around the British Museum's holdings of Greek cultural property, especially that in the Elgin Collection, but the principle could be extended to include much foreign archaeology held by museums throughout Britain. The resolution of the difficulties is likely to rest in small-scale and specific local agreements.

The United Kingdom has, in 1973, ratified the *European Convention on the Protection of the Archaeological Heritage*, a Council of Europe convention which requires governments to prohibit illicit excavations and to ensure that legitimate excavations are carried out by qualified persons and that the results are controlled and conserved. It also requires museums to avoid acquiring material from illicit excavations or material acquired unlawfully from official excavations. (This *Convention* could, of course, be applied to excavations inside, as well as outside, the United Kingdom.) The UNESCO *Convention on the means of prohibiting and preventing the illicit import, export and transfer of ownership of cultural property* (1970) has not been ratified by the United Kingdom, chiefly, it seems clear, to protect the activities of the great auction houses. However, a statement in support of the *Convention* was issued in 1972 by the then Standing Commission on Museums and Galleries in consultation with the British Academy, the British Museum and the Museums Association. This affirms the importance attached to the preservation and study of cultural material, and states that 'it is and will continue to be the practice of museums and galleries in the United Kingdom that they do not and will not knowingly acquire any antiquities or other cultural material which they have reason to believe has been exported in contravention of the current laws of the country of origin' (Lewis 1988). Many museums explicitly commit themselves to the observation of this *Convention* in their collection management policies.

Figure 5.2 demonstrates how reluctant many musems are to dispose of any of their material by any means (although a number of these will have agreed to the discarding of bulk excavation material before it reached the museum). Some have embarked on the difficult operation of discarding in the existing collection, but disappointingly few have begun to rationalize by disposal to other museums. Sales have been very rare, and this is more likely to be a problem for the future. It is clear that, in this whole difficult realm of disposal, the key question is the destruction of archaeological material, followed by the potential sale of collections. Very dubious transactions have happened in the past in both areas, and there are no easy solutions, but the best hope for the future rests with good professional management. Curators must not be afraid to occupy the high ground of principle, but they must be able to apply their convictions in detailed and practical ways, which demonstrate that all the necessary procedures have been properly followed and all the issues have been comprehensively considered, so that their judgments are accorded the weight to which they are entitled. Governing bodies (and directors) can sometimes be unsympathetic or erratic, and occasional disasters will happen, but against these steady professionalism is the best guard.

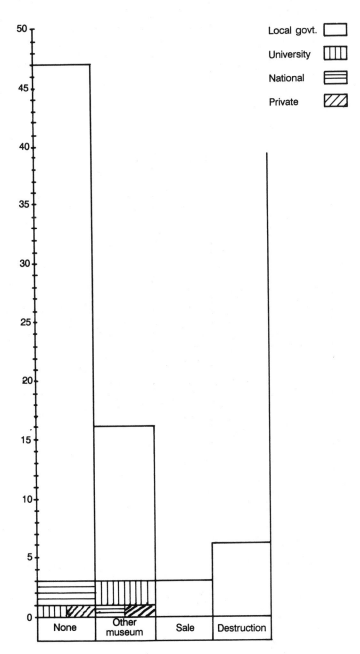

Figure 5.2 Disposal of archaeological material already part of museum collections

Collecting area policies

Whenever two or more archaeological curators gather together it is likely that their discussion will turn to the difficulties of creating and maintaining collecting area policies for museums holding archaeological material, and the obtrusiveness of the question demonstrates how complex the problem is, and how strongly individuals sometimes feel about it. The problem broadly resolves itself into three inter-linked issues: the cultural argument, the management argument, and the argument embracing political and economic affairs. Cutting across the potential resolutions of these conflicts on a local or regional basis, are the claims of the national museums.

The cultural argument rests upon two foundations, both of them part of our inheritance from the historic past. In the first place, most past societies in Britain were small-scale and therefore present appreciable regional differences, which form a focus for academic study and for interpretation and display. In each period in the past we are presented with a range of regional variations on a broad theme, and since these variations are the result of local differences in geology, ecology and earlier history, it is sensible and satisfactory for the surviving material culture to be held in the region which gave it birth and of whose traditions it is a part (however difficult it may be to define a 'region'). In the second place, the different areas or regions of Britain feel strongly about their own cultural identity, and their people undoubtedly believe that native material retained in local museums is one way in which regional culture can be strengthened and maintained.

Although the powerful sweep of regional ethnic feeling and pride of place is clear enough, its detailed application in terms of the legal placement of archaeological material is another matter. Occasionally, and Cornwall is a possible example, a case can be made for maintaining that the modern area which commands contemporary ethnic loyalty also bears a real relationship to the territorial area occupied by recognizably coherent societies in the past. Usually, however, the situation is much more confused and, as in Northern or Central England, both past and present show a conflicting picture where modern loyalties are of recent or relatively recent growth. These bear little relationship to the past communities from which much archaeological material comes, but they will be used to determine the destination of that material because of their contemporary cultural power, even though the material might be better placed elsewhere.

Community loyalty to a museum is an important force, and one which most museum services are at pains to foster, whether it works in terms of a county, a city, or a market town. Closely intertwined with this are the collecting traditions of the museums themselves. Most substantial museums are, and have been since their founding in the nineteenth century, placed in the important urban areas, while prehistoric and much Roman material, together with considerable quantities of medieval material, tends to come from the rural countryside and the smaller cities and towns. From their early days, for example, Sheffield Museum has acquired collections from the Peak District, and Plymouth Museum material from Dartmoor, while Liverpool Museum holds important pieces from North Wales. Where such traditions are established, there is clearly a good case to be made for continuing the collecting policy, even though it may cut across the interests of neighbouring museums.

The management argument centres around judgments which have to be made about the viability of an institution as an acceptable museum service, which is competent to hold collections. Opinions will differ here (see *Guidelines for a Registration Scheme* 1988), but an increased emphasis on professionalism is becoming apparent in, for example, the central government provision of some archaeological storage resources. Viability is likely to mean that the service has at least one paid, full-time professional (however difficult this may be to define) curator with sufficient resources to operate professionally, that is to say, with storage which fulfils minimum requirements, with access to a professional conservator, and perhaps also with some display and other interpretative facilities. Once these resources are in place, the scope of the museum, and consequently the quantity of material which it may acquire, are a matter for local negotiation and agreement; it is a fact of life that museums and resources are unevenly distributed and that some museums will not be able, and should not try, to take collections for which they have not the facilities, even though they may have a range of geographical and sentimental claims upon it.

It must be stressed that any museum which fails to meet these basic standards should not aspire to hold any archaeological material, and local larger museums should do all in their power to discourage the donation of collections to them. In practice, this can sometimes lead to a good deal of unpleasantness because the small museums without proper facilities are usually very anxious to develop their local role, and tend to see a stress on professional standards as a form of political manipulation. Since, as the law currently stands, local owners are perfectly free to donate their material wherever they choose, great tact is often necessary, and even so it will not always succeed.

The political and economic argument draws much of its strength from the regional loyalties and traditions already discussed, but it seeks to harness these cultural values to developments in the fields of leisure and tourism which will bring money and jobs. The experience of regional flavour, carefully arranged, is now a marketable commodity, and the place of museums in such schemes is well recognized and can create an alliance between local politicians, entrepreneurs and curators which, among other things, places great value on the acquisition and display of local material, and particular stress on local major artefacts and star pieces. This alliance is likely to become more important, and more effective, as future central governments of whatever colour are forced to face the problem of the north–south divide and the general movement towards broad regional devolution.

This whole, rather confused, inheritance is now being addressed by archaeology curators who are generally anxious that museum collecting areas should be established and agreed, at both the curatorial and the governing body/political level. The first step in each region is to find out what the various museums regard as their collecting areas, expressed probably in terms of districts or counties, although sometimes a very large museum may see itself as having a regional role. This kind of review has been undertaken in Yorkshire and Humberside, and in the East Midlands, among other areas. In the East Midlands, as White says,

> The results are illuminating: for the most part there is no clash of interest, and only in two cases is there a substantial degree of overlap (White 1979: 14)

and this notwithstanding the fact that in the East Midlands all the problems of uneven museum distribution and potentially conflicting loyalties are well developed. Once the various claims are clear, it should be possible to negotiate boundaries and compromises which can form the basis of a formal agreement entered into by all parties, even though some few definite and specific problems may be left outstanding. This agreement should be widely published, and it will form the basis for arrangements concluded between excavating units, landowners, and museums, and it is hoped also for acquisitions by other forms of donation and transfer.

Cutting across these regional agreements are the avowed collecting policies of the national museums. In Wales, the National Museum's charter of 1907 states that,

> The object of the Museum shall be mainly and primarily the complete illustration of the ... archaeology ... of Wales and the collection, preservation and mainte- nance of objects and things of usefulness or interest connected therewith (Green and Brewer 1987).

The Royal Museum of Scotland and the Ulster Museum pursue similar policies, backed by a supportive legal framework (see Chapter 3). In practice the difficulties are relatively simple in Ulster and Wales, where the number of non-national but competing museums is very small, but in Scotland the situation seems to be closer to that in England.

For England, the summary of the objectives of the Department of Prehis- toric and Romano-British Antiquities at the British Museum (Longworth 1980; 1987) may be quoted in full:

> 1. To acquire objects of outstanding artistic or historic merit in the areas and periods covered by the department.
> 2. To acquire material representative of the various regional aspects of British Prehistory and of the Romano-British period. In this the British Museum has a clear role as the only museum in Britain with the capability of offering the public, scholars and students the opportunity to compare, under one roof, these regional variations.
> 3. With regard to Europe in the later pre-historic periods and to the world in the earlier, to acquire, where possible, material representative of the major cultural groupings to enable British antiquities to be placed in their European and/or world settings.

These objectives are based on the belief that, 'the national collection of antiquities should be as broad and representative as possible in order to form a basis for meaningful judgments and comparisons' (Longworth 1987: 92). They are pursued with three basic requirements in mind: the need to identify material, which requires broadly-based comparative collections of artefacts so that the essential tasks of comparison and authentication can be undertaken; the needs of present and future displays, which require 'outstanding individual objects and good representative groups'; and the needs of present and future research, which requires individual objects or groups which will 'naturally provide essential data in any future consideration of archaeological problems' (Longworth 1987: 92).

Longworth's paper is a fair and reasonable statement of a particular position, but unfortunately this position is unacceptable to the great majority of archaeology curators, and to their governing bodies, and probably to their publics also (see Schadla-Hall 1987a). Politically, the time has gone when any London institution can automatically command a pre-eminent position, and the greatly improved resources given to regional museums, essentially as political gestures, mean that arguments about the quality of curation and collection management are no longer valid. There are no overwhelming reasons why 'outstanding individual objects' should go to the national collection, and local loyalty and identity provide good reasons why such pieces should stay at home.

The archaeological arguments are also powerful. The concept of 'representative material' is a potentialy dangerous one, for the only way to study bell beakers, for example, is to look at as many pieces as possible wherever they may be, rather than to assume that one central 'representative' collection gives an adequate sample. In the past, the desire to place 'important' material in the national collection has led to the splitting-up of many associated groups, but no professional is likely to advocate this today, even where large excavation collections are concerned. The application of Treasure Trove as it stands at present gives the national collection a favoured position, although most responsible opinion holds that this law is overdue for change.

It is obvious that solutions lie in mutual arrangements about the destination of finds from excavation, and from other sources where this is possible, and that these are most fruitfully conducted in an atmosphere of reciprocal understanding between the British Museum and the provincial museums. These agreements should be backed up by a much more considerable flow of loan material in both directions, both for long-term study and for exhibition, and the whole process will undoubtedly involve changes of attitude on the part of all concerned.

The present situation

Relatively little has been written which takes a broad view of archaeological collecting policies in operation, although a useful exception is Eyre's analysis of the situation in London (Eyre 1988) which includes a statement of the Museum of London's policy in relation to existing collections and future collecting (pp. 8–18) and similar statements from some twenty London Borough museums (pp. 19–47). All the interrelated problems of collection management are, of course, particularly acute in London, but a survey of this

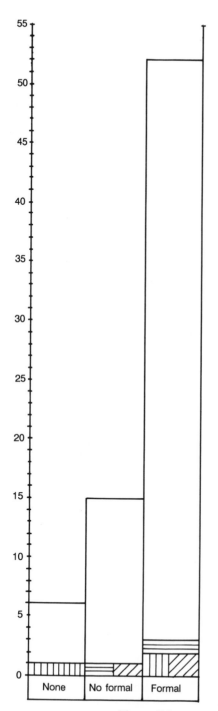

Figure 5.3   Collecting policies

kind presents some important facts, and serves, at least, to bring difficulties into the open. Similar detailed surveys for other areas would be very valuable.

As figure 5.3 shows some 75 per cent of the museums in the writer's survey operate under written collections management policies, although these are usually regarded (as they are in London) primarily as collecting or acquisitions policies, and are designed with this in mind. They are usually general policies, which either are taken to apply to archaeology with all the other collections, or have occasional specific paragraphs. Those museums who do not so operate, or who have avoided framing a formal policy, are probably influenced by fears that their curatorial discretion will be curtailed, and perhaps by difficulties which they anticipate will arise with their governing bodies. It is probable that pressure, particularly from neighbouring museum services, and perhaps to satisfy registration needs, will nudge these museums into better self-definition, and that this will happen sooner rather than later.

Eighteen individual archaeological acquisition policies were available for analysis, from a wide range of museums including six county services (e.g. Lincolnshire, Somerset, Powys), eight district and city services (e.g. Cotswold, Lancaster, Worcester), three smaller museums including private institutions and London boroughs, and one university museum (figure 5.4). It is fair to add that some of these at the time of writing were in draft state, or due to be updated. The general impression given by the policies is that they aim to provide professional, legitimate protection of the museums' interests, but

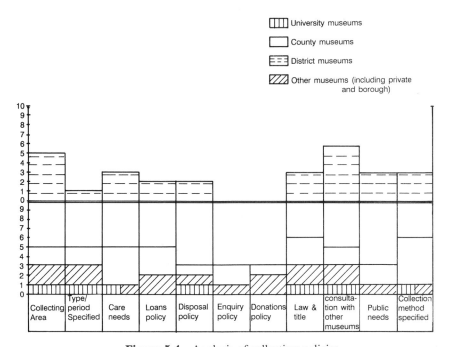

Figure 5.4 Analysis of collecting policies

that within this a number of different emphases are detectable, particularly where a museum is closely linked with a particular excavation unit.

Most of the policies (14) contained a statement on the collecting area, although this is often rather vague, and, in the case of some of the county services not very helpful to other museums within the county, although again most (15) of the total said that they were willing to consult with others. If the material type or period was specified it was usually described as 'everything' from the collecting area. A policy on legal title was usually carefully spelt out, and this was generally linked with an endorsement of the UNESCO convention. Loans policies usually covered the acceptance of material on loan, and restricted this to short-term loans or to particularly important items, but some also contain a reference to material loaned across a service from one museum building to another.

Specific policies concerning donations are rare, but this may well reflect their crucial role rather than the opposite and embody a desire to keep as many options open as possible. To be linked with this are the statements about desirable collection-forming processes. A typical statement runs,

> The majority of material will derive from properly controlled scientific excavations and surveys conducted by reputable bodies,

and sometimes adds that material is normally deposited as a complete archive. Some museums also took the opportunity to include a statement about enquiries, which embodied standard warnings about refusal to value or to deal with illegal material, which might include treasure-hunted objects.

Disposal is a nettle grasped only in eight cases. One full statement runs:

> The definition of a museum in paragraph 1.1 makes it clear that it is a key function of a museum or art gallery to acquire objects and/or works of art and to keep them for posterity. Consequently there must be a strong presumption against the disposal of any items in the collections of a museum.
>
> A decision to dispose of a specimen or work of art, whether by exchange, sale or destruction (in the case of an item too badly damaged or deteriorated to be restorable) should be the responsiblity of the governing body of the museum, not of the curator of the collection concerned acting alone. Full records should be kept of all such decisions and the specimens involved and proper arrangements made for the preservation and/or transfer, as appropriate of the documentation relating to the object concerned, including photographic records where practicable.

In one case, disposal was linked with an inability to guarantee safe storage and a substantial number of policies (10) contained references to the care needs of material, some in very uncompromising terms, for example, 'Items which cannot be adequately conserved or housed will not be collected'. In only a relatively few cases (7) was it thought appropriate to mention the needs of the public.

This overview suggests that archaeological museum services in general still have a considerable way to go in the written articulation of formal collecting policies, although in many individual cases curation will be supplemented by less formal, but very important agreements and guidelines, which might be easily bruised by heavy handling. Collecting policies are best regarded as a process rather than as a single act, and for this reason many collecting statements embody a review provision. The process may sometimes be slow and intermittent, but the need is now well recognized, which is, in itself, a substantial advance.

6. *Approaches to storage*

Introduction

Given the moral and intellectual—in a word the curatorial—case for the careful acquisition and retention of archaeological archive, which has been discussed in the preceding chapter, we must turn now to its practical care. The earlier section on *The Nature of the Archive* suggested that the archaeological material in museum collections derives from three main sources, which are excavations, large groups like private collections, and single items or small groups found by chance. To this material must be added the documentation, so that, physically, the archive embraces a very large range of types of materials, set out in detail in figure 6.1. Both these aspects of the archive play

Ceramic—	Sherds
	Kiln debris
Metalwork—	Precious
	Non-ferrous metals and alloys
	Ferrous
	Smelting and casting debris
Stone—	Small artefacts (axes, blades, etc.)
	Larger artefacts (querns, etc.)
	Worked stone (architectural frags.)
	Gem stones and decorative stones
Glass—	Artefacts
	Window glass
	Glass-working debris
Numismatic—	Coins
	Tokens, etc.
Bone—	Artefacts, waste
	Human skeletal
	Animal skeletal
Horn—	Artefacts, waste
Antler—	Artefacts, waste
Ivory—	Artefacts, waste
Shell—	Artefacts, waste
	Shell remains

Wood—	Artefacts (inc. amber, jet), waste
	Structural remains
Other organic—	Leather
	Textiles
	Basketry
	Rope, etc.
Structural remains	Bricks, tiles
	Plaster (inc. painted) etc.
Environmental—	Soil samples
	Organic samples (insects, snails, etc.)
	Inorganic samples (rock, clay, etc.)
Other—	Any material remains not included in the above
Site data—	All relevant excavation and/or survey records
	Catalogues of data
Drawings—	Published and unpublished drawings
(some large size)	Maps, site plans and sections
	Survey drawings, development plans, etc.
	Catalogues of drawings
Photographic—	Site slides
	Site negatives and prints
	Finds photographs (colour, b/w, X-ray)
	Other e.g. historic photographs
	Photographic catalogues
Finds data—	Small finds lists and record sheets
(all categories,	Analyses and drawings
as above)	C14 documentation, etc.
	Catalogues
	Storage location index
Environmental data	Sample information
(all categories,	Notes on methodology
as above)	Lists of preserved specimens and locations
	Analyses and drawings
	Catalogues
	Storage location index
Documentary	Copies of documents
material—	Relevant analyses, notes and drawings
	Draft reports
	Publication stages (reference lists, proofs, etc.)
	Final reports (incl. circulated interims, etc.)
	Copies of other relevant published material
Public relations—	Photographs
	Material for open days, etc.
	Press cuttings
Correspondence—	All correspondence relating to site other than that stored
	as above
Other—	Any documentary record not included in the above

Figure 6.1 Categories of physical materials in the archive.

a crucial part in the assessment of its storage requirements. In essence, good storage is the art of establishing the desirable organization of collections in store, and assessing the physical care needs of the material and its associated documentation, and then designing the strategies by which the best possible standard may be achieved.

Before these issues are reviewed, however, there is the all embracing difficulty of the name which should be given to the whole process. 'Storage' is rightly felt to be lacking in glamour, to conjure up exactly the wrong images and to handicap a number of strategic efforts, particularly those aimed at some governing bodies. The term 'reserve collections' can be used, but, as Hebditch points out (1981: 3) it carries an exclusive air which is not very helpful. 'Study collections' is another possibility, but is in some ways misleading for these collections are used for all kinds of interpretative projects. The traditional terms 'stores' and 'storage' will be used here, but in the consciousness of their limitations.

The organization of storage

By 'organization' here is intended the ways in which material can be divided up into various groupings, and physically arranged upon the storage units in order to satisfy its use requirements, although, of course, this must be done in conjunction with the environmental and other physical needs of the collections discussed below. The principle involved here is that of accessibility and there are three chief areas where organizational decisions have to be made: what parts of the collections are used most, how this should influence the ways in which the material is arranged, and how best use can be made of the available space, to ensure that material is as accessible as easily and safely as possible.

Archaeological curators have not yet embarked upon the development of use-of-collections measuring techniques of the kind which librarians call bibliometry. Ideas about differing levels of use among reserve collections are drawn from group memory and experience, fortified in many cases by the records which museums keep of the consultation of stored material, and it is upon such records that any more ambitious measurement of collection use would have to be made. Experience suggests that there are three classes of collection use. The first is material in use on a day-to-day basis, and this is likely to include the archive from an ongoing or recently concluded excavation, material which is the subject of an approaching exhibition, and material which is currently being studied in the museum on a (more or less) daily basis by a curator or research worker. The second class covers collections in steady demand by workers of all kinds. In theory, this material should have been catalogued and curated, but in practice some of it, at least, will be waiting its turn. The third class comprises material which is not often consulted and is unlikely to be displayed (see also Ford 1980). The documentation records associated with all this material must also be stored. The records for class one material, certainly, and probably also class two material, may be stored near the physical remains, but the record archive for class three may need to be more accessible than the material itself.

It would, in the light of this, be relatively easy to devise a use of space which put class one material in areas equipped as joint store and work rooms, class two material in the next most accessible stores, possibly linking them with the displays and offering them as visible storage (Ames 1977), and class three material in the more remote stores, perhaps those in a separate building if the rest of the collections are held in the museum itself.

There is, however, a major difficulty here. For good museological reasons of accession and documentation, there is a strong instinct to keep together the material from a specific excavation or collection and therefore to divide the whole into the three classes on a collections basis; but much research and some display is carried out on a period basis or an artefact type basis which cuts across collections (see also Chapter 8). Equally, the class three material is unlikely to comprise complete collections, but rather to involve, for example, the animal bones or undecorated body sherds from excavations whose other material may be frequently consulted. It can, of course, also often make good sense to store groups of small finds like coins, Roman brooches or Bronze Age metalwork, together from an environmental and security point of view, but most curators would hesitate before picking all the worked flint, for example, out of a range of collections and storing these together. Similar difficulties arise in the ordering of material on a chronological basis, to create, for example, an easily consulted typological sequence of Bronze Age pottery (supposing that any curator would be so foolhardy in the first place).

It is very difficult to devise a theoretical system which can absorb these conflicting needs (Watkins 1986), and any such system will prove to be very fragile when it is applied to actual museum situations. In practice, it is usually best to admit that neither hard organizational structures nor ideals of purity are helpful, and to treat the various potential groupings on their own merits, bearing in mind their particular requirements. Coins, for example, are likely to be abstracted from excavation collections and stored together in a cabinet. Excavation material from a medieval abbey may have its worked stone stored in one place and the rest of its building materials stored less accessibly, while flints from a field-working project will be kept together, both tools and debitage. Large items, like timberwork, will need special facilities.

This kind of mixed approach is also able to make the best use of the mixed storage, which many curators are likely to face. It does not, it must be stressed, mean that a curator does not organize the stores carefully according to their internal rationale, but rather that this will embrace a complex sequence of combinations and compromises. It does stress the importance of a proper system of storage location records which are kept up-to-date, linked with a facility to move material about within the whole storage system as it passes from one class of use to another.

This brings us to the relationship between flexible and accessible storage and the use of space, but very little work has been done on these problems in terms of museum storage. Librarians normally recognize that the top shelf should be no more than 6ft 4ins (1.93 m) from the floor, but even at this height boxes of heavy material can be extremely difficult to manipulate, and a solid pair of metal steps with a central rest is essential equipment. A library is reckoned to be unworkable once 86 per cent of the shelf space is taken up, and in order to allow for day-to-day expansion (but not a major acquisition for which special arrangements must be made) a newly-organized store should start with about 40 per cent of its space free (Loynd 1981).

In addition to the space earmarked for material remains, there must be record storage, and work space, which should be normally comfortable, and free from pets, plants and tobacco smoke according to the Museums and Galleries Commission requirements (1986). It is a sad fact that pressure on this study area is always strong, so that in the past it has tended to be one of the first sacrifices when problems of space arise.

Physical care

There is a large literature on the maintenance of collections in store which covers this complex subject in great detail (e.g. Thompson 1978, Leigh 1982 and the *Environmental Standards for the Permanent Storage of Excavated Material from Archaeological Sites* (1984) issued by the Archaeology Section of the United Kingdom Institute for Conservation (UKIC) as basic texts; for particular classes of material see McKinley 1981 (textiles); Horie 1981; Spriggs 1981 (metalwork); Kent 1981 (coins); Jones 1981 (organic samples); and Hartley 1981 (stonework)). Accordingly, only some basic ground will be covered here, and this relates to the standards laid down for grant eligibility by the Museums and Galleries Commission (see below, p. 98–102).

Standards have risen very considerably over the last fifteen years or so, but it is still necessary to make the fundamental point that the packaging and housing of materials to decent standards, and the constant monitoring of the storage environment, are crucial to the proper running of a museum service. There are two reasons for this. The first is the preservation of the physical object in a state which is no worse than that which it was in when it arrived at the museum, or, in terms of a modern excavation, when it was excavated (although old material always poses its own problems). The second is the maintenance of a crucial link in the chain of documentation, so that the object does not become detached from its data tag, and its tag or any associated labelling on bags and boxes does not deteriorate and become unreadable. If the museum has its own conservator, then he will be responsible for arranging the monitoring and for giving necessary advice, and UKIC has set up a Storage Study Group (Norman 1981), Otherwise, the duty falls on the curator, aided by a variety of assistance from bodies like the Area Museum Councils.

The whole storage complex is essentially a nest of boxes, where the largest is formed by the outside walls of the storage building, the inner ones are the separate rooms or areas, and the smallest are the individual boxes and bags which house the individual objects. The whole storage area should be structurally sound with controlled access, and not liable to leaks, flooding, pest infestation, gross pollution like boiler fumes, or excessive vibration. It should have good access, and if it is on more than one floor there should be lifts or hoists. If it is not on the ground floor, loading levels should be checked by qualified people. The store should be reasonably comfortable for staff to be in, and if it is in a separate building it should be equipped with wash room and telephone. It must be kept clean and should be fitted with dust excluders on all openings. Apart from bad handling, incorrect humidity levels are the main source of damage to objects, but because types of material differ in their sensitivity to humidity, it is economical to divide the material into two groups and house these in two separate storage areas.

The basic store will house most ceramics, most worked and unworked stone, most building materials, slag, and unworked bone, and will require humidity levels of between 45 and 70 per cent Relative Humidity (RH) with the smallest possible fluctuations. The temperature should not drop below 4 degrees centigrade or above 30 degrees centigrade, allowing a gradual diurnal movement of + or − 5 degrees centigrade. Daylight should be excluded and artificial light ultra-violet filtered. The material should be protected from dust by boxing.

The sensitive material store will house stabilized copper alloy, stable glass, worked bone and antler, other metals, and other organic materials including environmental samples. It will also take ceramic and stone material with special requirements. The RH should be between 45 and 60 per cent with a weekly fluctuation of no more than + or − 7.75 per cent and the temperature between 10 degrees centigrade and 25 degrees centigrade, allowing only a gradual daily movement of + or − 5 degrees centigrade. The lighting arrangements are as in the basic store, and all material should be boxed. Within this store it may be necessary to create micro-climates for iron, unstable copper alloys and organic materials by storage in sealed polythene containers with, for example, silica gel to keep iron dry. These micro-climates should be devised by a conservator and must be regularly monitored.

Both stores should be equipped with shelving or racking of baked enamel steel (as Dexion) or wood. Roller racking is often thought desirable because of the space which it saves (Plate 3). Material like flints or sherds should be packaged as appropriate in self-sealing polyethylene bags, perforated near the top and equipped with an opaque band on which documentation can be marked with a permanent, waterproof marker. A spun-bonded polyethylene label carrying documentation can also be bagged with the material. More delicate finds, and this includes all those in the sensitive store, should be kept in suitably-sized individual clear polystyrene boxes with snap-shut lids, carefully padded with materials like expanded polystyrene, and with the same documentation. The bags, and the boxes as appropriate, should be stored in cardboard boxes, which it is useful to have in two or three modular sizes, and these should carry a list of contents on the outside.

Objects of substantial commercial value, like coins or gold and silver, should be kept in a fire-proof safe with controlled access. The objects should be packaged as appropriate and their environments controlled and moni-

Plate 3   Roller racking installed in the Musem of London to house boxed archaeological archive. Reproduced by courtesy Museum of London.

tored. Objects on display should be kept to the same environmental standards as those described above, and cases should be regularly monitored.
Particular attention should be paid to the problems of dust and light,
especially if not all daylight can be excluded, and light-sensitive materials
should ideally experience a 50 lux level, with a minimum of 150 lux.

The record store will house the documentary archive (see figure 6.1) which
will be on a range of papers, film and electromagnetic material. Its environmental requirements are similar to those of the sensitive store, with which it
may be combined. Electromagnetic material should be stored in acid-free
materials and kept in wooden or plastic units, or purpose-designed data-
cupboards. All other records should be housed in acid-free containers and
stored in properly labelled baked enamel steel filing cabinets, of which a
large range are available on the commercial market (for photographs see
Tremain 1986; paper, Broughton 1986; and general records, Michelmore
1981).

Two main points emerge from this brief review. The first refers back to the
previous discussion on the arrangement of collections in store and, by
drawing attention to the difficult physical needs of the various materials,
reinforces the suggestion that these arrangements are best made on a
pragmatic basis. The second shows how professional and expensive
archaeological storage now is, and it is to the problem of resource levels and
their potential solutions to which we must now turn.

Storage strategies

What has been said hitherto describes, not the *ideal* storage conditions, but the *target* conditions which all museums who hold archaeological collections should intend to achieve. Contemporary realities present a varied picture. Figure 6.2 shows the relative proportions of museums who have 'good' and 'poor' in-museum store rooms, and those who have outside stores, either custom-built or well-converted ('good'), or 'poor'. A number of these outside 'poor' storage annexes will be redundant historical buildings, often churches, and old, temporary huts, and some of the in-museum stores will be in basements (the writer vividly remembers struggling in an historic house with one completely underground sub-basement store equipped with an open well) or attics, with all the problems of security, environment, access and so on which all such areas carry. Many museums operate with a range of storage areas, of mixed quality. The storage itself is likely often to be a medly of custom-built racking, old converted racking, and various non-standard cabinets and cupboards, some often under display cases (figure 6.3). The great majority of museums clearly regard steel racking as the best solution to their storage problems, linked with standard cardboard boxes. As figure 6.4 shows, the volume of storage space involved is often considerable, but, as would be expected, it differs considerably from one museum to another.

No curator would underestimate the problems which remain, but, nevertheless, as figure 6.2 shows, quite a number of curators are prepared to rate their storage as reasonably satisfactory, or as semi-satisfactory, and this cautious optimism reflects genuine overall improvements in recent years. A number of case studies have appeared in print, including the Grosvenor, Chester (Carrington 1981), Hampshire (Schadla-Hall 1981), Lincolnshire (White 1981) and Winchester (Lewis 1981).

Good storage requires resources and the principal sources are the governing authority of the museum, particularly in the case of national, university and local authority museums, and central government. Industry, where the commercial firm concerned could contribute towards the long-term care of finds as part of an excavation arrangement, should be another source, but this sort of development is still very embryonic. It is the curator's task to develop a strategy which will combine whatever resources of space and equipment he already has, with fund-raising from the governing authority and central government together, so that a better result can be achieved.

In general terms, this strategy is likely to involve the preparation of full policy reports, setting out the details of collection size and projected growth, storage needs and costings, and presenting possible solutions in terms of practical suggestions. The curator will need to encourage aceptance of the fact that storage is expensive, to be positive about the value of the stored collections to the community, and to be honest about his own convictions, albeit as persuasively and tactfully as possible. It is often helpful to bolster what is said with outside technical expertise, and the curator must be prepared for lengthy proceedings in which 'temporary' solutions must sometimes be rejected. The possible or imminent receipt of the finds from an

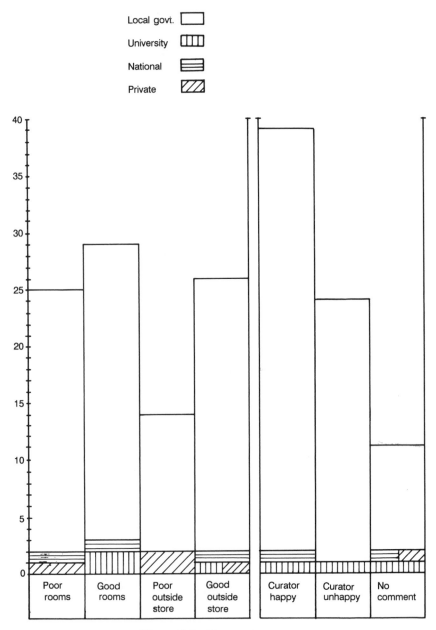

Figure 6.2 Nature of storage

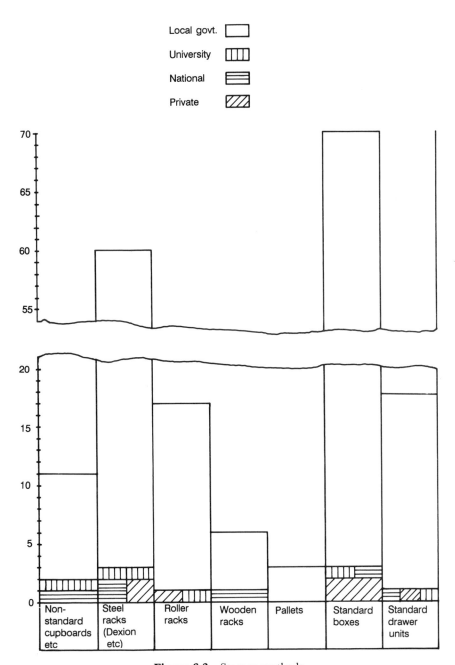

Figure 6.3 Storage methods

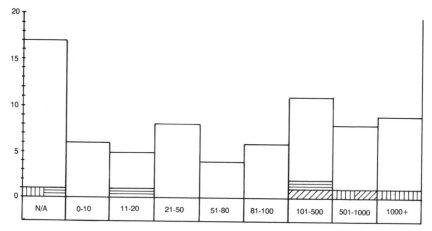

Figure 6.4   Storage size (expressed in m^3)

important local excavation frequently becomes the political issue which brings these proceedings to a head.

Central government money for archaeological storage has been available through the area museum councils for a number of years. These grants are paid in the normal AMC way, which involves a substantial contribution from the museum itself, and the money need not be tied to any particular class of material. More momentously, in October 1981 the Department of the Environment issued Advisory Note 31 which announced a scheme of grants to approved museums for the 'Storage of finds from Grant-Aided Rescue Excavations'. This grant scheme followed the policy implicit in the Frere Report (1975) with its recommendation that the whole excavation archive, 'properly organized and curated', should be housed in readily accessible form, and the Dimbleby Report (1978) which stated that archives should be held by museums and that relevant arrangements should ideally be made before excavation started. The grant-aid scheme applies only to England, and in the other parts of the United Kingdom the responsibility is left with the relevant government departments.

Advisory Note 31 confirmed that 'no museum should accept or request anything other than the complete archive'. The grant would take the form of a once-for-all payment, made at the time when the archive is handed over (although in practice the exercise can be split into several phases). Only certain museums may receive these grants, and so the then Standing Commission on Museums and Galleries drew up a set of criteria for the selection of approved museums, which in due course was issued by the Museums and Galleries Commission as *Eligibility Criteria for the Grant Aided Storage of Excavation Archives* (1986). This states as the general principles of eligibility that:

> The detailed criteria ... specify four classes of accommodation—General Store, Sensitive Store, Record Store and Study Area—and detail the required standards under the headings of *Premises*, *Equipment* and *Services*. Museums seeking eligibility need to demonstrate to the assessors that their premises and equipment meet the minimum standards set out, and that they can and will provide the services that the stored archive will require (1986: 3).

The document goes on to give in detail the responsibilities of the excavation unit, which includes prior consultation with landowner and museum, leading (if possible) to a joint agreement, and prior agreement with the museum over documentation systems, and over the treatment of finds. The criteria for museums are expressed in set standards and checklists covering the three headings. Under *Premises* the environmental and other requirements for the stores are those set out in the previous section, and the *Security* requirements follow normal museum good practice, but are set out in detailed specifications. Under *Equipment* the necessary environmental control equipment, lighting, perimeter alarms and fire alarms, furnishings and curtains and monitoring equipment are described. Under *Services* the necessary curatorial accessioning and inventory control procedure are set out (see Chapter 8) and monitoring detailed.

Access is counted as a service, and it is stated that the museum must be able to provide access to the archive to all *bona fide* visitors, including unheralded spot inspections by the local AMC or representatives of MGC. A working area should be provided for these visitors, where they will be invigilated by a member of staff, and there should be key control procedures, and handling procedures. In all these areas, the details which are set out are regarded as embodying minimum standards.

Museums seeking eligibility must demonstrate to the assessors that their premises, equipment and levels of curation meet these minimum standards. The eligibility of individual museums will normally be assessed by the local AMC, who must be approached by the museum for an assessment. If the museum's standards are considered adequate, the AMC will nominate it for inclusion on the MGC's list of eligible museums, but in any case the AMC will provide a report for MGC. If the standards are not met immediately, but are attainable at reasonable cost, a museum may be deemed eligible if its governing body agrees to carry out an appropriate programme of work, to be concluded within a three-year period. Three years after the initial conferment of eligible status, the AMC will review the museum to confirm that it still makes the grade, and thereafter further reviews will be undertaken at five-year intervals. The Conservation Grants scheme operated by MGC is sometimes able to provide funds for the upgrading of major archaeological stores in line with these criteria. Such grants were available in 1987–8 and at least one museum made a successful application.

In terms of the principles which it embodies, this document, in association with Advisory Note 31, is one of the most significant events in museum archaeology since the original formation of the museum collections. It is the acknowledgment by central government of the importance of the stored archive (albeit archive from only one source, centrally-funded rescue excavation), and of the fact that 'the proper repository for an archive is in a museum' (*Eligibility Criteria* 1986: 2). It brings the range of regional museums with archaeological responsibilities into a network which, in overall policy terms, begins to look something like a national framework for archaeology in the broad sense, and it backs this with storage grants.

Equally significant is the way in which this policy is to be administered. For the first time detailed, and relatively high, standards are laid down for the curation of archaeology collections, which, it is assumed, the museum and archaeological professions as a whole will recognize as suitable and appropriate. Each eligible museum must have at least one archaeologist with 'professional curatorial training' (1986: 2), a statement with profound implications for museums as a whole. Museums themselves are to be divided into two categories, the smaller group which conforms to the standards, and the larger which does not. This distinction, in effect, sets out to apply ideas about 'centres of excellence' which have been floating about in the museum world for many years, and the document takes a markedly more exclusive and generally tougher line than do the *Guidelines* which the MGC have laid down as the basis for the museum registration scheme (1988). The storage grant scheme will also have a major impact on the framing of archaeological acquisitions policies.

Very important, too, is the view of professional relationships which the policy embodies. It requires excavation managers to enter into proper negotiations with the appropriate museum, and states that this shall include agreement about documentation practices. It enhances the role of the AMCs who become the arbiters and monitors of archaeological curatorial standards in a very direct way. Last, but by no means least, the operation of the system as a whole, and of the 'three-year-programme of work' clause in particular, means that it can operate as a way of encouraging governing bodies to spend resources to bring their museum up to standard, both for reasons of pride, and in order to attract grants.

The implications of the policy, then, reach well beyond the actual provision of storage, and could play a substantial part in improving museum management as a whole. The picture on the ground, of course, is not so rosy, even bearing in mind that the scheme as it stands is only intended to apply to a limited class of collections. The scheme began slowly in 1982, with 49 museums initially chosen as eligible. Figure 6.5 shows the comparative numbers of excavation units and approved museums in each of the English AMC areas as it was in 1984 (Davies 1986). It is obvious that while the north and the south-west are reasonably well provided for, and the midlands is fairly well covered, provision in the south-east is very inadequate. This exposes one of the weaknesses of a system which works on an 'unto him that hath shall be given' basis, because it perpetuates existing problems rather

A.M.C. areas	Counties	Excavation units	Approved museums
North	4	3 1 University 2 County	6 1 University 3 County 2 District
North-West	5	6 2 University 2 County 2 District	5 1 University 1 County 3 District
Yorkshire and Humberside	4	4 3 County 1 District Trust	5 1 County 4 District
East Midlands	5	6 1 University 2 County 1 County Trust 1 District 1 Developt. Corp.	5 2 County 3 District
West Midlands	5	5 1 University 2 County 1 District 1 District Trust	8 2 County 5 District 1 Trust
South-West	7	13 1 Regional Trust 2 County 2 County Committee 5 District 2 District Trust 1 University Project	13 2 County 7 District 4 Trust
South-East	16	27 1 University 7 County 3 County Trust 1 London Borough 7 District 1 Developt. Corp. 7 District Trust	12 4 County 1 London Borough 6 District 1 Trust
	46	64	54

Figure 6.5 Comparative numbers of excavation units and approved museums in each English AMC area (after Davies 1986)

than assisting them, and in the south-east special arrangements probably need to be made.

Total grants made for storage purposes have been (Wainwright 1986 and Parker-Pearson, personal communication):

```
1981/2— £84,268
1982/3— £73,547
1983/4—£108,994
1984/5— £34,638
1985/6— £36,675
1986/7— £70,867
1987/8— £56,749
```

Individual grants have ranged between £14.00 and £59,655.00. The grant is calculated on the volume of material to be stored and the rate for 1988/9 stood at £8.55 per 0.017 cu. metre (a measurement of volume based on standard storage box size). In 1984 Wainwright was able to say that so far no grant had been refused on the grounds of shortage of funds (1986: 53).

The system has now been operating for nearly a decade, although there have been some internal developments during that time. Its effectiveness is difficult to assess. Some problems are clear, and have caused widespread disquiet. The distributional unevenness has been noted, and with this goes difficulties about the cover of conservation care (see Chapter 7). The system does not seem to help very readily with the problems which arise from excavation material already received into a museum before about 1980, so that a backlog remains. The range of eligible museums suggests that the fine detail of the criteria are being differently interpreted in the different AMC areas, together with a perceptible feeling that the criteria themselves are unhelpfully inflexible, and museums are, apparently, finding it difficult to claim the grants. Nevertheless, relatively substantial sums of money are available, and museums who might look to receive a grant should be able to integrate this into their overall storage strategies, in the ways which were suggested earlier. As to the more fundamental potential effects of the scheme, in terms of greater museum professionalism and the effective emergence of two recognized classes of museums, it is probably too soon to say. Here, the importance of the scheme is likely to be the part which it plays in the wider issues and changes, with which the museum world as a whole is coming to terms.

7. Issues in conservation

Introduction

Probably more has been written about various aspects of the conservation service, particularly the technical side of the service, than about any other area of archaeology in museums, and so it is not the intention here to review conservation practice in detail, either in terms of laboratory needs or of the treatment of actual materials (but for discussion of these areas see Pye 1984; 203–38). This chapter is concerned to look at the archaeological conservation facilities available in Britain, and the background to them, and to discuss the nature of the relationship between conservators and archaeological curators.

Archaeological conservation services

Archaeological conservation has been a major issue since the early 1970s. This was triggered by the enormous increase in excavation, most of it more or less specifically 'rescue', but also by the growth of intellectual interest in material culture and the information it can yield as a result of scientific investigation, and by the steady development of training and professionalism generally. From the archaeological point of view the issue has been uncontroversial, since the need for an adequate network of conservation services has been universally accepted.

In 1974 the United Kingdom Group of the International Institute for Conservation of Historic and Artistic Works published a survey of facilities in the United Kingdom, entitled *Conservation in Museums and Galleries*. This concluded that probably only about 20 per cent of then existing collections had had any conservation treatment, and that, allowing for the fact that some material will never need treatment, over 50 per cent of the collections were awaiting conservation. This backlog was, of course, growing steadily larger as more excavation material was acquired (1974: 87). Predictably, the survey concluded that improvement in storage facilities was a crucial factor, and it recommended that there should be a rationalization of salary grades and facilities based on more training and the creation of a network of regional centres (1974: 90).

By 1978 the pressure of excavation collections prompted the Department of the Environment to sponsor the report entitled *The Scientific Treatment of Material from Rescue Excavations*, usually known as the Dimbleby Report (1978). The Report was firm in its concern for standards, stating that, 'The important question is how much work can be carried out to an acceptable standard, not how much work can be carried out by lowering standards' (1978: 9). It stressed the need for planning and liaison between excavators, curators and conservators at a very early stage in a project, and noted that no excavation should take place without conservation. It underlined the truth that conservation is a valuable part of the research process, and that training standards and job levels should reflect this status. It pointed out that few of the conservators employed outside the national museums are responsible just for archaeological material, and stressed the difficulties that arise from the range of small and scattered laboratories which leads inevitably to an imbalance of services across the country. It, too, saw as the solution a scheme of regional centres, funded by central government, and assisted by a high-level Advisory Committee.

These large schemes, needless to say, did not come about, and the present conservation service shows a very mixed picture. Figure 7.1 shows the access to conservation services available to the museums who have provided information, many of whom use more than one type of service. It is clear that about 45 per cent of the total (37 museums) employ their own conservation staff, usually a single person responsible for more than solely archaeology. Another 48 per cent (40 museums) use the services provided by the AMCs. These services have to be paid for at a standard rate, so it is likely that they are normally employed for special pieces intended for display, rather than for the broad range of environmental monitoring and excavation material processing. Apart from these two types of facilities, a few museums have access to conservators on the staff of other local authority departments, or HBMC(E) and HBMC(S), or university departments. Very occasionally private, freelance conservators are used, and the Ancient Monuments Laboratory will provide advice. The national museums have their own conservation departments and they, too, will provide advice. Four local authority museums reported that they have no access to conservation facilities.

In 1984–5 HBMC(E) set up a number of extra archaeological conservation posts. These facilities are based mainly in museums, and they are located in Bristol, Manchester, Newham, Kent, Wiltshire, Durham, Yorkshire and Lincoln. The conservators provide a free service for material from HMBC(E)-funded excavations, but the system is geared to publication needs, and it is thought to deal with only 15–20 per cent of the total amount of material needing to be treated (Davies 1986). The untreated material then becomes the responsibility of the recipient museum.

In addition to these working conservators, there are two central government schemes which provide grants for conservation-related projects, although not normally for the actual treatment of material in the first instance. The first is the Grant-Aided Storage of Excavation Archives, operated jointly by HBMC(E) and MGC, which was discussed in the previous chapter; the capacity to provide adequate standards of conservation

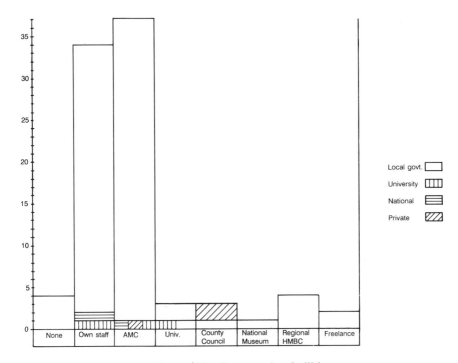

Figure 7.1 Conservation facilities

treatment is a grant criteria. The second is the Conservation Grants Scheme operated by MGC since 1984. This offers grant-aid to non-national English museums and related organizations for projects of national or regional significance where conservation practice generally can be improved, although the precise areas of interest differ from year to year. AMC directors have been brought into the scheme in an advisory role. As a means of monitoring the operation of all these facilities, the United Kingdom Institute for Conservation (UKIC) is conducting a survey of both conservators and their work, and of the conservation facilities available to archaeologists in England and Wales, which is intended to clarify the backlog of unconserved excavated finds to reveal the extent of backlogs in relation to staffing and material resources. It will also explore the relationship between conservators and archaeologists, and the role of the conservator in publication. A similar survey has been undertaken for Scotland (Ramer 1989).

Although all this is clearly an improvement on what went before, its effectiveness is difficult to evaluate. The present arrangements are a mixture of several funding sources, including the significant input from HBMC(E) and MGC, which demonstrates that central government is at last willing to admit a share of responsibility. The immediate impression is of a reasonably adequate country-wide network of conservation services of various kinds operating on recently excavated and old material. How far this represents the reality of collection management across the country is another matter. In her survey of archaeological collections in London, Richardson concluded, 'The system for conserving finds within approved (i.e. by MGC, see Chapter 6) museums is working well and to a very high standard, but other museums are not using the AMSEE service, presumably on grounds of cost, far too much unqualified conservation is carried out, and much work undone by poor post-conservation storage' (1988: 21). What is true for London is likely to be true for the other regions of the country, although London does have an unusually large number of small museums. Here we touch the soft under-belly of archaeological museum management, where resources are very poor, and real improvements hard to achieve.

Relationships between conservators and curators

Within the network of facilities, however patchy its operation may be, a number of principles are at work which create the interrelationship between conservators and curators. This relationship can occasionally be strained, but in the main the two groups of specialists seem to work well together, without the constant friction which can sometimes mar curatorial relation-ships with designers and educators. Both groups agree that there are three main areas where mutual needs and priorities have to be worked out: that concerned with evidence and interpretation; that concerned with the selec-tion of material for treatment; and that concerned with the preparation of objects for display (Keene 1980).

In 1983 UKIC issued to its members their *Guidance for Conservation Practice*, which defined the responsibilities of conservators in relation to the care and treatment of objects (see Ashley-Smith 1982; printed in Shell and Robinson 1988: 259–60). This *Guidance* makes clear statements on the need to preserve evidence rather than removing it during the conservation process, and on the desirability of undertaking only treatment which can be reversed. It defines conservation as, 'the means by which the true nature of the object is preserved', and uses the term 'true nature' to include evidence about the origin, construction and materials of the piece. It stresses, also, how impor-tant it is that both conservators and curators should accept this ethical attitude.

However, in the case of archaeological objects a number of difficulties arise. The object as it emerges from the ground is an encapsulation of its history up to that moment; but the unravelling of that history by the modern investigative techniques of the conservator inevitably involves the destruc-tion of evidence as much as the preservation of a version of the artefact. As Corfield has put it, 'while many general statements have been made about the importance of reversibility in conservation processes, the whole concept has been the subject of scrutiny as it has become more and more apparent that few conservation processes can be considered really reversible' (1988: 261). In other words, like archaeology in general, the processes of conserva-tion and investigation are, paradoxically, themselves inevitably destructive in the sense that 'an irreversible process is begun as soon as an object is removed from the soil, irreversibility continues as the layers of accumulated soil and corrosion are removed, consolidation may add another process of questionable reversibility, and finally it may be impossible to disassemble a reconstructed object' (Corfield 1988: 261).

The scientific study of material culture has been transformed in recent decades, and the analysis of an object by a conservator can now yield a mass of evidence about its morphology and style, its finish and decoration, the technology which produced it, and any organic material which may be a part of it or its context (see Black 1987). Linked to this are the range of sampling techniques now available for dating, and for petrological, metallurgical and other types of physical analysis. In a nutshell, the emphasis is now on finding out about a piece, rather than on cleaning it, because the information embedded in the various accretions or products of corrosion may be as diagnostic as the bare object itself. The object which emerges at the end of this process is not, and never again can be, the object which came out of the ground, and therefore a full documentary and photographic record is an essential part of the conservation process (Keene 1980). A most important element in the conservator's responsibility is, therefore, a judgment of the correct balance between the recovery of evidence on the one hand, and on the other the preservation of evidence through minimum intervention and as close an approximation as possible to the ideal of irreversibility.

Investigation in depth requires the closest co-operation between conservator and archaeologist (Cronyn 1980). Detailed work is very time-consuming, and so the choice of which objects should be examined in depth is a difficult one, and must be made on both archaeological and physical grounds, so that the yield in information is as great as possible. The conservators need to know as precisely as possible what questions require answers, and they prefer exact questions put to them about specific objects or groups of objects. Similarly, conservators need information about the context of the find and what structural interpretation the archaeologist would put upon it, the approximate date or period of the artefact, and who will undertake its study. Data sheets for individual artefact types, like those produced by Brown for Anglo-Saxon shields (Brown 1980: 11–12) and Lawson for stringed musical instruments (Lawson 1980: 12–13) are extremely helpful here. The framework for this kind of work is best developed jointly as part of the overall strategy for the excavation site, but it must be very flexible because it is the unexpected which will usually occur.

Equally difficult are the decisions which must be taken about the degree of attention paid to the great mass of excavation finds. Opinions differ about the need to have a conservator actually on-site during the excavation, and in any case this would not normally be possible. However, all excavation directors should ensure that the workforce follows basic guidelines for primary care and packing, like those embodied in the leaflet prepared by the Archaeology Section of UKIC, *Packaging and Storage of Freshly-Excavated Artefacts from Archaeological Sites* (1983), and the useful *First Aid for Finds* produced jointly by UKIC and Rescue edited by Watkinson (1987), with its ring binder format and waterproof plastic cover. Close contact with a conservator throughout is essential, and so is rapid but careful transport of sensitive material to the laboratory. This material, of course, is likely to feature largely among those specimens chosen for detailed work. The rest of the material will probably include large quantities of finds which will involve a range of the materials listed in figure 6.1. Sites always present very different conservation problems, and a programme to deal with finds which are largely ceramic is obviously easier to devise than one which must cope with considerable quantities of ironwork or waterlogged leather.

Limited resources mean that not all of this material can be given even the basic treatment which will ensure that its nature can be clearly revealed and its stabilization and survival assured, either from the point of view of initial conservation or from that of permanent storage, and, indeed, in terms of its value as evidence it is doubtful if such lavishness could be justified. Since there is little point in trying to store untreated metallic or organic material, the selection for treatment which is made at this point is tantamount in these classes of finds to a selection for retention; and the rest of this material may be discarded, a process which links up with all the problems discussed in Chapter 5.

The principles upon which materials are selected for conservation treatment will revolve around the quantity and quality of archaeological evidence which they embody and their potential for future study, together with their educational and financial value (Leigh 1982). It is important to remember that the significance of some material is revealed *only* as a result of conservation treatment, and this awkward fact greatly complicates the selection process. The selected material should then be cleaned and stabilized, and placed in permanent storage which meets, as closely as possible, the criteria laid down by the Museums and Galleries Commission. Some, but probably only a very small proportion of the selected material will need to be studied and drawn for publication and some of this will require more advanced treatment.

It is possible, then, to distinguish a hierarchy of conservation care. At the bottom comes material high in treatment needs but presumed low in evidential value, such as bulk finds of Roman nails: these will be recorded in the documentary archive but physically destroyed, all but a sample. Next comes material like ceramic, which in conservation terms is often not demanding and may have a high evidence yield, and other material considered of importance; this will be treated and stored. Then come the diagnostic finds selected for publication, some of which, particularly metallic and organic objects, will need a considerable investment of work. At the top of the ladder come those finds which, for specific reasons of context and character, can yield particular information, and these may well require very expensive and highly specialized work before their light can shine. The responsibility for deciding which material belongs where should be shared between the archaeologists and the conservators.

Besides this hierarchy stands another which is concerned with the choice and preparation of objects for display; and it is to this that we must now turn.

Objects for display

Only a very tiny proportion of the finds retained from an excavation are ever likely to appear in an exhibition gallery, and the responsibility for choosing which these finds are belongs with the curator, probably in conjunction with designers and educators and certainly with the advice of a conservator. The choice of objects is likely to depend partly on the way in which they can be used to convey information about the past, and partly on their intrinsic interest, rarity or attractiveness. These needs can sometimes cut across the scale of conservation requirements already discussed, because this is geared to the strictly archaeological demands of the documentation archive and publication. In archaeological terms, for example, a large quantity of waste material from a kiln is unlikely to rate much conservation attention and, indeed, might be a candidate for discard, but in display terms the demonstration of bulk waste material can make important points. The same may be true of large quantities of preserved timber or building materials, where their use in reconstructions may be an option. The key here is close co-operation, and if this can be linked with early decisions about the broad approach of an eventual exhibition then this is most helpful, although it is very difficult to achieve.

Single finds, which of their nature are going to receive considerable conservation attention, are usually also those which merit inclusion in a display, whether that display is geared to explaining methods of analysis, or the life of the past. It is around these finds that a range of ethical problems cluster, and at the heart of these lies the difficulty of deciding to what extent an attempt should be made to restore an object to its original appearance; what, in any case, constitutes the 'original' form of an object; and how the operative decisions should be arrived at.

The reason why the question of restoration to 'original' appearance arises is, of course, because more or less complete objects convey their messages much better, and are very much more intelligible to the visiting public, who, it must be admitted, find what they regard as battered oddments both dreary and ludicrous. Some degree of restoration is probably necessary for many objects if they are to be displayed successfully, and there is general agreement that two cardinal principles should operate here: the genuine parts should be immediately distinguishable from the reproduction, and the restoration process should be reversible so that if fresh knowledge make this desirable the piece can be stripped down and reassembled, although, as we have seen, reversibility is in reality an ideal to be aimed at rather than an easily accomplished state. It may be added that the extent of the restoration should be as limited as possible.

The problem of defining the 'original' form of the object is two-fold. In the first place, there is the archaeological question which involves the degree of knowledge held about the type of find under discussion, the quantity of available comparative material and the extent to which diagnostic features have survived, all of which will contribute to the credibility of any restoration. The second question revolves around the history of the piece itself. Many important objects have had complex histories of their own, which the scars or the reshapings that they have received embody. Which moment in this history should be chosen as that to be physically reproduced?

All these considerations are intimately intertwined, but each object will have its own unique combination of problems, and the way in which restoration work is to be approached will have to be decided individually. Such decisions should be taken jointly by curators, conservators and appropriate finds specialists, and also by any parties who have a legitimate interest, such as the owner of a piece which is on loan.

The problems appear, perhaps, at their simplest with finds like ceramic vessels. It is usually possible from the substantial excavated fragments of a bell-beaker or a fourth-century dish to form a clear idea of its appearance during its period of use. The pieces of the pot can then be glued together, and the missing areas made up with appropriate filler which can be coloured in a way which clearly distinguishes it from the authentic material. Both adhesive and filler can be dissolved away if any interpretative problems arise. Some metal objects, of greater importance in the art-historical sense, can be handled similarly. Corfield cites the bronze head of Lucius Aurelius Verus which was found crushed flat. The head was reshaped in the workshops of Smith and Plowden in such a way that the original intention and artistry of the sculptor was revealed. Evidence crucial to the understanding of the true nature of the object had been made plain, to both specialists and the visiting public, although at the cost of an irreversible process (Smith 1977; Corfield 1988: 262).

If, however, the head had been crushed as a deliberate political or ritual act, the decision to restore it would have been much more difficult. A group of Late Bronze Age phalerae in Devizes Museum, found at Melksham in 1976, had apparently been used as targets during their life in the Bronze Age, because they carried many of the lozenge-shaped holes characteristically dealt by contemporary spear-heads. These holes had left bent-back leaves of metal, with which they could have been filled, but clearly this would have been improper because the ancient damage was an important part of the history of the phalerae and of the historical evidence which they embody. The distortion caused by a mechanical digger at the time of their finding, however, was corrected (Robinson, personal communication).

The problems have arisen recently in an acute form in connection with the gold lozenge from the Bush Barrow, Wiltshire, acknowledged universally to be one of the most important pieces of material culture from the British Early Bronze Age. The lozenge forms part of the collections of Devizes Museum. It was placed on loan in the British Museum in 1922, and was returned to Devizes in 1985. The earliest published photograph of the piece appeared in Abercromby's *Bronze Age Pottery* (1912) which shows it to be considerably distorted and with a deep crease across it. Successive photographs show that the lozenge endured a number of vicissitudes over the years after 1912. Prior to its display in the *Symbols of Power* exhibition in Edinburgh in 1985, the piece was conserved or restored by the British Museum, and as a result, 'the lozenge plate was recognized as being now domed with its centre some 8–10 mm above the sides and a keeling introduced on the principal axes, and it had acquired a surface shine that was not previously apparent' (Shell and Robinson 1988: 249). The lozenge as it is now is shown in Plate 4.

The staff at the British Museum have endeavoured to show by careful metrical analysis that the restored shape of the lozenge is compatible with what appears to have been the intentions of the original goldsmith (Kinnes *et*

Plate 4 Early Bronze Age gold lozenge from Bush Barrow, Wiltshire. The keeling and shine is clearly visible. Reproduced by courtesy Wiltshire Archaeological and Natural History Society Museum, Devizes

al. 1988). Shell and Robinson, on the other hand, using similar methods, have come to the opposite conclusion, and believe that the convexity of the lozenge must have been caused by stretching the gold (1988). There is now no way of deciding between these two irreconcilable opinions because the only evidence was the distorted object, now irreversibly restored.

This history illustrates very well the problems which arise when adequate discussions between all those with a legitimate interest do not take place. It also highlights the genuine difficulties which can arise in deciding what the 'original' form of an object was, and suggests that therefore, in very many cases, it is better to give a piece only such treatment as it requires for physical stability, and not to subject it to an irreversible process in the interests of a more impressive display.

From all this, it is clear that the trend of recent discussion of conservation practice underlines a number of important points. The potential value of artefact studies and the crucial contribution which conservators can make to the better understanding of artefacts, becomes increasingly more obvious. Equally, resource restraints mean that difficult decisions about object selection must be made. Contemporary thinking recognizes that problems surrounding the nature of evidence are part of the preparation of material for display. The course which is likely to produce the most satisfactory results in all of these areas is close co-operation at all stages between conservators, curators and excavators, in association with educators and designers, all of whom are recognized as offering their own particular professional expertise. Viewed in this light, the conservator's role, far from being the passive one which earlier discussions suggested, becomes an important element in the active production of information and understanding.

8. *Documentation and research*

Introduction

The considerable resource which is required to store and conserve archaeological archives, and indeed to produce them by excavation or collection in the first place, can only be justified if the archives are available for use in the broadest possible sense: this cardinal principle means that the material itself, and all the related information which pertains to it and is embodied in it, should be accessible, and in turn implies that the information is held on an organized documentation system.

Good documentation also ensures that collection handling and recording is monitored and controlled, and it gives clear proof of the ownership of the collection. It helps to establish a sensible acquisitions policy which takes account of existing holdings and monitors the adherence to that policy, it offers satisfactory accounting to interested parties like auditors and insurers, and it provides the information needed by museum staff for exhibition, education, conservation and research, and by outside researchers and the general public. The documentation of material, and research into the significance of that material, however 'research' may be defined, are two aspects of the same process because the way in which the information is organized is fundamental to the ways in which it can be interpreted, but in order to ease the discussion, documentation as data-handling is here discussed first and research second.

Information technology is one of the primary concerns of our day, and this is reflected in a considerable quantity of recent literature on archaeological and museum documentation, both in general terms and specifically in connection with computerization (e.g. Martlew 1984; Richards 1987; Orna 1983, 1987; Roberts 1985; Cooper and Richards 1985; Lock and Wilcock 1987; Richards and Ryan 1985; Stewart 1980a, b). There are also a number of specialized groups and journals including *Archaeological Computing Newsletter*, *Computer Applications in Archaeology* (the proceedings of an annual conference produced from 1973 onwards), and the Museums Computer Group, which organizes twice-yearly meetings and produces a *Newsletter*. In North America, the corresponding group is Museum Computer Network, which produces its quarterly newsletter, *Spectra* (Moffitt 1989). The subject is a huge one, and its boundaries and landscapes are constantly altering, so rapid is the pace of change. All that can be attempted in this brief compass is a simple overview of some of the more obvious features as they appear at the time of writing.

Museum archaeological documentation: the problems

Museum archaeological documentation shares many problems with all the other museum disciplines, and the size and scope of the recent literature highlights one of the most basic of these. Many collections are very large, and the creation of a complete documentation archive is so formidable and so resource-consuming a task that it has to be conceived as a long-term project which will take years to complete and must be serviceable for many more years. On the other hand, information technology, and especially computer capacities, are developing very rapidly so that it is extremely difficult to select systems which will be satisfactory for the longer term. This strategic problem, linked with the immediate difficulty of choice from a large and competing market, acts as a deterrent to the creation of a modern documentation system in many museum services, particularly the smaller ones.

Once a choice of system has been made, the pressure on resources created by the workload is very considerable. Data-entry is highly labour-intensive and highly skilled, and it is not an area where the employment of volunteers or workers on Manpower Services Commission type schemes is likely to be very successful unless the participants are highly motivated and well trained, as many museums have found to their cost. Documentation work can be very dull if it is carried out for a long period without any variety, no matter how committed to the task the staff may be, and, like all 'back room' work it does not greatly commend itself to the members of many governing bodies or private funders, who prefer to see a more obvious 'front-of-house' product for their money, especially, again, in a smaller service.

General problems of choice and resource are matched by difficulties inherent in the archaeological archive itself. The normal presumption is that each item in the collection will have its own unique number and accompanying record. In most museums since early in this century this number has taken the form of, for example, 100/1988/1–5 in which 1988 represents the year of accession, 100 shows that it was the hundredth accession in that year, and 1–5 is an extension series showing that the group consisted of five objects. However, the extension series system was often in the past badly used, leaving large, poorly recorded groups, and old excavation collections were often scarcely documented at all in museum terms because they presented such difficult problems.

Much important material comes from very old collections whose sketchy documentation usually consists of an entry in an early day-book, ledger or register. A typical example from Exeter City Museum (Plate 5) shows a page from the old Antiquities Register in which miscellaneous material was entered between about 1868 and 1886, and given a running accession number. Numbers 4145 to 4147, two bronze spearheads and a flat bronze plate, and 4190, a sword recorded separately, refer to the Worth (Washfield) weapon hoard, which is a crucial find for the interpretation of the later

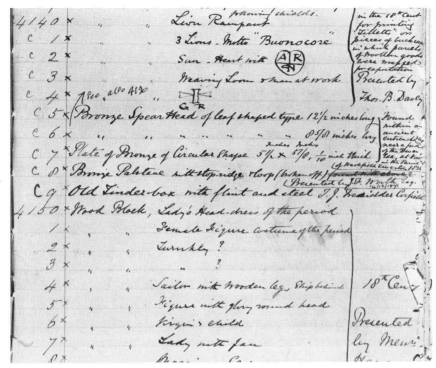

Plate 5 Page of early Museum Register, showing the original acquisition record of the Worth (Washfield) Bronze Age hoard. Reproduced by courtesy Exeter City Museum.

Middle Bronze age, while 4148 refers to a palstave, known from other records to be the sole survivor of a different hoard, which was apparently found fairly near, but not with, the Worth find. Other pieces of information are added in the margin. The documentation on to a modern system of this kind of information can only be done satisfactorily by a curator who knows the material and its various records very well, and even so choices have to be made which may well not show up as such in the system and will therefore be misleading. Most museums will have a stratified sequence of successive accession systems, and these mixed records are likely to be both specific to the archaeology section and part of the general museum record. They will probably not be to a modern standard, and they will include all kinds of incompatibilities. They can turn the creation of a new system designed to modern standards into a very thankless task.

A further problem implicit in the history of acquisition at many museums revolves round the very mixed nature of the collections, and means that priorities must be established so that the documentation of some material is worked up at the expense of others. For most archaeological museums this is likely to mean that local material takes precedence, followed by other British material, leaving Mediterranean or Northern European collections with a low priority.

A quite different set of difficulties is concerned with the desirability of integrating museum documentation with that created by other archaeological record-making. The most important of these concerns the integration of current excavation and field work records with the documentation system of the museum to which the excavation and fieldwork archive will go, and this is discussed in a separate section. Clearly, the better museum records can be cross-referenced to the county Sites and Monuments Registers (Burrow 1985), the better the whole data-bank will be, and the same would apply to national registers like those maintained by the National Monuments Record, English Heritage and the National Trust. Sadly, however, this kind of link is in a very embryonic state, and is not likely to develop much in the foreseeable future, considering the variety of format and approach employed, for example, just by the Sites and Monuments Registers.

Mutual integration of records across archaeological museums would be equally desirable, but faces similar problems. Museums have had, and most still do have, their own design of record system, whether this is on paper or on computer, and although museum records cover similar ground, they differ widely in design, content and approach, so that they could not be used together in a simple fusion even if this were physically possible. It was this infinitely various situation which the introduction of the Museum Documentation Association's (MDA) cards was intended to standardize (see below).

Finally, there is no standardization of archaeological terminology or of necessary techniques like measuring or colour-coding, and no thesaurus of archaeological terms has found general acceptance, in spite of efforts to provide such a system (or elements of such a system) by the Council for British Archaeology and RCHM(E) (*Thesaurus of Archaeological Terms*, 1986), and by pioneers like the Oxfordshire Sites and Monuments Register (Benson 1972). Many archaeologists would argue that the nature of research and interpretation in the discipline requires a high degree of flexibility in the terminology, with the scope to create new categories at will and to refine the meaning of old ones, but this, of course, means that a standard database can never be created, and any worker approaching a fresh data source will always need to know when it was compiled and, probably, under whose instruction. Nevertheless, the creation of a detailed set of keywords which can go into general use (eventually, because, of course, there will be a very large backlog) is an urgent priority for British archaeology, even though its creation presents major conceptual and practical problems (Lavell 1986, 1987), and it is a priority which the establishment of the MDA-Museums Terminology Group is beginning to address.

The current state of archaeological documentation in museums must be viewed against the background of these thronging problems, which arise from the nature of the collections, from incompatibility, and from resource limitations (figure 8.1). Four museums are still using bound registers of the most traditional kind, and these are, of course, not computerized. Over a third (36) of the museums are using, or beginning to use, MDA cards, a

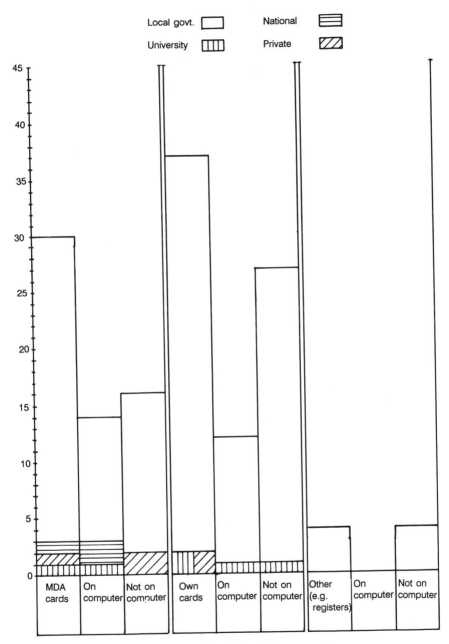

Figure 8.1 Archaeological documentation

surprisingly large proportion, and of these about half have already embarked upon computerization while a number of the rest plan to do so. The remaining museums, however, are using their own cards, or sheets, and relatively few of these, mostly the largest, are in the process of computerization. Generally, these are the medium-sized and long-established museums with a sound tradition of manual record-keeping, while those using MDA cards are either newer services (often emerging as a result of various reorganizations and so inheriting a mixed bag of records) or smaller museums intent on creating a professional database for the first time.

Documentation: manual solutions

Traditional manual systems usually involve a suite of printed (or duplicated) forms on which documentation proceeds, beginning with the arrival of the object, and the completion of the entry form and the entry in the Day Book or Initial Register, continuing with the allocation of a permanent accession number, and concluding with the completion of the Accession Form and any necessary insurance updating (Stansfield 1988). Systems differ considerably in detail, and in many museums each subject department will maintain its own records as well as completing those required for general museum purposes. Comparison across a range of archaeological record forms shows that these differ very considerably also, but all carry boxes for standard information about owner, date of accession, accession number, object name, acquisition method, description, location or provenance, and history of the piece. Some allow for further entries relating to insurance and valuation, conservation treatment, storage location, photographic record, and exhibition and publication history. Record sheets or cards of this kind are often duplicated so that the multiple copies can be used to create indexes of period, location, donor and so on. These relatively simple systems can, of course, be entered into a computer provided that the necessary software package can be acquired, but they are primarily intended for manual use.

Record systems designed by individual museums and primarily intended for use with a computer can, of course, generate a range of paper records which can be used manually, but the most important system which includes manual card indexes linked with computerization is that created by MDA, and as figure 8.1 shows, a number of museums do use MDA cards as a purely manual system. MDA's own literature is considerable (see Roberts 1988; *Practical Museum Documentation* 1981 and the material on *The MDA Museum Documentation System* 1976–87), and includes a regular bulletin, *MDA Information*. MDA also offer an advisory service and welcome responses from users. MDA catalogue cards are designed to hold the full master records about objects in collections, and all the cards in the range are based on the same all-embracing data standard and are therefore fully compatible with each other. The cards are highly flexible in the diversity and depth of information which they can accept, and they can be cross-indexed for information retrieval. Because they are designed for manual and computerized use they incorporate the rigorous form of punctuation known as the separator convention, and using this can be very irksome for the manual operator.

Each discipline object card is accompanied by its own instructions book, and that for archaeology is *Archaeology Object Card Instructions* issued in February 1980. These give detailed information about the conventions to be used and line by line instructions which define the meaning and use of each part of the card. They offer lists of possible key words and suggest the adoption of internal conventions, although it is made plain that these suggestions are not intended to be restrictive. The information the cards hold is similar to that on most museum cards, but more comprehensive than many. MDA cards, like all manual systems, are time-consuming to use and can only be consulted in the museum, unless catalogues have been published, but, properly organized and maintained, these manual systems can and do operate perfectly satisfactorily.

Documentation: computerized solutions

Two inter-linked choices surround the computerization of museum archaeological records: that of appropriate hardware, the computer itself, and the necessary peripherals such as printers; and that of suitable software, that is the operating system and user-written programs or commercial packages which include the database that will give the desired information retrieval, and probably facilities like word processing, graphics and statistics (for general discussion, see Abell-Seddon 1987, and Richards and Ryan 1985). The Information Retrieval Group of the Museums Association (IRGMA), from which MDA developed in 1977, had hoped to create a national computer archive of museum holdings on a single central machine, and this would have involved the use of a mainframe computer and a single database package with an input of records from all museums in the United Kingdom. The desirability of such a unified archive is obvious, but by 1971 IRGMA had had to decide that it was unrealistic, and that the way forward in computerization would involve a more fragmented system implemented on local computers, using a standard of data structure which would, in theory, allow the exchange of files between machines. It is this concept of data structure which the MDA system embodies.

County museum services are frequently in a position to make use of county council mainframe computers, although access can be a problem. Here, as in Leicestershire, the museum will have the help of county council programmers to design suitable accessioning programs. The facilities will include large-scale information storage capacity. Other museum services and excavation units are more likely to use one from the available range of micro-computers and the applications of these have been discussed in two recent publications (Stewart 1980a; Light and Roberts 1984). IBM compatibility for micro-computers is now the industry standard and many mainframe database packages are producing personal computer versions, such as ORA-CLE, which are IBM compatible: this development is helping to ease the problems created by the use of different systems in contemporary working life (but does not, of course, solve the problem of incompatible backlogs). Micro computers are now cheap enough to be within the reach of many museum services. The storage capacity of these machines was limited, but is now increasing rapidly, thanks to the relative cheapness of 100 mg hard discs, and the possibilities offered by networking which allows central storage with multi-user access. *Computer Usage in British Archaeology* (Richards 1987) gives the results of a survey into the types of computers and software in use in British archaeology, but the information concerning museum archaeology is incomplete.

MDA offers two software packages which are compatible with its cards. The Museum Object Data Entry System (MODES) runs on a wide range of popular micro-computers and offers the rapid data entry of museum records. MODES has sparked off a Modes User Group (MUG) which works to keep MODES users in touch with each other by means of a newsletter, events and demonstrations, and to provide an organized forum for feedback to MDA on future developments of the system. TINMUS can work on its own or interface with MODES, and is a multi-user cataloguing and retrieval system in which the results of a search can be printed out to a number of different formats. It holds catalogue records in a form which allows fast access by object identify number, people, places, dates, events (e.g. exhibition), proces- ses (e.g. conservation, acquisition) and documents, and all these may be explored by a process of navigation. MODES was released in 1987 and began to establish itself in museums quite rapidly, while TINMUS, released in 1988, has yet to prove itself. A mainframe package which can process large quantities of structured text records and set up information retrieval systems which will access catalogue records by keyword descriptions is MUSCAT. This package can also be run on the larger range of modern micro- computers, and several museums are showing interest in it.

After strong early hesitations through the 1970s, the computerization of museum archaeological records would now probably be regarded as desir- able by most curators, for whom the advantages of easy access and automatic cross-referring, coupled with the development of micro-computers and better user-friendly systems, outweight the difficulties of unfamiliarity and change.

Museums, excavation and fieldwork

The satisfactory integration of the excavation or field survey archive and the museum retrieval system presents one of the greatest challenges to curators and fieldworkers, because only if this is achieved can the archive, usually all that is left of its site, be used satisfactorily for post-excavation projects of all kinds, and the original work justified. This is true of all field survey work, although the archive product here is usually relatively simple, and it is true also of excavations undertaken before *c.* 1960, although here, of course, both the work itself and the succeeding archive were often sketchy (however the published report may read) and any retrieval correspondingly unsatisfactory. It is acutely true of more recent excavation programmes undertaken by field unit teams, where standards of work are generally high, where the archive is correspondingly large and complex, and where, in accordance with contemporary thinking, the published report often represents a synthesis rather than a detailed account (for a discussion of the nature of archive, see Chapter 5).

The difficulties which surround the integration of excavation and museum documentation have been relatively little discussed, given the extent to which documentation problems generally have been canvassed, but Rance addressed the question in the 1970s (Rance 1973, 1976, 1978, all published typescripts) and more recently it has been usefully reviewed by Stewart (1980b) and in some of the papers published in the volume *Dust to Dust: Field Archaeology and Museums* by the Society of Museum Archaeologists (1986).

The question can be broken up into a number of specific problems, quite apart from the ever-present resource constraints of money, time and staff. The size and scope of the whole archive has increased hugely over the past three decades, but only in the county and larger district museum services have the organizational structures developed correspondingly. The history of the relationship between excavation units and museums has not always been happy (see Chapter 2) and although this is improving steadily there are still sometimes residual difficulties. Most curators pride themselves on their detailed knowledge of their collections and stores and this expertise is immensely valuable, but it becomes dangerous when it is used as a substitute for formal documentation. Unprofessional practices of this kind, on the part of curators and excavators, are much less common than they used to be, but they have frequently left a poor legacy behind them.

Legal questions must be borne in mind. Museums normally expect that archives given into their care will be donated to them and on this assumption integrated documentation can be considered at an early stage; but some landowners, especially private ones, are unwilling to give up their title until they know what kind of material is involved and this, although very understandable, can hamper the archiving process. Auditors' needs must be taken into account, just as they are in all forms of museum accessioning.

The most fundamental problem, however, is the fact that the documentation system normally used by an excavator, and that habitually used by a curator, are quite different, and that the two systems work reasonably well in isolation but do not marry up very easily (Stewart 1980b). Excavation systems usually assign each small find (defined as an item deemed worthy of separate recording within this particular excavation strategy) a number within a single continuous numerical sequence linked to a site and year code. This can be further broken down in various ways but typically it yields an item documentary reference like

NAB.1955.25/1 (= site.year.context/item number)

The total finds from a site may therefore include a range of separate number sequences which record their strategraphic provences, and each item (or sometimes group of items) will carry its own number. This nest-of-boxes approach to documentation is at odds with a museum accessioning system which, as we have seen, depends on a continuous date-linked system giving

27/1973/1-14 (= year number/year/extension numbers given to items in the same group)

The problem is made more difficult for the curator because he will probably be dealing with the material from a range of different excavation sites, probably produced by more than one field unit, each of whom will have their own idiosyncratic habits and traditions. The effort to standardize recording and descriptive techniques across excavation units has made little progress as yet. When manual systems are replaced by computer systems the problems are further compounded. There are at least seven computer programs for excavation documentation, all of which operate on different machines, and the receiving museum will not have access to the necessary range of hardware and software, although the acceptance of IBM compatibility will improve this situation.

There is no easy or obvious solution to this range of problems. The simplest way of absorbing the excavation number runs into a museum system is to allot the excavation an accession number (or block of numbers if necessary) at the very beginning of the excavation. Each excavated item can then be given its museum number at the same time as its excavation documentation. This is the general method used in practice by most museums who may receive mixed material from a range of units, and in any case, may lack the facilities for a more sophisticated documentation service. Even this simple approach, of course, depends upon a pre-excavation agreement between landowner, unit and museum, and, failing this, the curator will find himself faced with the task of working over each excavated item in order to add its museum number; usually, he compromises and adds it only to the outside of the storage boxes.

This is, in any case, only a very superficial procedure unless it is carried to the length of using museum numbers, or creating extension numbers, of each context and its linked item group, accompanied by the integration of the excavation archive into the normal museum cross-referenced indices, so that retrieval can be made under headings like 'amber' or 'Trevisker Ware', and the whole system is so arranged that these can be physically located in the store. This type of thorough-going approach to museum documentation, which may be applied in a number of ways, is only possible if the curatorial department and the field unit are elements in the same organization, or are independent but willing and able to work very intimately together, so that a detailed documentation policy can be worked out before the excavation begins. All the marking of items with their documentation can then happen at the same time, and the excavation and museum records can be created together.

Systems to this level of integration and complexity are used in only a small number of archaeological services. The Museum of London has put considerable effort into designing a system which includes an Archive Directory, which briefly states the main findings from each site and lists the archive reports on site, finds and environmental material, and a more detailed finds data-bank which can give information organized according to types of object (Schofield 1986; Rhodes 1986; and references in both to detailed manuals produced by the Department of Urban Archaeology, Museum of London). The National Maritime Museum has produced an integrated fieldwork and museum record (Booth 1986).

Oxfordshire Department of Museum Services works in close co-operation with the Oxford Archaeological Unit (Hassall 1979) and the Museum Services have produced their own *Procedures for the organization of excavation finds and archive* which covers the organization and storage of archival material and the accessioning and storage procedures for find material. The *Procedures* include a detailed description of the allocation of a museum accession number to every unit of excavation material, and the way in which this should be applied to all items in the archive, in association with organized storage and the maintenance of five categories of catalogue and index (archaeology group records, accession records, collection detail record sheets, computer files and parish/site index). Similar systems are in use at St. Albans (Stone 1978, 1979).

Archaeological research in museums

There are a number of ways in which a policy for archaeological research in museums might be formulated (see Davies 1984; Pearce 1974; Renfrew 1967), and the discussion here divides the topic up into curatorial research, research assistance, information flow, local research strategies, and pure or academic research. Although the last is usually given pride of place, this discussion is not intended to place these activities in any kind of hierarchy, but rather to identify elements which together make up a research policy in conjunction with a properly formulated documentation policy.

Curatorial research involves knowing enough about the museum's holdings and the related archaeology to be able to document the material satisfactorily, so that an appropriate record can be maintained, and the curator can plan exhibition briefs, write information leaflets, answer enquiries and give an assortment of general lectures. This is easier said than done, because it involves making time to keep abreast of recent literature, including local and national periodicals, to attend a variety of archaeological meetings (usually on Saturdays), and to maintain links with a local university or similar institution. Curatorial research should make possible the publication of catalogues of archaeological holdings (although this can also, of course, involve the curator in 'pure' research) and it will include liaison with the various petrological and other materials analysis projects, and with the activities of the growing number of small specialist groups like the Small Finds Research Group, the Lithic Studies Group and the Society of Bead Research.

The increased archaeological activity of recent years has made it clear that this kind of collection-linked curatorial knowledge needs to put on a more uniform and accessible basis and, at the time of writing, is leading to discussions between the Museums Association and the Society of Museum Archaeologists with the view of setting up a national collection research project to identify British and foreign archaeological material in British museums. Pilot projects of this kind are under way in Yorkshire and Humberside, and the West Midlands, where David Symonds has organized the West Midlands Archaeological Collections Research Unit (WEMACRU). The unit is working on a linked geographical/material type basis and has circulated forms on which museums record the number of objects they hold according to country/county, site, and material (stone, clay, glass, and so on). This is intended to provide the fundamental raw data which, for example, will tell a student that a particular museum has five clay vessels from Cyprus, as a starting point for further enquiries. A country-wide data-bank of this kind would be very valuable, and it is hoped that problems of definition and terminology, and of data collection and collation can be overcome.

Every curator has a fundamental duty to assist the research of others by making material and its whole documented record available to *bona fide* students, who will be drawn from a vast diversity of people, ranging from post-graduate students looking for particular groups of material to biographers interested in a particular collector, or artists looking for inspiration in the design of a book jacket (but not embracing school children for whom different provision needs to be made).

Renfrew (1967) suggested that the scholastic researcher needs accessibility of material linked to good store location, which are requirements common to all disciplines, and also specifically archaeological information relating to association, material type, grid location and 'archaeological taxonomy', that is a classificatory ordering of 'type' and 'culture'. This poses problems of terminology standards and also of collection organization (see also Chapter 6). Traditionally, excavation collections are stored as a single unit, divided into stratigraphic sub-units, but more research work is done by category, so that if, for example, a student wants to look at Black Burnished Ware, he will be directed towards the massed archives of several excavations and left to go through the boxes and the documentation in order to pick out what is wanted from the whole. Probably the root reason for this is the curator's unwillingness to break up an excavation collection and loose the physical links which still exist when objects excavated together are stored together in the same bag, because such a link, once lost, might be difficult to reconstitute. There is no theoretical reason why excavation collections should not be reorganized by categories provided that the documentation attached to each piece is adequate, correct and secure, but in practice, through weaknesses of both excavator and curator, this is by no means always the case, and so the less risky, but less helpful, course is usually pursued.

As every curator knows, all these kinds of research enquiry, whether they involve a written letter or a personal appointment, are extremely time consuming, with a suite of knock-on problems involving the provision of samples, photocopies and photographs, all of which must be ordered in accordance with the general policy of the service. A students' room with a range of useful maps, literature and work tables large enough to spread material out, where the collections and the student can be brought together, can help to ease many problems.

The researcher should also realize that he will gain much more from a museum if he approaches the curator sensibly, by stating needs as clearly as possible, by making and keeping firm arrangements, and so on: the ways to achieve a successful visit have been pertinently and humorously described by Cheetham (1987). A problem here, but one perhaps more often discussed than encountered, revolves around the desirability of passing on to a researcher unpublished information which may be part of the curator's own research work. Any strict ruling is unlikely to be helpful, and in practice most curators (although not all) are perfectly willing to pass material on providing they receive due acknowledgment, recognizing that second-hand work is seldom as authoritative as the eventual primary publication.

The maintenance of a flow of information from the museum to a range of other bodies is a similarly basic duty. This involves the transfer of information from enquiries and donations to Sites and Monuments Records and perhaps to record holdings in a planning department, national park or reference library. This will add to the body of information held in a data-bank, and it may be usual for a museum also to publish an account of new material annually in a county journal or a museum annual report. All these activities add to the body of information available in the research workplace.

Equally fundamental is a curatorial influence on local research or information gathering strategies, of the kind which involve excavation and fieldwork programmes, the setting up of conservation projects of various types and, on occasions, the preparations for a Public Enquiry called in advance of development. Each county or region usually has a range of committees which are concerned with such matters, either steming from archaeological societies or acting as advisory bodies to local authorities. It is important that the museum should have a voice on these bodies, even though local problems or technicalities arising from local authority arrangements sometimes make this difficult, so that the museum is seen to be a part of the regional process of discussion and consensus, and that when policies are designed, museum factors of collection management are taken into account from the very beginning.

'Pure' or academic research is usually defined as work which creates new understanding, either by producing new knowledge or by synthesizing existing information in ways which give fresh interpretations. Clearly, there is no sharp line between this kind of work and all the other activities which have been discussed here, including, most fundamentally, the way in which the museum orders its documentation system and the kinds of knowledge which this makes possible, through the application of various statistical and other analytical programmes. However, work recognized as pure research is generally considered to give great personal satisfaction, to develop the potential of the collections (since it will usually be based, at least in part, on the museum's own holdings), to attract funds and events, and generally to add to the respect in which the museum is held.

Figure 8.2 shows that a substantial proportion of museums give a high priority to research, taken by most museums to mean that curators are

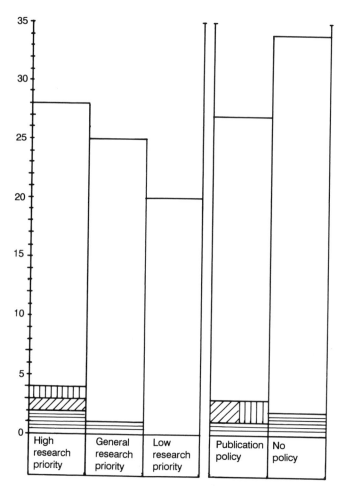

Figure 8.2 Research and publication

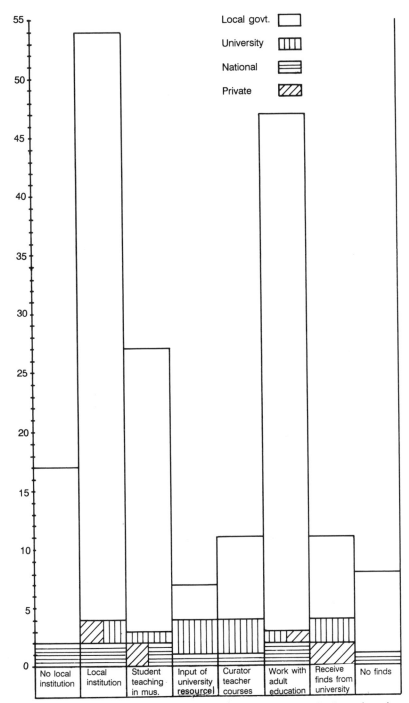

Figure 8.3 Relationship with local institute of higher or further education

allowed to carry out such research during working hours (if they can find the time) with varying degrees of encouragement. A number of museums, however, confine research to general activities of the kind defined here as providing help to others, and a third group give a low priority to research in relation to other objectives, a policy usually bitterly resented by the curators concerned. Nearly half the museums contacted have considered publications policies, although these will embrace the whole range of academic publications and information sheets.

For curators, academic research is likely to involve liaison with a university (or college of higher or further education with an archaeology section) as a higher degree student and tutor, and also as a recipient of finds from university fieldwork and perhaps of some help from university resources in the shape of grants (increasingly unlikely) and jointly-appointed short-term staff. Figure 8.3 sets out the present relationship between higher education establishments and archaeological museums, and shows that mutual involvement is relatively substantial, particularly in the areas of adult extension courses and student teaching. Curators tend not to make many applications to the research-funding bodies, and it may be that the establishment of the Forum for Co-ordination in the Funding of Archaeology, which is intended to stimulate co-operation so that the most productive use can be made of the available resources, will act as an encouragement.

This whole area has an important bearing on the kinds of people whom museum services may wish to recruit as curators and on the ways in which their careers are perceived. It is often argued that more staff interchange between national and regional museums, and between museums, universities and similar institutions, would benefit all concerned. The achievement of this requires a range of mental adjustments, in which the proven ability of curators to undertake research plays one part.

Publication is a crucial element in all these activities and has attracted a corresponding amount of recent attention. The Council for British Archaeology's *Signposts for Archaeological Publication* (1976) is still useful and Cambridge University Press produces a valuable series of authors' and printers' guides. The Department of the Environment through various agencies has put out a number of guidelines relating to excavation publication (e.g. Young 1980, Frere 1975). Computer firms like IBM and MacIntosh now offer desk-top publication systems and the archaeological applications of these have been discussed by Sutton (1987), and by several authors in the volume edited by Ruggles and Rahtz (1988). Increasingly, report elements are likely to be published on microfiche, with all that this implies (Mytum 1986a).

General conclusion

The interrelated operation of documentation and research is clearly one of the most crucial areas of museum policy, in archaeology as in every subject. The installation of new and sophisticated systems, whether or not they are computerized, is expensive in resource terms, but the expenditure is worse than wasted if it is not accompanied by well-thought-out programs backed by considerable expertise, because without these expensive mistakes will become enshrined in the system, creating endless difficulty and frustration.

These problems notwithstanding, the range of the archaeological archive, as it has come to be understood over the last decade, will require a more informed and more complex documentation system than the traditional approaches could offer. 'The well-tempered archive', to borrow Stewart's phrase (1980b: 22) would encompass the actual transference of finds and documents to the museum numbering systems, the application of satisfactory documentation and data standards, and the provision of well-organized storage, all expressed in an archival policy. Such a policy would aim to translate into physical premises and working practices all the aspects of collection management which have been discussed in this part of the book. This must be operated in a climate of genuine co-operation between curators and excavators, and between the curators of different museum services. A few museums, ranging from the very largest like the Smithsonian with its Museum Support Center organized into storage pods and other facilities (Duckworth 1984), to enterprises like the Northamptonshire Archaeological Archive operated as an extension of the museums service, are putting an integrated approach to archaeological collections into practice. Such systems, no doubt, represent the ideal rather than the present reality for many museums, but it is the ideal to be aimed at, so that collections are not just held, but truly managed.

Part three.   Museums, the public and the past

9. Our public

The term 'general public' is capable of a range of interpretations, not all of them flattering, but here it is taken simply to mean all those people who do not regard themselves as professional curators or archaeologists, and therefore constitutes, as we should never forget, the huge majority of the population. Within this majority there are three fairly clear groups. The greater proportion of the adults includes those who have no regular commitment to the past, or whose interest takes a form which professionals often consider unfortunate or improper. The smaller section embraces those adults who do take an informed interest in the past. The third group are the children, whose interests are not yet fixed. Cross-cutting these distinctions are the cultural differences which result from the fact that Britain is now a multicultural society.

The way in which the past is viewed by the general public, and how those views should or could be changed, is one of the most difficult areas to confront modern archaeologists and, perhaps, particularly museum archaeologists. Its importance is undoubted: both museums and archaeology depend wholly upon public support, mediated in a variety of ways, for their operation, and as Fritz and Plog have succinctly said, 'we suspect that unless archaeologists find ways to make their research increasingly relevant to the modern world, the modern world will find itself increasingly capable of getting along without archaeologists' (Fritz and Plog 1970: 412). The chapters in this part of the book set out to explore the nature of the relationship between the public and museum archaeology.

The gulf between the majority of the public and those who take an informed interest in the past is significant, and, needless to say, the dividing line broadly follows that which separates the well-off and better educated from the rest, as the chart (figure 9.1) produced by Merriman for museum visits as a summary of the main demographic tendencies in his recent survey shows (Merriman 1989).

The nature of this divide has been perceptively analysed by Bourdieu, one of the few sociologists who discusses museums and galleries (e.g. Bourdieu 1984). He argues that individuals are socialized primarily by their families into ways of thinking and feeling, which he calls 'the habitus', and that this exerts a strong influence on achievements at school. Since school culture is constructed in terms familiar to the middle class, the middle-class child will be better able to decipher the code and assimilate what is on offer. The same applies to museums and to what they display:

a work of art has meaning and interest only for someone who possesses the cultural competence, that is, the code, into which it is encoded (Bourdieu 1984: 2).

Visitors	Non-visitors
'Middle' age group (35–59)	The over-60s
Owner-occupiers	Council house tenants
Car owners	Non-owners of cars
Students or those in employment	Retired, unemployed or part-time work
Attended selective school	Attended non-selective school
Stayed on at school	Left school at minimum age

Figure 9.1   Tendencies of typical museum visitors and non-visitors (after Merriman
1989, Table 14.3, 156)

Lack of training in the objects on show means that they are assessed only
in terms of colour, size, and unfamiliarity, as anybody who has spent an
unobtrusive ten minutes in his own gallery knows, and so boredom soon
results from an inability to make the objects mean anything. Possession of the
code may be described as a form of cultural capital, which is closely linked
with economic capital, because an investment in culture pays dividends on
the school, university, job and marriage markets, and capital is, by definition, a monopoly of the middle class (although, nevertheless, in many
families among the economic middle class culture is more or less despised).
The inevitable result of this is a popular argument which runs: why should
we spend large sums of money maintaining institutions, collections and
pleasant jobs for which we have no use?

This question is much more difficult to answer today than it was a century
ago, when satisfactory reference could be made to the great European
tradition of science, humanism and high culture, to which, quite specifically,
the museums were intended to give access to all. Those on the lay side of the
divide now have their own justificatory theory which revolves around a
perception that culture and the use of leisure, together with ideas like
'respectability', have been controlled by the establishment in its own interests, and that academics and curators have maintained a magic circle of
esoteric lore, which is chiefly designed to enhance their own separate
superiority but which, at the end of the day, is no more 'right' or 'wrong'
than any other view. This is the stand of many ley-line enthusiasts, Stonehenge cult-makers, and treasure-hunters, whose alternative archaeology has
been described as, 'a kind of popular repossession of the past' (Williamson
and Bellamy 1983: 57). This line of thought is wholly alien to the present
writer and, probably, to most who are likely to read this book, but it cannot
be answered by argument; only a prolonged endeavour to teach the cultural
code will serve.

A realization of these issues, and an understanding that the first necessary
step is to find out more about popular attitudes to the past, has led to two
recent surveys. The first was organized from the Cambridge Department of
Archaeology and Anthropology, and in its final form gathered data from
Cambridge, York, Lancaster and Southampton (Cambridge Research Co-
operative 1983; Stone 1986a,b). It was intended to collect information on
how people's concept of the past is formed, and on people's archaeological
interests, attitudes and awareness. The full results of the survey have not yet

	Frequencies (%)
Visiting the site/area	20
Guided tour of site/area	19
Watching a TV programme	16
Reading a book about it	13
Listening to a talk by an expert	12
Enquiring in a library	7
Visiting a musum	7
Going to evening classes	6

Figure 9.2 The most enjoyable way of finding out about the past (after Merriman 1989, Table 14.10, 162)

been analysed and published, but four general conclusions seem to emerge. Firstly, there is a basic and wide-spread interest in the distant past; secondly, the information which people usually have about this past is on a level with the film *One Million Years BC* which shows Raquel Welch fighting dinosaurs; thirdly, the more middle class the respondent the better his/her information is likely to be, but not necessarily his/her basic interest; and fourthly, women tend to be less interested and less informed than men.

The second survey has been carried out and published by Merriman (1989) and was addressed specifically to the social basis of museum and heritage visiting. From the results of his survey Merriman identified three major clusters in museum visiting: 68 per cent who have visited a museum in the last five years, 18 per cent who have never visited, and the rest (13 per cent) who are very occasional visitors. The main demographic tendencies of these visitors and non-visitors have been given in figure 9.1.

Of these people, 89 per cent of visitors and 65 per cent of non-visitors thought that it was worth knowing about the past, a large and encouraging proportion, but as figure 9.2 shows visiting a museum comes equal seventh in popular preference for ways of finding out about the past. This evidence of interest in the past is borne out by the huge visitor figures which some of the main 'ancient' heritage attractions in Britain achieve (in 1987 Stonehenge had 656,000 visitors, Jorvik had 897,000 and Bath, including the Roman site and the Pump Room together, had 900,890), and underlies the economic importance of heritage visiting (Myerscough *et al.* 1988). The low preference for museum visiting as a means of satisfying this curiosity presumably reflects both the inherited image of museums as forbidding 'temples of culture' and a dislike of the kind of archaeology which is usually presented in them. The analysis of participation in 'heritage' activities (figure 9.3) shows that active engagement, especially in the person's own area or family, are the preferred activities, and Merriman's cross-tabulation of these activities by status tells its own story of alienation from a formal or academic relationship with the past (1989: 165, table 14.13).

The survey overall shows that museum visiting reflects social divisions which lie deep in British society, and suggests that the elements which most people find most rewarding in giving a sense of the past are objects and sites in their own setting, preferably out of doors, with an element of self-discovery, and ideally connected by some form of personal link to their own

'Have you ever done any of the following things?'
(% of respondents participating)

Been a member of a local history or archaeology club	4%
Been a member of a local collectors' club	3
Used a metal-detector for 'treasure-hunting'	7
Gone on an archaeology dig or gone field-walking for pottery	10
Researched your family tree	15

Figure 9.3　Participation in 'Heritage' activities (after Merriman 1989, Table 14.12, 164)

family or area. This would suggest museum developments like community centres, self-directed trails, and discovery rooms, where visitors can be assisted by professionals who can give advice about fieldwork and local research points. However, these developments are likely to attract more of the kind of people who already participate in heritage activities, rather than extend the participation to a wider group. The survey suggests that the members of this wider group are best reached first in their own homes and through the media, especially television (for discussion of archaeology on television, see Hill, c.1987; Stone 1986b; Sutcliffe 1978; Jordan 1981; Norman 1983).

A number of areas of direct interface between the archaeology museum and the public can be identified, all of which operate within the perimeters suggested by the surveys and the broader context. Exhibitions and the cultural resource management of open-air archaeological sites are two of the most important of these, and they are discussed separately in Chapters 10 and 11. Chapter 12 considers the role of formal education and the broad issues of reaching out into the community. Equally significant are enquiry services, and relationships with the treasure-hunting fraternity, and it is to these that we must now turn.

Enquiry services

Enquiry services (taken here to mean the identification of objects brought in by members of the public, variously called enquiry, identification and opinion services, and letters requesting similar information) are probably the one area of museum activities which do genuinely involve the general lay public, and the willingness with which people penetrate the formalities of entrance hall, attendant staff and enquiry forms is a true index of the power of their curiosity about the past. Of all museum areas, also, it is perhaps the one where least literature has been published, and none specifically on archaeological enquiries. Such information as there is focuses on the organization of these services, rather than on their underlying principles, or on the nature and number of the enquiries themselves (see Young 1972; Clarke 1984; Pearce 1988), although Trustram has completed an interesting short survey of history museum enquiries with special reference to the Museum of London Modern Department (1987). The Rayner Report on the Victoria and Albert Museum and the Science Museum was critical of the amount of curatorial time expended on enquiries and attempted to discourage 'less serious' enquiries (Rayner Report 1982: 41–2). Very few curators are likely to be in sympathy with the tone of the Report's recommendations.

The broad problems of operating an enquiry service, involving matters of staff organization, administration and security, need not be repeated. More relevant here would be a discussion of the kinds of archaeological material which is brought in, the quantity of this material, and the amount of curatorial time which dealing with it involves. The answers to these questions undoubtedly differ from one type of museum to another and from one area of the country to another, and no co-ordinated information is available. The writer's own experience, and her discussions with colleagues, suggest that a large museum like Merseyside perhaps receives some fifteen or twenty enquiries directed towards the archaeology staff every week, while a medium-sized museum like Exeter, Worcester or Norwich receives perhaps six or eight such enquiries each week. The most striking feature of this material is its extremely miscellaneous nature, ranging across Middle Eastern or Mediterranean material, most of it bought in the tourist market and much of it fake, assorted curios of all kinds, some artefacts which a professional would count as 'genuine archaeology' like worked stone or medieval sherds, and coins.

Coins, in the absence of a specialized numismatist, usually fall to the archaeologist, and they probably account for well over half of the total number of enquiries received. Archaeologists soon learn that the Standard Catalogue of British Coins published by Seaby of London (Mitchell and Reeds 1985) and the other volumes from the same firm, together with the standard works on Roman coins (e.g. Carson 1982) are very useful. A potentially large proportion of all enquiries do, of course, come from treasure-hunters, but this is a separate issue which is discussed later in this chapter.

The number of enquiries does not remain constant: It is heavier at some times of the year than others, and especially heavy around the bank holidays. It can increase dramatically if the museum has decided to pursue a policy of active encouragement, rather than passive acceptance. The amount of curatorial time involved is very difficult to quantify, because this depends upon the level of response which is deemed satisfactory, and the experience of the staff (in museums where there are several archaeology curators enquiries tend by tradition to fall to the most junior). Probably in the largest museums a single member of the curatorial staff may spend up to 50 per cent of his time working on enquiries, while in a medium-sized institution a curator may spend a rough average of some five or six hours each week. Individual arrangements are highly idiosyncratic, and will affect these figures considerably, but it is clear that even a passive policy is a considerable commitment of curatorial resource.

It is highly significant that the critical literature on enquiry services is so sparse, and that virtually no museums seem to have a policy on enquiries which extends much beyond their practical administration, to cover questions like the depth to which they should be researched and the time which the curator should spend talking personally to the enquirer. Enquiries usually have a lower priority than documentation, collecting or exhibition. This clearly reflects the traditional cleavage between the curator, for whom archaeology and its artefacts are to do with the nature of past societies and the process of change, and the enquirer, whose interest concentrates upon 'how old' the object is, 'what is it' at the crudest level, and how much it is worth, all in the context of personal possession sometimes expressed in unattractive terms.

Contacts with enquirers can often be pleasant and fruitful, but a curator talking to an enquirer sometimes senses an uncomfortable knot of emotions, which entangles a resentment at the curator's acknowledged authority, especially when an unwelcome opinion has to be given, a trust which has sent the enquirer here rather than to a dealer, and a consciousness of personal standing as a ratepayer and a citizen. The curator traditionally tolerates all this for the sake of sometimes recording information of value, sometimes receiving significant donations, and occasionally making an important new discovery (for the writer this was the recovery from an attic of the late Bronze Age hoard of cups, axes, armings and amber from Glentanar, Aberdeenshire, Pearce 1970–1; all curators can tell such stories). The whole process is rendered much more difficult if, as sometimes happens, delicate issues of title and legality are involved. If, as often happens in many systems, the enquirer does not speak directly to the curator, then he may well be very disappointed, and the museum has no idea whether or not the information given on the written sheet matched expectations.

It is true that the gulf of interest between curator and public is frequently deep and genuine, that much of the material brought in is of little interest from any informed point of view, and that any substantial extension of the enquiry service which gave the layperson more contact with the curator would have a major impact upon time and resources. It is, however, also true that the act of making the enquiry is often more important than the enquiry itself, and that an improved enquiry service would be one important way of making the museum service more accountable and more responsive to the needs of the public. One suggestion is the provision of an 'enquiries room' which would have a range of reference books of the more accessible type, maps, and perhaps handling specimens of all the more common kinds of enquiry, backed up by free fact sheets and similar information. The enquirer could be encouraged to discover more about his object here, although he would probably need curatorial assistance, and perhaps he could help the curator to complete the records which are needed for the museum, the Sites and Monuments Register, and so on. This could be a valuable extension of the enquiry relationship, and indeed often happens informally in the curator's office; but its formal implementation would undoubtedly be very demanding.

Treasure-hunting

If enquiry services are one of the most important interfaces between the wider public and museums, one of the most difficult areas here is the whole broad question of treasure-hunting, which often surfaces in the most direct fashion across an object brought in for identification. Treasure-hunting as a phenomenon has been discussed in some depth in the archaeological press, with an increasing degree of sympathy in some quarters in recent years (Gregory 1983). Gregory, for example, speaks of the problem as being, 'an ethical and social one'. He discusses the middle-class, serious, polite and university-educated style of archaeology and describes 'the inevitable result' as 'the evolution of alternative, working-class archaeology born of a coalition of the detector-manufacturers, collectors and detector-users revolving around the collection of material ... with an emphasis on its monetary value depending on the individual involved' (Gregory 1986: 25–6).

The treasure-hunters see themselves as pursuing a legitimate hobby, motivated not primarily by financial gain but by a desire to find out about the past and to come into tangible contact with it, which makes them equal and equivalent to other kinds of archaeologists. Olive Portsmouth, editor of *Treasure Hunting*, wrote, 'I genuinely believe that there is little difference between archaeologists and readers of *Treasure Hunting*. Treasure hunters' methods are different, but we are all striving towards the same aim: a greater knowledge of the past', and added that 'the low esteem in which treasure hunters have been forced to regard many archaeologists has cost museums a great many finds which otherwise would have been gladly donated' (Portsmouth 1979).

Faced with this kind of genuine conviction on the part of the hunters, the fundamental problem resolves itself into the intellectual gulf between those who understand and appreciate the philosophical and methodological concepts in which professional archaeology is grounded, and those who do not, with all the misunderstandings of the value of contextual evidence, systematic recording and site integrity which inevitably follow. The polarization of interest in the past on a class and education basis is a fundamental difficulty which has already been touched upon. It is one for which archaeologists must bear their share of responsibility, but this must not be allowed to obscure the essential significance of the intellectual stance about the nature of our understanding of the past. Once this has been said, however, we are left with the difficulty of finding solutions to daily problems, in museums as elsewhere, and of working out practical relationships.

In an interesting survey, Crowther endeavoured to discover the attitudes towards treasure-hunting held by the hunters themselves, by field units, and by museums (Crowther 1983). The treasure-hunters are well organized into a network of local and national clubs, embracing perhaps some 100,000 people (Portsmouth 1979). Crowther sent questionnaires to some 62 of these clubs, receiving replies from 43 per cent, which explored attitudes to archaeology, to codes of practice and to museums. Most clubs seemed to agree that the recording of finds was necessary, although they did not have a satisfactory means of monitoring their members, but a group felt that archaeologists 'made too much fuss' about their activities.

Most clubs felt that affiliation to a national body would help to maintain standards, although the emergence of the Detector Information Group (DIG) in direct response to STOP (see below), with its aim of countering 'archaeological propaganda' is, from the archaeologists' point of view, not a helpful step. Most clubs followed a 'Code of Conduct', theoretically at least, usually based on that published by *Treasure Hunting* (reproduced in Council of Europe 1981). This Code states that archaeological sites or ancient monuments should not be interfered with, that permission should be asked for access to private land, that all unusual finds should be reported to the local museum, and that all finds of gold and silver should be reported to the police. Eighty-nine per cent of those who replied claimed some kind of contact with their local museum or archaeological society, and of these 70 per cent would be willing to liaise in finds plotting and information exchange schemes, although the remaining 30 per cent seemed to regard the whole idea as largely 'a waste of time'.

Crowther received responses from 114 museums (59 per cent) and 26 units (68 per cent). Of these, 43 per cent of museums and 39 per cent of units had no liaison with local treasure-hunters whatever. Museums and units were offered four means of approaching the problem and could select one or a combination of the following: (1) banning the sale and use of metal detectors; (2) greater legislative protection of sites; (3) introduction of licences to control use of metal detectors; and (4) establishing liaison. The results of this selection are shown in figure 9.4, where it is clear that a liaison policy is favoured by most, in one form or another, although often regarded sadly as a pragmatic necessity which inevitably undermines the moral and intellectual case, and gives treasure-hunters a mantle of respectability which they should not have. Punitive measures tended to be the least popular.

Two supplementary questions were asked of museums: whether they would be willing for treasure-hunters' finds to be deposited for an agreed period for identification and record, to which only 38 per cent said they would be willing; and whether they would be prepared to help the clubs to borrow surveying equipment. This last was extremely contentious, going as

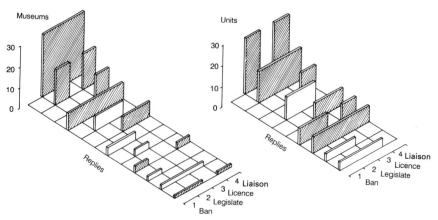

Figure 9.4   Approaches to treasure-hunting: four possibilities were offered, and the popularity of each chosen combination of approaches is contrasted for museums and units. Shaded combinations are those which include 'liaison' as a possibility (after Crowther 1983)

it does into liaison well beyond the exchange of information, with 39 per cent in favour and 34 per cent against. Generally those who had had some experience of liaison were more interested in developing it, than those who had had little or none.

The survey shows, therefore, that a considerable proportion of treasure-hunters declare themselves ready to abide by a code of practice, and that a substantial number of museum archaeologists are willing to work with them, albeit with varying degrees of reluctance. This hope of a more useful mutual relationship has led to a number of initiatives. The Museum of London has a good working system with the Thames Mudlarks who hunt over the river banks. In Norfolk, liaison led to the production of a leaflet *Archaeological Finds: Some Suggestions about the Use of Metal Detectors* which encouraged hunters to bring finds into the Norfolk Museum Service. This resulted in a link between the local club and the museum, by means of which areas of land could be checked against the Sites and Monuments Register before club members detected over them (Green and Gregory 1978).

Recently the Museums North Archaeology Panel has prepared a proposed Code of Practice for curators to employ when dealing with treasure-hunters. This covers the recording of objects brought in for identification, the passing of information from one museum to another, the recommendations that antiquities should not be purchased, and the need to keep a record of known treasure-hunted sites. The proposed Code suggests that if an object is donated, the donor should sign a form transferring title to the museum (both the Museum of Antiquities at Newcastle University and the Museum of London use such forms), and that enquiries should be dealt with in person, with any written identification given on plain paper so that it cannot be used to enhance an object's monetary value (Allason-Jones 1987). The gains of this approach for archaeology are clear—goodwill is generated, finds are recorded, and the treasure-hunters can be made aware of legal restraints like that in the 1979 Act, which restricts the use of detectors on scheduled monuments (see English Heritage advice leaflet *Users of Metal Detectors*, 1985).

The opposite view, which prizes archaeological purity above liaison, has been represented by the STOP (Stop Taking Our Past) campaign which was founded in 1979, with the support of the Council for British Archaeology and a formidable band of organizations, including the Museums Association and the Society of Museum Archaeologists. STOP's stated policy is that, 'treasure hunting constitutes a great threat to the country's archaeological heritage, and is thus contrary to the national interest' (STOP leaflet, undated). The STOP literature cites cases like that at Mildenhall in Wiltshire where a Roman coin hoard was removed by hunters from a scheduled site, and where eventually, after three hunters had been apprehended by the police, much damage was done to the site and the remains of two coin hoards hopelessly confused. Such cases, and those arising from doubtful legal title, seldom result in prosecutions which are satisfactory from a strictly archaeological point of view. The case against any liaison with the treasure-hunters has been stated most ably and forcefully by Henig (1987) who makes the fair point that there can be no such thing as an 'alternative working class archaeology' in Gregory's phrase because, 'archaeology is a science, the accumulation of a body of knowledge, and its alternative is not' (1987: 13).

The attitudes represented by STOP and Henig, and by liaison are essentially unreconcilable, but there seems to be a growing sense that no stricter legislation is likely to be forthcoming, and that, as Crowther puts it, 'polemic is no substitute for dialogue' (1983: 19). Useful co-operation between museums and others with the treasure-hunter clubs seems to be a possibility, and offers the chance that known archaeological sites will be respected and finds properly recorded. The clubs, of course, house the 'respectable' hunters, who are willing to abide by their Codes. Beyond and outside are the 'rogue' hunters, primarily concerned with profit and with the looting of known sites. Indeed, a distinction is beginning to develop among archaeologists between 'metal-detector users', meaning those with whom it may be proper to associate, and 'treasure-hunters' who are beyond the pale. The rogue hunters are recognized almost everywhere for what they are, but since they can only be stopped by the force of public opinion, and since the responsible hunters make up an important part of that opinion, it would be foolish to let the best be the enemy of the good.

10. Exhibiting archaeology

Introduction

Over the last two or two-and-a-half decades all archaeologists have come to recognize their obligation to the public (with various degrees of willingness), and archaeological exhibitions are one of the most obvious ways in which this debt can be discharged. Accordingly, the great majority of museums in Britain with substantial archaeological collections, and many of those with smaller collections, have mounted new archaeological displays during this period, sometimes more than one such display. Figure 10.1 shows the date at which current permanent exhibitions (in the usual sense in which curators use that phrase) have been installed throughout the country, and makes it clear that most museums have relatively up-to-date displays.

Each exhibition will have been the result of intensive planning and careful work on the part of the museum staff concerned, and as figure 10.2 shows, in the majority of museums the curator was responsible for the overall approach and the text, but usually with professional designers, who helped to create the story line and build the actual display. The gallery space devoted to archaeology is also substantial: there are small displays at a few museums like Cheltenham and Edinburgh, and a few very large ones, but the general range encompass a substantial floor area, and all of this, relative to the size of each museum, represents a considerable commitment of resource to the display of the distant past (figure 10.3).

In addition to these permanent displays there have been a number of very interesting temporary exhibitions (figure 10.4), many of them shown at the larger museums, like *Capital Gains* at the Museum of London (1987), *Symbols of Power at the Time of Stonehenge* at the (then) National Museum of Antiquities, Edinburgh (1985), and *Archaeology in Britain: New Views of the Past* at the British Museum (1986). The Museums and Galleries Commission is now operating a *Grants for Travelling Exhibitions* scheme which may help to tour exhibitions like these to other museums. Considerable attention, too, has been paid to the public response, particularly by Merriman (1989) and others discussed in Chapter 9, and, in an *ad hoc* way, by museums like Jorvik or Danebury, who keep a careful eye upon their visitor figures.

Clearly, very considerable effort has been, and is being, put into the exhibition of archaeology, and a corresponding effort of thoughtful design, in the broadest sense, has been directed towards the need to make archaeologi-

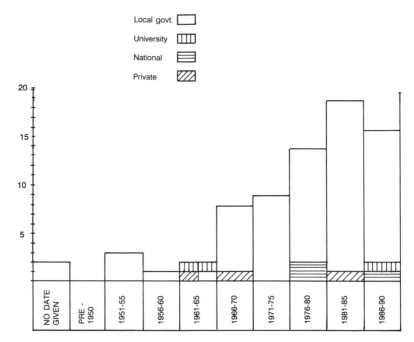

Figure 10.1   Date on which current permanent archaeology exhibitions were installed (final date given, but limited revision not taken into account)

cal information intelligible. However, apart from the publications accompanying the exhibitions, which are very mixed in quality, all this activity has
generated little literature other than reviews in the *Museums Journal*, notorious
for their generosity, the Society for Museum Archaeologists' volume of
collected papers *Archaeological Display* (White 1985), which is disappointing,
and a few other scattered articles like that by Schadla-Hall and Davidson
(1982), and chapters in general books like that by Margaret Hall (1987).
Pirie's analysis of archaeology exhibitions, now in progress, promises to be
interesting, and Ian Jenkins' discussion of the history of the Greek and
Roman Daily Life Room at the British Museum should stimulate further
papers of this kind (Jenkins 1986). For discussion which is concerned with
the fundamental nature of exhibitions, we must turn to studies being carried
out at the Royal Ontario Museum (1976), at the Polish Academy of Sciences
(Swiecimski 1987), at the Bartlett School of Architecture and Planning,
London University (Peponis and Hedin 1982), at the University of Brno,
Czechoslovakia (Suler 1988) and at the Department of Museum Studies,
Leicester University (Pearce 1987a).

    The substantial body of post-war thinking (see Hawkes 1977), which is
aimed at elucidating the nature of communication and of our use of signs and
symbols in the broadest sense, is very relevant and helpful here, because
writers like de Saussure and Barthes (to name only two very influential
thinkers) can give us what hitherto we have lacked, a range of fundamental

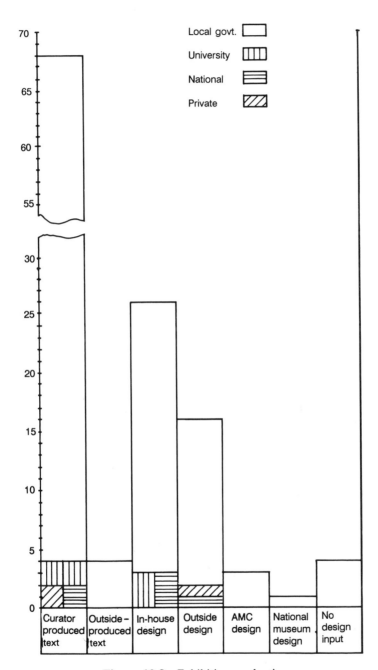

Figure 10.2 Exhibition production

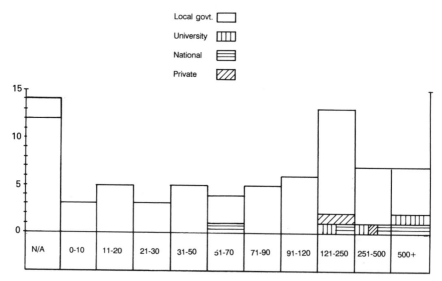

Figure 10.3 Size of exhibitions of British archaeology (expresesd in m² of floor area)

theory about the nature of objects and texts as communication systems, through which the discussion of exhibitions can be articulated. In semiotic terms, exhibitions are clearly a 'language' system of their own, albeit a complex one, which combines objects of all kinds, label texts, graphics, hardware like cases and agents like lighting, all put together in a specific form. The subject is a large (and fascinating) one, but a taster is offered here of some of the ways in which this analysis might work.

Saussure's original distinctions can be applied very fruitfully to the material culture of the past, interpreted in its widest sense to include structures, environmental samples and so on, and its subsequent life in a museum collection and exhibition (see Pearce 1989b). He showed that each society 'chooses' from the large (albeit limited) range of possibilities, the forms which its communication systems, like language, accepted 'knowledge', kinship, food, and objects, will take. This communication material must, however, be structured according to the society's rules of use in order to be intelligible and useful, so that language is a combination of vocabulary and grammar, food of raw foodstuffs and prepared meals, knowledge of information and interpretation, material culture of objects and their use categories: this structured body Saussure called a society's *langue*. Each actual event, each spoken or written sentence, each meal, each object put to its own use, is drawn from the *langue*, and Saussure called this usage *parole*. Any analysis of any sequence of events, or of any society, depends upon analysis of *parole*, since this is all that is available to us. Our efforts to understand the 'real' structure of an event, or a human group, are bound to be inferences drawn from collected *parole*, which may enable us to come to a view about the nature of the *langue*.

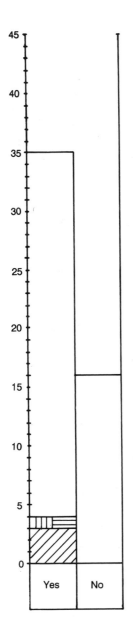

Figure 10.4 Temporary archaeology exhibitions

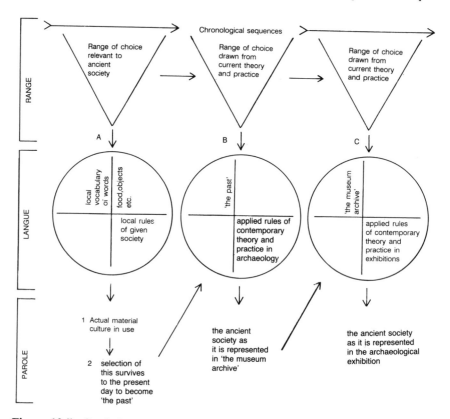

Figure 10.5   Semiotic analysis of the relationship between ancient material culture, museum collections, and exhibition

Figure 10.5 applies this model to archaeological material and its display. A shows the relationship which the surviving material of the past bears to the society which created it. This *parole* becomes the communication material of archaeologists, to be structured according to contemporary knowledge in theory and practice, from whence it will emerge as the museum archive, part of the *parole* of the day (B). In the third phase, C, this archive shifts to become again *langue*, this time of the museum workers, who restructure it to produce their *parole*, the exhibition. Among other points, it is obvious that the body of material which represents 'the past' appears in a sequence in which the *parole* of the previous form becomes the *langue* of the next. We might say, using Barthes' terms (but rather crudely), that we see a chain in which the physical embodiment, the *signifier*, and the concepts which it embodies, the *signified*, (that is, the operation of the *langue*) together constitute the *sign* (the *parole*), which then goes on to become the signifier of the next stage. The exhibition is the final sign in this chain, and it bears what may be called a metaphorical or symbolic relationship to the processes which have preceded it.

Analysis of this kind is considerably more than a mere playing with terms and diagrams, however irritating the technical vocabulary can often be. The continual creation and re-creation of meaning, by which existing signs and symbols go towards the making of new ones appears to be a fundamental aspect of the way in which humans understand the world and come to terms with their place in it. It is an important part of the imaginative process by which we make sense of our common past and our present activity, and within this museums and their exhibitions play a significant role. It follows that every exhibition is a communication event in its own right, a medium which embraces many different media but in which the whole is richer than the sum of its parts; it is a specific work of culture, a synthesis whose content may be analysed at a number of levels and from a range of standpoints.

Exhibitions, in their morphological juxtapositioning of plan, selected objects and graphics (in the broadest sense) create their own kinds of knowledge, and may therefore be analysed in such epistemological terms. All human history exhibitions are representational, and so provoke questions about the nature of their relationship to 'a past reality' and to historical change. Archaeological exhibitions are intended to interpret material culture, or perhaps to demonstrate how material culture can be interpreted, and therefore face familiar problems surrounding the study of artefacts; and further difficulties revolve around the transmission of all these messages to a viewing public. These ideas will be pursued in the following pages.

Exhibition morphology

Work at the Royal Ontario Museum has confirmed that, since the majority of people take the shortest distance between two points when they walk through a gallery, the floor plan of an exhibit has a crucial influence upon how much of it most people will see (1976: 107–13). This kind of approach is capable of generating thoughtful displays structured around hierarchical sequences of information (figure 10.6). Exhibition morphology, however, has a more fundamental effect upon the way in which knowledge is produced, and the kind of knowledge which is generated, than this approach to spatial organization is able to demonstrate. Peponis and Hedin (1982) have shown that to capture the relationship between spaces in an exhibition gallery, two points of view may be adopted. On the one hand, the longest straight lines that can be drawn on the plan without crossing a boundary (e.g. a display case) can be considered, and on the other hand, the plan can be studied from the point of view of its convex organization by drawing the largest and fattest convex spaces that are needed to cover it, again without crossing boundaries.

These viewpoints generate three relational properties, in terms of which transformations in exhibition morphology can be described. The first concerns the relative separation of spaces: when exhibition plans are compared it becomes clear that the number of spaces, defined by the lines and curves, which must be crossed to get from one display unit to another, is greater in some than in others. The number of spaces that need to be crossed to move from one point to another may be defined as the *depth*, and the aggregate of spaces separation shows that some exhibitions are deeper than others.

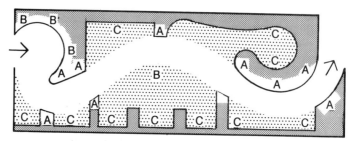

LEGEND   A Constant flow   B Crowd Stoppage   C Variable

Figure 10.6   Exhibition plan and information hierarchy in relation to visitor flow (after Royal Ontario Museum 1976: 107)

The second property concerns the provision of alternative ways of going from one space to another, that is the number of *rings* defined in the plan, a ring being a series of spaces connected in sequence so that a visitor can return to his/her starting point without back-tracking. Syntactic measures show that some gallery plans are more '*ringy*' than others. The final property bears on the ease with which a visitor comprehends and uses the structural pattern of the gallery, and this relates to the number, and the simplicity of plan, of the straight, axial lines; this property is known as *entropy*, and the more entropic a gallery plan is, the less it is structured.

The social connotations of this morphological analysis are important, because the whole process crystallizes what many curators and visitors feel in an intuitive way when they walk round a gallery. To put it rather crudely, exhibitions with strong axial structures, shallow depth and a low ring factor present knowledge as if it were the map of a well-known terrain where the relationship of each part to another, and all to the whole, is thoroughly understood; while exhibitions whose plans show a high degree of entropy (or a weaker structure), considerable depth and a high ring factor show knowledge as a proposition which may stimulate further, or different, answering propositions.

An analysis of two contrasting exhibition plans shows what this means. For a period the British Museum was showing both the temporary exhibition *Archaeology in Britain* and the permanent display known as the *Early Medieval Room*. *Archaeology in Britain* was an ambitious project intended to present the new approaches to archaeology and the new information which these have yielded, and embraced a chronological stretch from the Mesolithic to AD 1600. The subject matter was broken up into fifteen units, together with the sixteenth, *Lindow Man*, intended to act as the exhibition's climax in the popular sense. Figure 10.7 shows that the exhibition plan has, generally, a strong axial structure, with shallow depth and a generally low ring factor, interrupted by three areas with a greater ring factor, at sections 7/8/9, sections 12/13/14 and section 16, Lindow Man. Archaeological knowledge in this exhibition was presented as a known sequence which the visitor might learn. The same note of information presentation was struck in the individual section units, all through the employment of a polished technology (Plate 6).

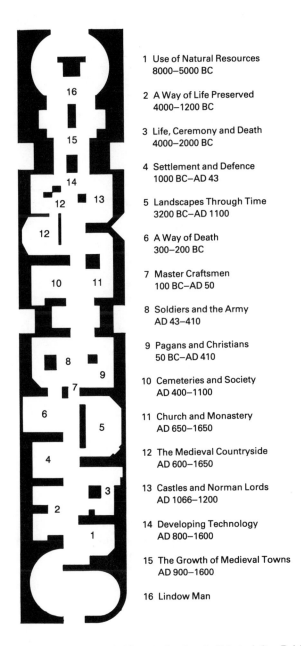

1 Use of Natural Resources
8000–5000 BC

2 A Way of Life Preserved
4000–1200 BC

3 Life, Ceremony and Death
4000–2000 BC

4 Settlement and Defence
1000 BC–AD 43

5 Landscapes Through Time
3200 BC–AD 1100

6 A Way of Death
300–200 BC

7 Master Craftsmen
100 BC–AD 50

8 Soldiers and the Army
AD 43–410

9 Pagans and Christians
50 BC–AD 410

10 Cemeteries and Society
AD 400–1100

11 Church and Monastery
AD 650–1650

12 The Medieval Countryside
AD 600–1650

13 Castles and Norman Lords
AD 1066–1200

14 Developing Technology
AD 800–1600

15 The Growth of Medieval Towns
AD 900–1600

16 Lindow Man

Figure 10.7 Ground plan of exhibition *Archaeology in Britain* (after British Museum teaching material, 1987)

Plate 6   View of *Archaeology in Britain: New Views of the Past* exhibition, 1986, British
Museum, giving a view of 'The Medieval Countryside' with 'cinema' booth
behind it, Section 12, (rear) and part of 'Castles and Norman Lords',
Section 13 (foreground). Reproduced by courtesy of the British Museum.

The *Early Medieval Room* is a considerable contrast (figure 10.8). It traces
the rise of Medieval Europe from its roots in the Late Antique world, and it
does so through 45 cases which include a series on the migration and post-
migration tribes *c* AD 400–1100 (cases 1–15), a series on the Late Antique
and Byzantine World (cases 16–28), a sequence on the Germans, Anglo-
Saxons, Celts and Vikings with a strong British emphasis (cases 29–50), and
a separate section on the Sutton Hoo ship burial (cases 51–56) which ensures
that this will be one of the most popular galleries in the museum. The
material on show is predominantly 'fine' work, particularly in metal.

The plan shows a pattern of axials which creates a lattice work structure
within the room, so that from any position a visitor can be attracted to a
range of possible movements. At the same time, the plan has considerable
depth and offers a very complex series of overlapping and concentric rings.
All this means that the chronological sequence is well-nigh impossible to
follow and, indeed, it is not greatly stressed in the display content, but that
the visitor is encouraged to look at the material as he chooses and to form an
opinion, for example, about how classical forms influenced early medieval
craftsmanship.

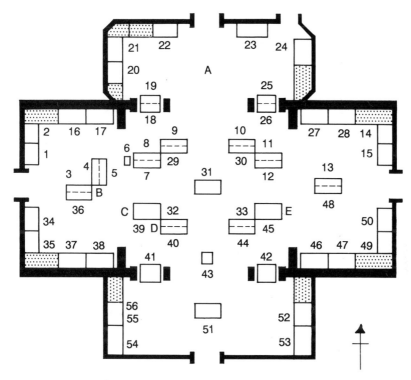

Figure 10.8 Ground plan of *Early Medieval Room* (British Museum, as in 1989)

The exhibition entitled *Victims of Time* at Dorset County Museum, Dorchester, created by Roger Peers and Robin Wade Associates, one of the most important commercial firms in the business, makes these points very well (figure 10.9). The choice of Maiden Castle as the focusing theme meant that the story of the multi-period hill top occupation could be used as a kind of microcosm of the early history of Dorset, and brought in important early archaeologists like Wheeler. The combination of specific theme and related broad chronology generated a particularly cunning gallery plan, in which a central spine tells the history of Maiden Castle in a coherent, chronological exhibit of its own, and displays which radiate from the spine broaden the story out to include Dorset generally, period by period. The visitor has good axial views outwards from the centre which encourage movement, and although there is a high ring factor, the structure is strong enough to maintain the sequential pattern (Plate 7).

The two sorts of exhibition plans offer different models of knowledge, and create a different relationship between the curator and the viewer. Both are potentially didactic, although the more rigid plan is more obviously so, and is better placed to impart a complicated story. The ethical basis of the didactic exhibit is grounded in the belief that knowledge is morally good, partly in an absolute sense and partly because it helps to develop socially responsible

Plate 7   View of *Victims of Time* exhibition, Dorset County Museum, showing part of
the central Maiden Castle display (right and centre left) and the displays
radiating from it (far left and centre back). Reproduced by courtesy Dorset
Natural History and Archaeological Society, The Dorset County Museum,
Dorchester, Dorset.

citizens who identify constructively with their community and its traditions;
it looks back to Victorian ideas about self-betterment, tainted though these
are with much political and social hypocrisy. The didactic approach con-
trasts with the emotive or mood-making exhibition, grounded in the rather
different conviction that an experience of the ancient, the exotic and the
beautiful is good because it enables us to share in the common scope of
human experience, to live more interestingly and to accept more easily the
essential precariousness of life.

Again, both types of exhibition can be emotive; feeling may flow more
easily in the fluid arrangement, but an exhibit like that of the Sacred Spring
and Temple Site at Bath, for example, combines a strongly axial and low ring
factor plan with, essentially, the single intention of generating response to the
temple by means of careful spotlighting and display, uncomplicated by any
intention of interpreting the very complex history of the site. The difference,
in fact, is usually only one of degree. A burial group, for example, that
commonplace of archaeological display, has elements of both the emotive

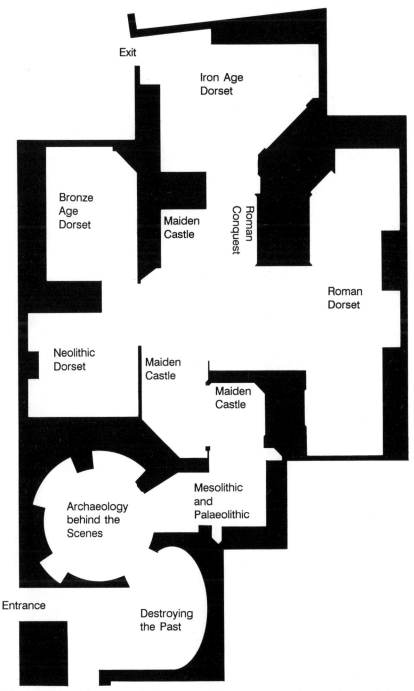

Figure 10.9 Ground plan of *Victims of Time* exhibition, Dorset County Museum (DCM 1988)

and the didactic, and most exhibitions try to combine both kinds of understanding, either throughout or in different parts.

The interpretation of material culture in exhibitions

An equally crucial area is the way in which an exhibition approaches the
interpretation of material culture. The discussion of theoretical archaeology
in Chapter 2 pointed out that objects can be viewed in three ways: as
artefacts, that is as physical constructions produced by the application of
technology to raw material in order to provide the commodities which
sustain life; as signs and symbols, that is as messages which create social
distinctions; and as meaning, that is as physical embodiments of ideological
statements and the feelings which these induce in us; and that all objects
embody elements of all these attributes. Exhibitions, similarly, draw on a
blend of these interpretative stances, but usually one of the three comes to the
fore.

The functionalist stance, which sees material culture as objects, is the
rationale behind the many exhibitions which show how various craft techniques were operated in the past, how the land was worked through ancient
farming practices, how buildings of all kinds were constructed and, also, how
the archaeologist knows about these things through the (supposed) straightforward application of techniques like excavation, dating, and physical
characterization. Exhibitions like this are popular with curators because,
since they show supposedly 'hard' or 'positive' facts, they are relatively
uncontroversial, and because by the same token, they are believed, with good
reason, to be intelligible and interesting to the visitors: essentially this is the
stance taken by Jorvik. Archaeological exhibitions seldom try to bring
together the separate elements of functional analysis into the coherent
picture of a whole mechanically-functioning society, partly because of gaps in
the evidence and partly as a result of intellectual cowardice which balks, for
example, at presenting the medieval parish church in the museum's town in
classic marxist terms.

In theory, it is possible to detach the discussion of artefacts as signs and
symbols from the ideological constructions which they signify and symbolize,
but in the display of actual concrete objects it is difficult to do this because
the nature of the symbol and the nature of its meaning are made apparent at
the same time. Much effort has gone into elucidating the role of objects as
symbols, as messages which can say the unsayable and symbolize fear of
death or sex, represent social processes, carry with them social distinctions
and function as vehicles of political manipulation (for discussion, see Pearce
1986b, 1987b). *Symbols of Power at the Time of Stonehenge* was an exhibition built
around this approach. It was intended, in the words of its organizers,

> ... to present [an] approach concentrating on aspects of a single theme, the
> manifestation of power, prestige and status in the third and second millennia BC.
> Influenced, however indirectly, by the view of Marx it is not perhaps unexpected
> that we should choose to look at the material in terms of the ideology of

domination but in selecting this particular aspect we would not attempt to deny either that the evidence we have chosen is capable of alternative interpretations or that its contribution to our understanding of the past is limited to this particular theme. . . . But we are here concerned with the use of material culture as symbols of power for it is this aspect which provides archaeologists with access to the strategic patterns involved in the creation, maintenance and collapse of power among groups (Clarke *et al.* 1985: 3, 4, 5).

Symbols of Power was an interesting exhibition which repays careful thought, but so far it seems to be the only major exhibition of its kind (Lawson 1987). Displays of archaeology, particularly classical archaeology, as 'works of art' are, by contrast, very common. Here the aesthetic of exhibition depends upon the acceptance that the objects embody a very particular kind of symbolic power with a universal significance, and that this is offered to a visitor not as an interpretation, as *Symbols of Power* showed Bronze Age gold, but as a matter of faith. Exhibitions of this kind face all the obvious theoretical difficulties which this stance entails.

A rather different approach to the interpretation of material culture, especially that from the medieval periods, entails the use of objects as essentially the visible authentication of the historical narrative, which is derived from documentary evidence and offered to the visitor as a story told in labels, graphics and photographs, backed up by genuine three-dimensional artefacts. The artefacts are used to legitimize the narrative; their concrete properties serve as 'proof' that what is being said about the past is true. From a strictly archaeological standpoint, this is a misuse of material culture, since the discipline stands on the ability of the archaeologist to interpret human artefacts in terms of themselves alone and to derive significance therefrom; but a purist answer of this kind is unhelpfully exclusive, and fails to face the limitations of material culture as evidence from which a view of the past may be constructed.

All the various stances have their potential for the creation of exhibitions. The point is that the study and exhibition of material culture, like any other social study, has its own insights and perspectives to offer, and that these are not right or wrong, objectively true or subjectively dubious, except in the crudest sense, but interesting, perceptive and intellectually exciting.

Representation, reality and the passage of time

Different kinds of gallery plans, different interpretative approaches, and stances which are variously didactic or emotive, may create different kinds of knowledge in the hearts and minds of the viewers, but the way in which this knowledge may bear any relationship to a 'real' past is one of the principal questions preoccupying archaeologists today, and as such has already appeared in this book. The trend of the times is to suggest that, although there is a positivist element in our information about the past (a Norman army invaded England in 1066; a large hill fort was constructed at Maiden Castle during the Iron Age), the questions which were posed to produce this information, and the constructions which are put upon the answers, derive from the political contexts of the researchers, and are a reflection, not of the past, but of aspects of the present. Moreover, archaeology is rhetorical study, in that its practitioners are actively involved in the effort of persuading others, both fellow professionals and the public, to share a particular view of the past, and so, by implication, to share a particular view of the present.

It follows that exhibitions are perpetually involved in restructuring the past through a series of persuasive presentations grounded in the present; but because exhibitions have to be intelligible to the visitors in the most basic sense, that is to say they have to be close enough to general experiences and assumptions to 'make sense', they tend to take a comfortable choice from the range of contemporary options, and to include ideas about moral progress and the absolute value of technological change. In this way, exhibitions usually end up preserving a stereotyped idea of the past, and confirming a particular political view of the nature of the present. The designing of an exhibition is an act of interpretation which opens up meaning, and in a political world this is a political act which needs to be handled with great care.

A rather different aspect of the production of knowledge stems from the fact that, of their very nature, archaeological exhibitions, like all human history displays, have to try to show man in the past and his passage through time. Two ways in which this difficult problem has been approached can be distinguished. The first of these is '*static*', while the second may be called '*dynamic*'. Static displays are those which, fundamentally, evade the problem of realizing social change through time by taking a theme like *Life in Ancient Egypt* or *Daily Life in Roman Britain*, by means of which a segment of the past is frozen into a kind of 'archaeological now' (to borrow a phrase from the anthropologists) and is treated as if it had no future, no past, and no internal movement. These displays, which are often mounted in order to show collections which are good in themselves but lack any particular cohesion of time or place, tend to be very general in their cultural content. They assume a cluster of norms through which 'Ancient Egypt' or 'Classical Greece' can be realized, an assumption which lies at the base of all historical display as of all historical writing, but which emerges in exhibitions of this kind in a particularly crude form.

Some exhibits of this sort can perform the tasks for which they were designed very well. The re-creations of Roman rooms at Cirencester come to mind here, a display technique which has been deservedly influential, and so does the Roman Villa display at Ipswich Museum, where again there are reconstructions of a villa kitchen and drawing room, and a contemporary rural scene, supplemented by didactic display panels. At Ipswich, the reconstructions are linked to specific villa excavations, although these did not provide sufficient detailed information on which to base the reconstructions and in the rural scene, for example, gaps had to be filled from a stock of general ideas about what Roman Britain looked like. This is fair enough if it is done carefully, and relatively simple displays of this kind, especially on accessible topics like villas, can work well for the public and for school parties. It is no accident, either, that the form of the Ipswich exhibition is highly unstructured, allowing free exploration.

An interesting extension of this static approach, sometimes attempted with contemporary anthropological material, and occasionally tried with British prehistoric finds and collections of much more recent exotic material, is the display which juxtaposes the two groups, inviting the viewer to understand the one in the light of the other. This is usually done in order to explain primitive technologies, so that, for example, British Neolithic flint work can be displayed in front of a photograph of an Australian aborigine making a missile head out of bottle glass. However, used more thoughtfully, it can suggest that human life *is* essentially static in the sense that human beings do not change, and that the insights of the psychologists and of some of the sociologists offer interpretations of human activity which is always applicable across time and space. Viewed from this perspective, it would make better sense to show British Early Bronze age material beside that from the nineteenth-century Polynesian chiefdoms, than to follow it with Middle Bronze Age finds.

Most archaeological exhibitions are dynamic in concept, viewing history as a linear process in which one set of circumstances gives rise to the next, creating a sequence which moves human societies chronologically forward, leaving their pasts behind them. This dynamic view of history has a long intellectual pedigree going back to Marx and Hegel, and it has two distinct moral tones: the pessimistic, represented among archaeologists, perhaps, by Gordon Childe, which tends to see the process of history as steadily increasing the exploitation and oppression of most humans, and the optimistic, represented primarily by the British liberal tradition, which sees enlightened self-interest leading to steady general improvement. Most exhibitions adopt the optimistic view, not stating but usually implying that, for example, life was better in a medieval town than it was in the migration period; one cannot help but feel that the Victorian base of most of our museums and many of our buildings encourage curators and public alike to adopt appropriate attitudes within them.

The *Anglo-Saxon and Viking Life* gallery (Hartley 1985) at the Yorkshire Museum is a good example of a classic dynamic display (figure 10.10). The exhibit is principally on the ground floor of the museum, and here the plan includes a first part (sections 1, 2 and the beginning of 3) which has a strong axial structure and low depth and ring factors, a central part (sections 3, 4 and 5) with greater depth and more rings (although so arranged that some visitors will undoubtedly skip section 4), and a third part broadly like the first. These correspond to the chronological sequence which takes us from the end of Roman Britain, through early Anglo-Saxon settlement, and into Christian Northumbria in the first part; Christian Northumbria and the closely related Golden Age of York (with all the value judgments that that title implies) and contemporary weaponry in the central part, and the Viking progress in the final part. It is obvious that a strongly structured plan fits with the production of knowledge in a strongly sequential mode, while the greater depth and ring factors in the central part go with the range of broadly contemporary material on display there (Plate 8).

One fundamental problem emerges from exhibitions of the York type, which is common to the study of material culture, and to archaeological research in general, and that is the difficulty of demonstrating the passage of

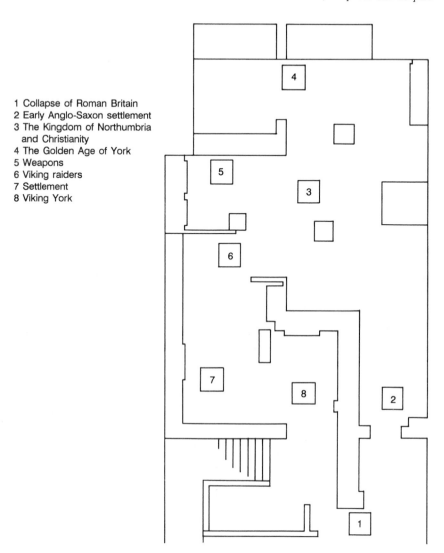

1 Collapse of Roman Britain
2 Early Anglo-Saxon settlement
3 The Kingdom of Northumbria
  and Christianity
4 The Golden Age of York
5 Weapons
6 Viking raiders
7 Settlement
8 Viking York

Figure 10.10 Ground plan of *Anglo-Saxon and Viking Life* gallery, Yorkshire Museum (after Hartley 1985)

time and the process of social change; although exhibitions framed around a linear dynamic set out to show social change, what they usually do in practice is to give a series of spatial snapshots of the past which are arranged in chronological order. The problems involved in interpreting change, and the limitations of material culture as evidence, have been much canvassed in recent years, and by drawing on this work, it might be possible to devise an exhibition which could link successive typological and distributional patterns

Plate 8   View of *Anglo-Saxon and Viking Life* gallery, Yorkshire Museum, showing Anglo-Saxon settlement (foreground) and 'The Golden Age of York' (rear). Reproduced by courtesy The Yorkshire Museum, York.

to historical and social change. This would be an improvement in display terms, but it would not, of course, help to resolve the basic difficulties inherent in archaeological method and evidence.

Communicating archaeology in exhibitions

Archaeologists who have had experience in the production of exhibitions, are well aware that some areas of the past are difficult subjects in which to create an interest among the general public. Roman Britain and a few medieval topics are relatively accessible but the prehistoric past, in particular, presents problems, and this general statement is not belied by the popularity of television programmes such as *Chronicle*, for which subjects from the distant past are rare and are chosen with very great care. Faced with collections composed chiefly of pot fragments and worked stone, enlivened by a certain amount of metalwork, curators have, for the last twenty-five years, usually worked within three broad principles: the archaeology displays should concentrate on the local area, eschewing universal subjects like the descent of man popular before the war (and leaving the susbtantial non-local material, which many museums hold, in store, or using it for separate displays); the displays should be as welcoming and accessible as possible; and they should employ a range of the mixed media techniques which help to bring the real people back into their curated remains.

The last two of these principles show a developing appreciation of the idea of the exhibition as a communications system, a concept which has attracted a considerable amount of discussion (Cameron 1968; Knez and Wright 1970; Strong 1983). The system embraces the sequence transmitter–medium–receiver, in which the transmitter is the exhibitor (curator, educator, designer, etc.), the medium is the whole exhibition content (that is, those aspects already discussed) and the receiver is the visitor. It is obviously important that the exhibitor and the visitor should share the same codes, that as far as the exhibition is concerned, they should be speaking the same language. So, for example, if archaeological fragments are shown, it cannot be assumed that the visitor will necessarily mentally complete the fragment and perceive the whole object as a specialist would do. The visitor needs help in the form perhaps, of accompanying drawings as is done in the Yorkshire Museum, or with the objects displayed against an outline of their original shape.

Some objects, thoughtfully displayed, can say a good deal for themselves, about their design and craftsmanship and about the human interest which they embody as grave goods or toys, but important information about time, place and social significance must be conveyed in other ways, and this means the use of text labels, perhaps accompanied by other audio-visual media. Museums have not yet come to terms with the findings of studies like that by Sorsby and Horne (1980) which concluded that 'on average about three-quarters of visitors to museums will be unable to pay attention to at least two-thirds of the labels because the vocabulary and sentence structure are too difficult'.

Similar points are made by Serrell (1983: 1–24, 60–80), yet a glance around almost any archaeological display will show labels carrying all the classic communication faults. The reason probably lies in the way in which curators expect labels to do too many jobs at the same time. It would be better to recognize that one label can do only one task, and that therefore several levels of communication are necessary, either through the use of a label hierarchy, accompanied perhaps by cunning exhibition design, or through a series of information sheets and catalogues. Audio-visuals can be fitted into a scheme of this kind. The communications strategy for a single exhibition should (ideally) be part of a strategy which embraces the design approach of the whole museum.

What, then, for the visitor constitutes a good experience in an archaeology gallery? What makes an archaeology exhibition successful? There is a broad level of agreement about the ways in which the effectiveness of exhibitions generally can be assessed and the success of exhibitions evaluated (Miles *et al.* 1988; Griggs 1984; Stansfield 1981), and these involve detailed procedures of observation and feedback linked to very specific recommendations of gallery layout and design. Processes like critical appraisal and market research leading to front-end evaluation and the statement of exhibition objectives, formative evaluation as part of development and production, and summative evaluation undertaken after the exhibition is open, provide a framework through which the operation of the exhibition can be monitored.

In broader terms, which are admittedly difficult to monitor, a successful archaeology display has to be one which, like a good television programme or book, keeps the visitor attracted until the show is finished; if the visitor is carried along with his interest caught, then he will go away with some enlargement of knowledge or sympathy, and that is success. Surveys like Merriman's (1989) have shown that the public has a poor expectation of enjoyment from archaeology exhibitions, which come low on the scale of preferred ways of finding out about the past. This, we must hope, is not something inherent in the nature of exhibitions as such, but rather our inheritance from early poor display.

It has been recognized since the early 1950s that visitors respond well to galleries which have differing light levels and contrasting colours, in conjunction with impressive graphics like large blown-up photographs. The new post-war tone was set by the opening of the archaeology display at Jewry Wall Museum, Leicester Museum Service, in 1966 (Plate 9). This exhibition was very influential and much copied, with its glass wall open to the Roman Bathhouse Jewry Wall site immediately outside the building, its specially

Plate 9 Archaeological exhibition at Jewry Wall Museum, Leicester, opened in 1966, showing the then new wall-hung display units, the free-standing units and part of the Anglo-Saxon family group (far right). Reproduced courtesy Leicestershire Museums Service.

constructed ramps from which the floor-laid mosaics could be viewed, its irregular arrangement of display units (rather than just 'cases'), and its lavish use of large graphics, photographs, and eye-catching ancillaries like the famous period family models originally created for the Festival of Britain in 1951 (Cruickshank 1972). Most of these features reappear, so far as resources permit, in most of the local or regional-based exhibitions discussed had graphics like the placard announcing 'Baptisms every Sunday' to show interpretative techniques like models, audio-visual presentations and computer generated graphics and games, like those incorporated into the British Museum *Archaeology in Britain* exhibition.

Curators are beginning to experiment with labelling in the hope of breaking down the dislike of 'the book on the wall'. *The Lost Kingdom* exhibition at Scunthorpe Museum (Leahy 1988) on the theme of the Anglo-Saxon kingdom of Lindsey, produced by Kevin Leahy and Catherine Coutts, has graphics like the placard announcing 'Baptisms every Sunday' to show the coming of Christianity to Lindsey, and the cartoon with the caption 'Norman, that's a nice name' to introduce the arrival of the Normans. The genealogy of the kings of Lindsey came to Friothulf Finning and continued with 'Good Lord, you're actually reading this' before pressing on with the list, and a strip of bronze from a grave at Manton was labelled, 'God knows—but we don't—Sixth Century'. Visually, the exhibition was more traditional, but the material was clearly presented to make a strong impact, and it was accompanied by a well-written and designed guide. The exhibition achieved a thousand visitors a week, and shows that real archaeological quality can be combined with visitor appeal (Plate 10).

Parallel to this kind of exhibition runs those created by Heritage Projects at Oxford, Canterbury, and the Jorvik Viking Centre at York (Addyman and Gaynor 1984; Addyman 1986). The 'journey' around the Viking Centre is made in a number of distinct stages, beginning with the Orientation Hall which sets out to explain who and what the Vikings really were, and continuing with the time-car ride of about 13 minutes which takes the visitor through the full-scale reconstruction of the tenth-century York Coppergate complete with sounds and smells. The visitor proceeds through a reconstruction of the Coppergate excavation of the 1970s where the original timbers are displayed, and on to a conservation laboratory exhibition and the Skipper Gallery, where the finds are on display, and finally to the shop (figure 10.11). The Viking Centre literature suggests that Jorvik succeeds because it makes learning fun, and because, without in any way endangering academic integrity, it presents the complicated story of an excavation and its interpretation in a way that people can grasp, using innovative and highly imaginative interpretative techniques. The Coppergate reconstruction has not been without its critics, who argue from archaeological, feminist (Chabot 1988), aesthetic and educational angles (Schadla-Hall 1984), and there is a startling contrast between the innovative reconstructions and the classic, not to say archaic, museum displays in the (overcrowded) Skipper Gallery, though most interest here will concentrate on the hologram of the Coppergate Helmet. What is clear is that Jorvik is a success, and from it lessons must be learned (Plate 11).

Plate 10 View of the *Lost Kingdom* exhibition, Scunthorpe Borough Museum, showing display of Anglo-Saxon grave goods and settlement material. Reproduced by courtesy Scunthorpe Borough Council.

Another valuable approach involves 'hands-on' experience, not just of interactive games, but of actual objects or live discussion. A number of museums have experimented with the use of (disposable) archaeological artefacts placed at intervals in a display so that the visitors can handle them, but the experience can be disappointing if the visitor does not understand what the object is. More successful is the idea used at Manchester University Museum in 1983–4 (Prag 1983) where the exhibition about the activities of the Greater Manchester Archaeological Unit featured archaeologists at work in the gallery, who were willing to talk about what they were doing.

Some implications

Archaeological exhibitions are seldom discussed in the general archaeological literature, but an exception is the recent extended discussion published by Shanks and Tilley (1987a: 68–97). They take a low view of the present state of the art, suggesting that, 'In the museum the past becomes the death mask of the present' (p. 97) and setting out the inherent flaws in museum presentations of the past, which have already been touched upon here, by

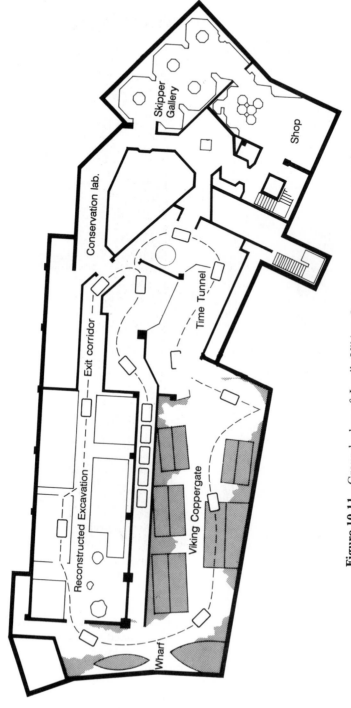

Figure 10.11 Ground plan of Jorvik Viking Centre, York (after Jorvik Viking Centre publicity material, 1988)

Plate 11 Part of the display in the 'Viking village', Jorvik Viking Centre, York, showing silversmith and customers. Reproduced by courtesy York Archaeological Trust.

contrasting them with their more desirable opposites in a set of binary pairs:

spatial	temporal
closed, completed	open, unfinished
past	history
eternity	history
reified	relational
repetition	particularity
identity	difference
presence	absence
homogeneous	heterogeneous
coercive	explorative
passive	active
monologic	dialogic
forgetting	remembrance
conservation	redemption

The museum display supposedly fixes the past as a passive and completed act, suppresses differences in order to create uniformities, and conserves a single view which forgets disagreements and dislocations. It does this in order that the present may recognize itself and be justified, because it is an ideological institution. Accordingly, the exhibitions may be redeemed by the introduction of political content into displays to show how the past may be manipulated for present purposes, by creating montages of de-contextualized objects to which the visitor may respond as he pleases, by introducing irony and absurdity into displays as a means of de-mystifying their authority (as was done at Scunthorpe), and by encouraging people to construct and present their own pasts by giving them access to collections and galleries. These are radical ideas, most of which await trial by practice, but they do capture some of the fundamental problems in exhibiting the past.

There may be a stance which brings some resolution to these curatorial difficulties, and this leads us to the final major point, which will draw together some of the threads of this discussion. By their nature, archaeology exhibitions, like all others, are normally conceived by their originators as works of art in the traditional European sense, which is to say that, like a novel or a play, they address themselves to a chosen set of human circumstances. They set out to convey an intelligible, if complicated message, and they do this by selecting elements from the flux of muddle and experience which we call life, and composing these into a pattern which seems intellectually and emotionally satisfactory (more or less) to the originators; as we have seen, this pattern will often be chronological, but it may be static, or include elements of both. It will involve a choice of artefacts and of the way in which their interpretation is approached, and a choice of graphics and other media. It will include decisions about the underlying exhibition morphology, with all that this implies. It will also include a choice of stance, optimistic or pessimistic, sexist or racialist, 'modern' or 'reactionary': in other words it will draw from the ethical and political problems discussed in Chapter 4 and in the foregoing pages. It may well involve choices about exhibition themes, which result in a concentration upon a particular site, or region, or famous archaeological figure. The pattern will seem satisfactory to other people in varying degrees, depending upon their age, and experience, and on the power and integrity of the exhibition itself.

The sum of these selective and structuring processes, which emerges as the public exhibition, clearly does not represent a picture of any society which is 'true' in an objective sense, but rather a reflection of the curator's and designer's mind, to be refracted again through the mind of the viewer. Provided, of course, that external facts about the material—dates, provenance, raw materials, characterization and so on—are correct; provided, in a word, that the curator has done an honest job, how much does the intensely subjective nature of museum interpretation matter? Its character as art should give us a clue. At a fundamental level, artistic creation of every kind supposes that people share a common mind capable of grasping poetic truths about the human condition which are expressed in social artefacts, including material culture (and, of course, in an exhibition itself, which is equally an artefact). If a work of art departs so far from this norm that it makes no sense to a viewer prepared to bring a degree of sympathy to its understanding, it has failed, and so has an exhibition. If, however, the work on show strikes a chord in the viewer's responses, then it has begun to succeed, and it is at this level of common human understanding that our interpretations of past people find their legitimacy, from the subtlest appreciations aroused by a presentation of social organization, to the direct emotions evoked by dog-paw prints in Roman concrete.

This discussion has deliberately tried to concentrate upon the underlying philosophies and meanings of archaeological exhibition, rather than upon the detail of display techniques and modern gallery requirements. The writer is grimly aware that philosophical speculation tends to falter in the face of intractable galleries, poor resources and requirements like fire exits; but nevertheless, display decisions must be and are taken, and the more consciously they are taken, the better the displays are likely to be. To borrow a word from the vocabulary of literature or art, exhibitions are our genre, and for our sake and for that of our public, we must make of them as much as we can.

11. Open-air sites

Introduction

The past, we are all agreed, is a valuable resource and that aspect of it which can be experienced in the open air has recently been treated in a veritable flood of public debate and published discussion (e.g. Cleere 1984; Price 1984, 1986; Stone 1986a; Lambrick 1985; Emery 1987; Darvill 1987). The reasons for this lie in a sharpened awareness that political goodwill, public funding, and the potential involvement of the very many people who do, or may, see a site visit as a good day out, are all interlinked, and that this places upon archaeologists a responsibility for making their field-work and excavation as accessible and intelligible as possible. This new climate of opinion is embodied in the new shape and purpose given to English Heritage, with its stress on the public enjoyment and the entrepreneurial management of the monuments in its care, a fresh thrust to which many museum curators seem ready to give a cautious welcome. It is clear that a substantial number of museums are already involved in the management of open-air sites (figure 11.1), and many more have curators who are giving advice and help to those who do, and it seems obvious that this aspect of museum work is likely to increase over the next decade or so (see Southworth 1988).

The management of monuments in the landscape, often called cultural resource management, is a very large subject, and much of it lies outside the scope of this book; but it may be helpful to review briefly some of the more conspicuous areas of discussion and, especially, the approaches to the presentation of open-air sites, because these overlap with the interpretative approaches used within the museum walls. The debate really resolves itself into three main areas: the ethical or conceptual issues which the representation (rather than simply the preservation) of ancient sites poses; the practical or management difficulties which surround the presentation of a specific ancient site; and the choice of strategy to render that site intelligible to the visiting public.

Conceptual issues

The value inherent in sites of past activity has recently (1984) been analysed by Lipe into four areas:

*   aesthetic/artistic values (cultural materials which give aesthetic pleasure);

170

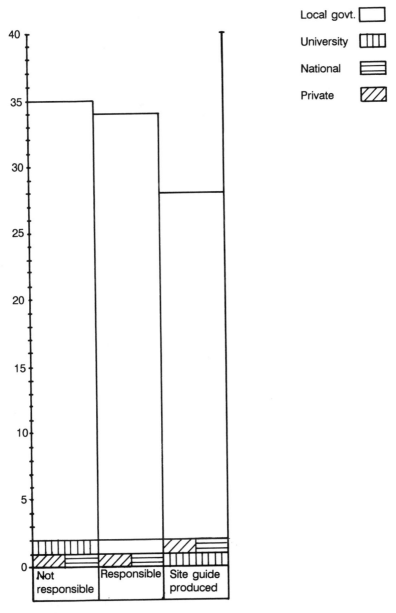

Figure 11.1   Museum involvement with open-site management

* associative/symbolic values (cultural materials as visible symbols of the past, which may be given a range of romantic, traditional, personal or political meanings);
* historic/informational values (cultural materials as unique sources of information about past societies, to be experienced now, and/or to be preserved for future educational or research purposes);
* economic/utilitarian values (cultural materials as market-place commodities, commanding a sale value and capable of generating income through re-use or tourist visiting). This value depends upon the three previous values. We should add that many archaeological sites have an economic value which has little or nothing to do with ancient activity, and much to do with perceived modern industrial and social values.

Lipe's review gives a useful summary of the wide range of human responses to ancient sites, and from them arise a series of tensions, all of which have an important bearing on the whole problem. In terms of archaeological politics, the immediate choice between 'rescue', the *ad hoc* excavation of a site threatened by development, and 'research', the excavation of a site as the result of a carefully conceived and problem-oriented design, may not be as difficult as it has sometimes seemed, given the better liaison with planners and developers which archaeologists in most areas have succeeded in creating, but a 'rescue' site will probably have a much poorer chance of surviving as an interpreted site for visitors, and the quality of the information derived from it is likely to be poorer also.

More fundamental still is the extent to which excavation can be justified against the need to preserve sites untouched for future generations; again it may be that a site which has seen some excavation can be made more intelligible to the visitor, but this is not necessarily always true, particularly where tracts of ancient landscape are involved, like those surviving from the Bronze Age on Dartmoor or Bodmin Moor. In the past, the advantages of a site from the public display and access point of view have seldom played a part when decisions about excavation, or survey, or complete non-interference, have been taken, but there are signs that this attitude is changing substantially, and that archaeological work programmes are now often becoming one element in a larger policy which includes the creation of open space, the regeneration of a run-down urban area and an interesting visitor focus. These plans may link in with income generation, either directly through charging for entrance or for informational material and souvenirs, or indirectly through the encouragement of local enterprises, including businesses and housing.

A good example is the inner harbour and quay area at Exeter, where the built environment ranges in date from Roman to modern, and where, with various inputs from the City Museum, the independent Maritime Museum, the City Planning Department and local business, the interesting but semi-derelict wharfage and waterway complex has been turned into a leisure area with a range of activities, and shops and private housing (and where any voice of dissent is not in tune with the times). Schemes like this are coming to fruition in many towns and cities, and their rural equivalents range from the grand designs being canvassed for Stonehenge or Maiden Castle to smaller enterprises in country parks, often centring upon Iron Age earthworks, which offer a range of country pursuits geared to the needs of modern families.

This sort of archaeological and developmental project is bound up with the debate between 'conservation' on the one hand, and 'preservation' on the other. Conservation is taken to mean that a new context may be created for the monument, in which it may well function as something more than just a ruin, so that craft shops may be developed in eighteenth-century warehouses, or what was once a priory and then a private house may operate as a community centre. Churches, of course, have been doing this kind of thing for a long time. The preservation ethic hinges on the concept 'preserved as found', and tends in practice to mean embalmed at one chosen moment in history, which is of particular interest to the archaeologists or historians of the day, much as the Victorian ecclesiologists endeavoured to preserve the Gothic phase of a church in preference to, say, an eighteen-century phase. 'Conservation' involves the acceptance that 'authenticity' is a very dubious concept because no one phase in the history of an ancient site is more authentic than any other, including its modern phase, and also accepts that a site may need to operate simultaneously on several levels of value, which include, of course, due respect paid to the historic/informational value which it embodies.

This leads to a further difficult area. The 'conservation' of a standing-building site in this sense may entail a certain amount of reconstruction work, or even rebuilding or new building work. The encouragement of visitors to a monument, or a series of monuments in an ancient landscape, will almost certainly entail a degree of consolidation, quite apart from the provision of footpaths and access points which many visitors may well confuse with the monument itself. Again, most visitors are likely to find an incomplete monument considerably more rewarding if its earlier appearance is made clear; this can be done for ground plans quite easily, provided the information is available, by the use of marker blocks set in turf or pavement, but the appearance of an elevation is more difficult to convey without a degree of reconstruction which most scholars would find unacceptable.

Between preventative consolidation and reconstruction there is a continuous scale of intervention (Stubbs 1984) along which the degree of interpretative input steadily increases, and hence there is the need for 'the development of a conservation/restoration theory to provide a philosophy and a set of criteria by which to judge restoration work' (Price 1986: 6). Basic to this work is a thorough understanding of the site in its original 'whole', that is, its context and its history. This achieved, a choice has to be made as to which phase(s) are to be restored or reconstructed and how this is to be related to the physical contexts, and to the overall strategy of interpretation: very difficult decisions are involved, especially where multi-phase monuments like castles, abbeys or elaborate prehistoric ceremonial sites are concerned, and each solution must be judged separately on its own merits.

At the root of many of these problems lies a fundamental dichotomy, which surfaces very frequently when actual sites and developments are being discussed, and which may be summed up in the phrase *history/ archaeology : heritage*. The issue has already appeared in Chapters 4 and 9, and it resolves itself into questions like 'What is the cultural heritage?', 'Who expects to get what from it?', and 'Are the expectations justified?'. Archaeologists and historians regard themselves as engaged upon an examination of the past, a critical discourse which has as one of its principal aims the de-mystifying of past events and the debunking of myth-making and special pleading. The management of the heritage, on the other hand, sometimes called 'heritization'—an unpleasant word for an unpleasant process— stands in great danger of reinforcing popular mythology or creating new myths, because by its nature it simplifies and institutionalizes particular moments in the past.

The problem is not simply that a castle site, for example, is shown as quiet, sweet-smelling and grass grown, although this sort of difficulty is important. More fundamental is the problem of selection, whereby the sites preserved and displayed are usually prehistoric tombs, stone circles and hill forts, Roman villas and military installations, and medieval abbeys and castles, rather than settlement sites and field systems, and so the view of the past presented is grossly imbalanced. This is partly because the sites of this type are often already in public ownership, so the legal problems are easier and a momentum of pressure for interpretation can build up. Partly it is because such sites usually involve surviving structures which are often impressive and can be reconstructed in varying degrees and are therefore easier for a non-professional to understand, and partly it is because they are perceived as 'important' in their own right, by virtue of their 'quality', their rarity value perhaps, and the superior position which they seem to have held in the past. All of this, of course, means that their economic potential in the present is enhanced.

This whole line of argument itself presupposes that ideas about the virtues of balance and of the 'de-mystified past', that is the ideas of historical scholarship, are themselves legitimate in a sense which goes beyond a desire to protect expert as opposed to lay status, even though 'the message conveyed by the past and revealed by the expert, and the system of values associated with rational method are further legitimated in this recognition of value [attached to objects in the past]. The sins of archaeology (dependence on values) are confessed to salve the guilty conscience of the origins of its values in contemporary capitalism' (Shanks and Tilley 1987a: 65).

The development of some archaeological sites in the near future seems likely to show the link between heritization and contemporary capitalism in a particularly vivid form; and archaeologists may have to accept that the public wish to experience the cultural heritage is not really about understanding the past at all, but rather about feeling better in the present. The heritage, in this sense, is a commodity like any other, to be sold in the ways in which people want to buy it, and may perhaps be distinguished from 'cultural inheritance', which implies the transfer of traditional values, and some, at least, of the preserved sites which these values identify, on to the next generation. All these are thorny problems to which no simple solutions exist, but their difficulties at actual sites can perhaps be negotiated by helpful approaches to management and display.

The management of open-air site presentation

A substantial body of literature is developing around the management of the preservation of ancient sites in general (e.g. Darvill 1987; Lambrick 1985; HBMC(E) 1984a, 1984b; Countryside Commission 1980, 1983, 1984, 1986) but much less has been written about the management of the presentation of ancient sites, although the number of bodies now involved in this is considerable, and includes, apart from museums, HBMC, the Countryside Commission, the National Trust, the National Parks, county councils, and district councils and boroughs. Some excavation projects, like that at Sutton Hoo (1986), are now building a presentation aspect into their overall strategy. This is clearly a very large question, involving as it does the ethical considerations already discussed, the developing impetus in the tourism and leisure fields with the corresponding political goodwill which the public presentation of open-air sites now attracts, and the difficult choices between the creation of 'honeypot' sites to absorb large numbers of visitors, or modes of presentation which disturb the site and its landscape considerably less.

A management approach to the development of a presentation strategy for each individual site is needed, and figure 11.2 gives in flow diagram form the kind of sequence which this development might take. The choice of a presentation strategy, the different forms which this may take, and the different kinds of success which may be achieved, is the area to which we must now turn.

Interpretative strategies

The extent to which museums are becoming involved in the presentation of open-air sites has already been mentioned (figure 11.1), and a random sampling of the literature shows how varied this involvement is. The City Museum, Stoke-on-Trent, for example, is responsible for the site of Hulton Abbey; Bromley Museum operates the Romano-British bath house and Anglo-Saxon cemetery site at Povenest Road; Woodspring Museum (Weston-super-Mare) manages Worlebury Iron Age Hill Fort; Lancaster City Museum is responsible for the Roman bath house and the coastal site of St. Patrick's Chapel at Heysham; Edinburgh City Musum has plans for a history park at Cramond which would include a display of Roman structural remains; and Harlow Museum manages a range of some seven ancient sites and offers Old Town and New Town heritage trails.

All these sites, and all the many others, entail the effort to make intelligible to the public the nature of ancient monuments. This happens sometimes in the context of modern development which has obliterated all but the monument itself in the narrowest sense, sometimes with the advantage of a

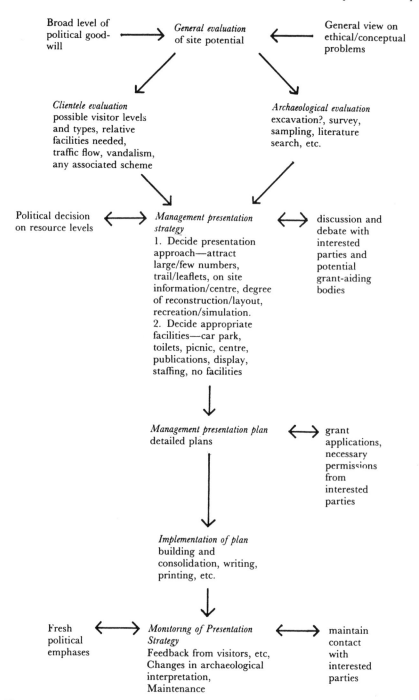

Figure 11.2 Flow diagram showing the development of a site presentation strategy

fuller preserved context which gives a better 'feel' and allows some scope for interpretative installation, and occasionally through the survival of large tracts of ancient landscape showing a sequence of features. In each case the approach must balance the choices set out in figure 11.2, and arrive at an appropriate individual interpretative strategy.

For many monuments, the strategy often involves the basic tidying and consolidation of unmanned sites, linked with the production of descriptive leaflets which can be purchased at the museum, and sometimes at other outlets, but not usually at the site itself. Leicestershire Museums produce the excellent *Guide to Twenty Archaeological Sites in Leicestershire* (Liddle 1983) which, for a selection of the best-known and most easily understood monuments in the county, provides for each site a good plan (or plans), a succinct description of its history and significance, a further reading list, and sometimes an illustration. This *Guide* can be linked in with the museum's Archaeological Reports series to give a substantial account of the local archaeology. Broadly similar strategies have been adopted by Lincolnshire Museum Service. Cleveland County Archaeology Section produce a good series of leaflets on excavation sites like Church Close, Hartlepool and the Saxon Cemetery, Norton, and visitor sites like the hill top of Eston Nab. They also have a series of smaller leaflets like that on *Bronze Age Burial Mounds* which describes a route to be followed by car that takes in some of the large barrows of the county. The reasons for this approach are obvious; it is relatively inexpensive, it creates the minimum of disturbance on and around the sites themselves, and yet it makes very adequate information available to those who want it. Its chief disadvantage is that it requires a very high level of interest and understanding on the part of the visitor.

A more positive approach to on-site interpretation can be more rewarding for the visitor, and this normally takes the form of a site trail, usually embodied in a leaflet, but sometimes backed up by sign boards, and occasionally by the full panoply of interpretation centre, shop and picnic site where the size of the site and the number of expected visitors makes this worthwhile. At Worlebury hill fort, an area with both local visitors and seasonal tourists, Woodspring Museum has adopted a policy of scrub clearance from the walls and ditches, and from some internal areas where hut platforms and pits are visible, linked with an interpretation programme aimed at raising people's awareness of the site through information panels, a teacher's resource pack and a small travelling display. The Stafford Castle project, operated by Stafford Borough Council who do not run a museum and seem to regard this as an alternative, involves the excavation of the castle and the nearby medieval deserted village, and their interpretation within the landscape. The interpretation of large areas of ancient landscape need different treatments, and one of the most successful ventures has been that at Roystone Grange in a remote valley of the Peak District where, in 1984, a trail was set up to link the well-preserved prehistoric, Romano-British, medieval and post-medieval sites in a walk of some 7 km (Hodges and Smith 1987).

Another very important area which needs public interpretation is that of the excavation itself, that is of the nature of archaeological techniques and of archaeological evidence, and of the inferences which may be drawn from them, so that an understanding of the whole archaeological process may be acquired. All this is potentially very exciting to the public, but it has proved difficult to perform, in part for practical reasons like insurance and safety standards, especially on urban sites, and the shortage of excavation manpower and other resources. However, the new English Heritage publication *Visitors Welcome* (Binks *et al.* 1988) describes how the presentation of excavations can be managed, and the important project at Castell Henllys in Dyfed (figure 11.3) shows what can sometimes be done (Mytum 1985; 1986b).

John Ruskin's comment on reconstructions, 'Do not talk to me of reconstructions, the whole thing is a lie from the very beginning', notwithstanding, the success of archaeological reconstruction in Scandinavia, at sites like the reconstructed Iron Age village at the Archaeohistorical Centre, Lejre, Denmark (Kristiansen 1984) has prompted a number of similar ventures in Britain over the last decades. A group of these relate to Roman military sites, like the rampart section, timber gateway and granary at The Lunt, operated by Coventry City Museum, the sections of Hadrian's Wall at Vindolanda, and the gateway at South Shields fort operated by Tyne and Wear Museum Service. Others are prehistoric, like the Castell Henllys round houses and the Iron Age houses at Groby built by Leicestershire Museum Service. More ambitious than any of these is the Butser Ancient Farm Project in the Queen Elizabeth Country Park near Horndean, where the Iron Age houses are set in reconstructed contemporary farmland, appropriately managed with ancient tools, methods and species (see e.g. Reynolds 1978). Most of these have taken actual excavated remains from specific sites as their starting points.

The proper term for this kind of activity has proved difficult to pin down. Hobley, responsible for The Lunt, says, 'The words reconstruction, restoration, reconstitution, recreation and realization all give a sense of replacing what is known to have existed. The writer strongly prefers the word 'simulation' to 'reconstruction' since it accords more closely with the spirit of The Lunt experiments (1982: 223). Problems of terminology point to a deeper unease within the archaeological community at the validity of such schemes and the way in which they may be presented to the public. In fact, many of them, like Butser (Reynolds 1982), began as research rather than as primarily public projects, intended to assist in the evaluation of excavated data, to test hypotheses about craft techniques, and to discover information about man hours, qualities and types of materials and skill needs, in order to throw light on social and economic organization. Also, it was hoped that they would illuminate the ways in which ancient structures may have decayed. Usually, though, there has been an idea of public presentation running in parallel with these archaeological aims, to provide support and to extend the usefulness of the result.

A major re-creation of this kind has been undertaken at West Stow, between Bury St. Edmunds and Icklingham, Suffolk, on the site of the excavated Anglo-Saxon village, as part of the development of a country park, bordered by the Icknield Way and the River Lark (West 1985). The park includes an area of Breckland Heath, designated as a site of Special Scientific

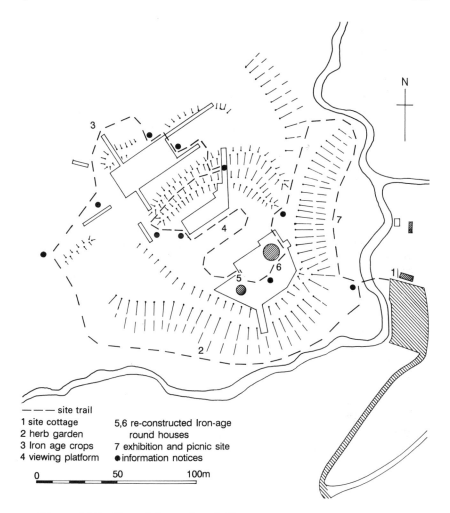

Figure 11.3 Plan of site at Castell Henllys, Dyfed (after Mytum 1985)

Interest, a nature trail, and facilities which will soon include a visitor centre with information and exhibitions (Plate 12).

All these re-creations of the past, including perhaps Butser, suffer from the same range of problems. Archaeological knowledge and theory moves forward rendering older ideas unsatisfactory, so that the simulations themselves become fossils of their own periods. Practical problems of intelligible demonstration sometimes mean that various elements have to be shown as co-existing when, in fact, they were probably chronologically separate (a problem which arises equally acutely in more traditional exhibitions). There is always a certain air of unreality, and the twentieth-century wear and tear which the buildings develop does not seem to be like that which they would

Plate 12   Reconstructed Anglo-Saxon village at West Stow, Suffolk, showing a view
of the hall and houses with a 'grubenhaus' style building in front of them,
and in the foreground timber splitting. Reproduced by courtesy West
Stow Anglo-Saxon Village Trust.

have had in their own time. Also, of course, they can be over-exploited in
unacceptable ways. Nevertheless, they undoubtedly offer to many people an
experience of past life styles which is more vivid than that which they could
receive in any other way, shown perhaps most clearly in the often-heard
surprise that past people lived so comfortably in such substantial homes, and
this must give them a high potential value.

None of the problems raised by the public presentation of preserved
archaeological sites, and their simulation, offer easy solutions, but several
clear issues do emerge. The choice of which sites to present is difficult and
will result from a mixture of archaeological and political pressures, all of
them slightly different in each individual case. The choice of which strategy
to adopt in the interpretation of the chosen site is equally difficult. It seems
clear that there is a considerable, and wholly legitimate, appetite amongst
the public for visiting sites, and that people get most from those sites which
carry on-site trails backed up by well-conceived information panels and by
reconstructed simulations. Archaeologists must come to terms with the value
of this response, and with its nature, which is admittedly limited and
impressionistic from a professional point of view. The presentation of open-
air sites is one of the most important interfaces between the committed
archaeologist and the public, and it needs to be treated with a corresponding
degree of serious attention.

12. *Reaching out into the community*

Introduction

'The community' may be defined here as those people who are neither professional curators nor professional archaeologists, and, as has already been said, these divide into two very uneven sections: those who have a genuine interest in and commitment to the study of the past, and those who do not, while underlying, as it were, all these individuals are the school children they once were. This chapter will review the relationship between the committed 'amateurs', the school children, and the archaeological curator, and conclude with a discussion which draws together all the aspects of the public relationship which have been discussed in this part of the book.

The 'amateurs'

The relationship between archaeological curators and those people committed to an interest in the past goes back to the beginnings of the museum profession, and has, in general, been an extremely pleasant and fruitful association, which continues to work well. Amateur archaeologists of this kind are often gathered into county or local archaeological societies, national organizations like the National Trust, and a large range of local interest and amenity groups. Figure 12.1 shows how close the relationship between museum and local archaeological society usually is, encompassing most aspects of the lives of both. Museum archaeologists, indeed, seem to have retained rather better relationships with these groups than many specifically excavating organizations have done. The archaeological press has seen over recent years a good deal of mutual bitterness about amateur limitations in the face of modern excavating methods and standards on the one hand, and poor, patronizing treatment of those who offer their labour and enthusiasm for no payment on the other (Corti 1988).

The Congress of Independent Archaeologists has been set up as a forum for those amateurs who feel that they need a united voice, other than that which has been provided for many years by the Council for British Archaeology with its range of publications designed to keep people in touch (Selkirk 1985; Porges 1987; Cleere 1986). Museum curators frequently serve on the committees of local societies, provide lectures and open days, give access to

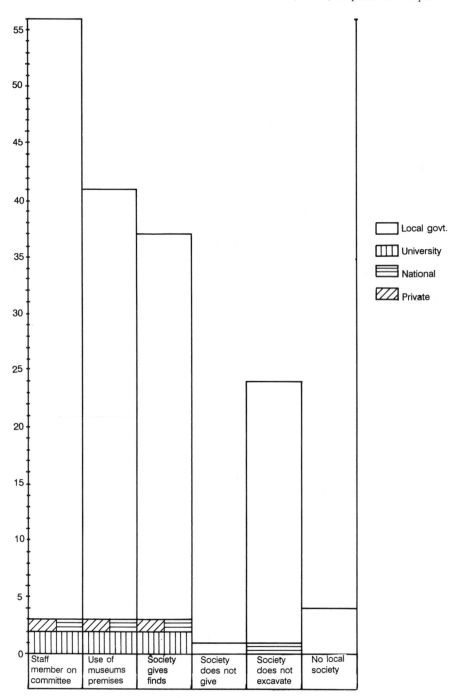

Figure 12.1   Museum relationship with local archaeological societies

equipment, offer storage facilities, and so on. The curator is likely, also, to be involved in a similar relationship with the local university adult education department, the WEA, perhaps the adult education section of the local education authority, and, of course, the Friends Organization of his own museum; and he will receive regular requests for talks from a very large number of organizations, ranging from village clubs to the summer meeting of the Prehistoric Society.

In practice, the membership of these groups tends to overlap, and in most areas there is a central core of some twenty or thirty people who appear at all the events, and carry much of the responsibility. Some of these are also willing to spend time on a regular basis working as a museum volunteer. As figure 12.2 shows, most archaeology departments find that a group of up to five volunteers works best, in terms both of available people and of organization, although some museums work with more, and some have none, usually as the result of a policy decision. Museum archaeological volunteers usually fall into one of three groups. Some are retired people of either sex; some are married women whose families have left home; and some are young people, often archaeology graduates, who put in volunteer time in the hope that this will help them to a full-time paid job. The volunteer groups are very flexible, with people dropping in and out, and spending a greater or smaller number of hours across a spread of months. At some times, a curator may have several people working with him, but at others it may fall to a couple of stalwarts.

The problems and benefits created by volunteers have been usefully discussed recently, together with approaches to their organization (Mattingley 1984), and need not be recapitulated here. In archaeology departments, they frequently work on projects like data retrieval from published sources, washing and accessioning large pottery collections, cataloguing, and assisting with exhibition work. The relationship is sometimes categorized as 'middle-aged, middle-class and extremely cosy' but these criticisms, if criticisms they are, do not do justice to the immensely valuable work performed by such people, for which most curators have good reasons to be grateful.

The volunteer principle has been carried to one of its finest expressions in Leicestershire where an integrated county museum and archaeological service has, through the sterling work of Peter Liddle, developed the concept of 'community archaeology'. This is based on the principles that the past is the property of the whole community, that people have the right to be informed about their community's past but also the right to participate in its discovery, and that any failure—real or perceived—to achieve this will lead to alienation and the growth of alternatives. The community archaeology programme operates through a county-wide network of groups and individuals who run their own fieldwork research programmes and check planning matters, backed up by regular newsletters, meetings, publications, training courses, an identification service and general help and advice provided by the museum. In Leicestershire amateurs and professionals have worked happily together to demonstrate how rich the archaeology of the area is, and how successfully the 'level of archaeological consciousness' in the community can be raised (Liddle 1985). A range of broadly similar projects

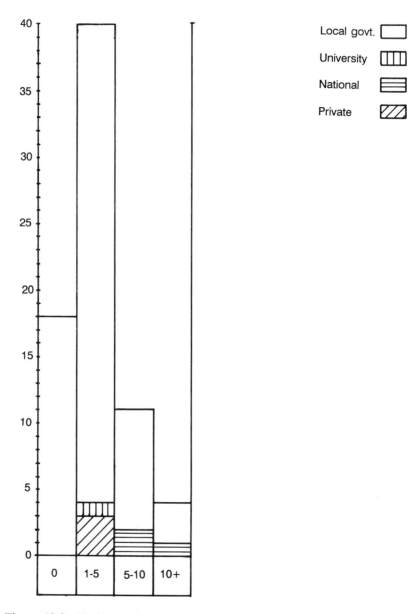

Figure 12.2   Numbers of volunteers per year (including students) between 1985 and 1987

are being developed from other museum bases, singly or jointly with other organizations, across the country.

Archaeology, education and museums

It is now time to turn to the area of museum archaeology and formal school-based education, the crucial importance of which for curators of archaeology (and for museums and archaeology in general) need not be laboured. For a number of years now, educators have understood education to be the transmission and development of skills rather than the accumulation of facts and bodies of knowledge, and the kinds of skills involved have been set out in matrix form by Richard Doughty (figure 12.3). The skills are transmitted through a range of student-centred activities, including interactive learning, projects and self-discovery modes of all kinds, and the methods of teaching will include team-teaching and small group work.

There is, of course, a danger in this that school children, while developing considerable expertise in asking questions, will lack the necessary information to give their questions any substance or significance; as E.H. Carr said nearly thirty years ago, 'The historian without his facts is rootless and futile; the facts without their historian are dead and meaningless' (1961: 24). This is not the place to discuss current political stresses, but much of the sharpness in the present debate on education revolves around the tension between skill learning on the one hand and the acquisition (and testing) of knowledge on

Skills	Definitions
1. Reference Skills	Ability to find, select and abstract information
2. Interpretation Skills	Ability to understand information
3. Communication Skills	Ability to structure information and express it in different modes
4. Translation Skills	Ability to take information received in one form and express it in another form
5. Inference Skills	Ability to think in hypothetical and deductive terms.
6. Synthesis Skills	Ability to bring parts together to form a new pattern
7. Evaluation Skills	Ability to make value judgements upon information in the light of stated criteria.

Figure 12.3 Matrix showing the skills which working with objects can help to develop (after Richard Doughty)

the other, and it is to be hoped that teaching programmes can be created which will combine the best of the post-war learning modes and the need to acquire hard information. How this is achieved will differ according to the various age groups, and as far as secondary pupils are concerned the new General Certificate of Secondary Education (GCSE) will clearly play a crucial role.

The internal debate within archaeology about its relationship to the broader world has combined with the public debate about the nature of education as a whole, to generate a stream of publications (Dyer 1983; Corbishley 1983; Cracknell and Corbishley 1986; Adams 1986; Corbishley 1986; Cooper 1986; Planel 1986; Suffield 1986; Holman and Burtt 1987). Activities like the *Archaeology for Schools* series produced by CBA, and the teacher training courses, teaching packs and *Remnants: Journal of English Heritage Education Service* produced by the considerably increased education staff of English Heritage, are being developed. The 'Archaeology in Education' Unit, organized by the Department of Archaeology at Southampton University, is generating very valuable data and theory, together with a series of archaeology and Education projects on topics like *Dead men Don't Tell Tales: A Graveyard Project for Schools* (Hill and Mays 1987) and *Porchester Castle* (Wilson and Planel 1987). The Unit, with sponsorship from CBA, the British Institute of Field Archaeologists, Rescue and the GCSE Southern Examining Group, also organized the first international conference on *Archaeology and Education* at Southampton in 1987, the papers from which are to be published. The archaeological communities in the universities of Cambridge and Sheffield are involved in similar concerns: the Archaeology Department at Sheffield has produced impressive teaching packs, slide packs, videos, artefact kits and replicas.

Most county and district museum services now have education officers (listed in Corbishley 1983: 69–77) but it is sadly still true that in some museums, especially in some of the national and other large museums, the relationship between educationalists and curators is strained, with curators apparently taking an over-protective line with their collections and an over-academic view of their exhibitions. In some of the regional museum services, the fact that Education Officers are often employed as local authority teachers, with appropriate working hours and holidays, does not help liaison. In all museums the ordinary problems of collection management and object handling need to be tactfully arranged, so that teachers and students are not made to feel that they are always fobbed off with collection debris, and the provision of a proper schoolroom reasonably equipped with the materials the teacher needs, is an enormous help. Teachers from local schools, also, need to appreciate that normal administrative courtesies must be observed. Nevertheless, in spite of some lingering problems, it is true that at the fundamental level of staff and space provision, museum education services have been, and still are, a major growth area.

How much of this museum educational activity is directed to archaeology is unclear, nor is it easy to discover the extent to which archaeology appears in school work, in either the primary or the secondary age groups. Most museum educators do not have any special training in, or interest for, archaeology, and the situation is similar in the schools. Adams has analysed the education services and the availability of archaeological resource material like postcards, slides, booklets and replicas in museums, and shows that the range is considerable (Adams 1983: 65–77), but this provision is likely to be rather patchy in most places at present. Some museum education services, like the staff at Southampton, Warwick (who organized the seminar published as Cracknells and Corbishley 1986) and Worcester (who mounted the exhibition *Archaeology and Education* in 1988) are very active in the field, but these are the exceptions.

It seems clear that, while museum educators are well placed to work with an increased demand for archaeology from primary groups (allowing, of course, for all the usual problems of resource), they are unlikely to be able to offer what secondary groups need, particularly those involved in archaeology at GCSE level. Teaching here would need a considerable input from the curator, and quite how this can be organized in practice remains to be seen; but it is obviously in the interests of archaeology as a whole to encourage museum-based school work. At the moment this depends on the accidental presence of curators and teachers who happen to have the particular interest, but it is an area which needs development, in terms both of theory and practice.

There is beginning to be a climate within which the nature of the relationship between archaeology and education, and between archaeologists and teachers can be analysed, and some pointers are emerging. An interesting survey undertaken by the Southampton *Archaeology in Education* team covered 117 children of ages 10–12 years from a variety of backgrounds in Southampton, in an effort to understand how children conceive of the past and its people (Emmott 1987). The findings of the survey showed that the children were only just beginning to understand time as an abstract concept, and that they tended to think of history as about Kings and Queens. Nevertheless, 80 per cent of the replies said that the past was important. The children tended to see past people as less clever than us because they lacked our technology, and they seemed to take a similar view of non-western cultures. These images of the past 'originate in the content of school curriculum, childrens' books and television programmes' (p. 139) that generate 'a distorted, ethnocentric and sexist view of the past, which forms a lasting impression and impinges on their images of the present' (p. 139).

This links up with other investigations. J.D. Hill has shown (1987: 144) that archaeology sees education as a commodity, as a way in which archaeologists can communicate what they regard as the important results of their work to the public, and so justify the public money spent on them in a highly visible and obviously responsible way. Teachers, similarly, see archaeology as a commodity, making some use of the scope for skills learning and for projects which it offers, but failing to understand the nature of the discipline. Hill found that 'the over-whelming majority of teachers have little understanding of modern archaeology so the result of their use of the discipline is largely mis-representative, perpetuating dubious stereotypes of what archaeology is and what it can do. The stress placed on teaching the right methods is often at the cost of fact. Several teachers have suggested to the author that it does not matter if the facts are completely wrong, so long as the children learn to use their historical skills correctly' (1987: 144). As a result, neither teachers nor archaeologists understand what the other is trying to achieve, and the product is potentially both bad archaeology and bad education.

This dislocation between the aims of the two groups will not be overcome easily, but since archaeologists probably have most at stake, the responsibility is primarily with them. Archaeology places an emphasis on the critical evaluation of a range of kinds of evidence to a much greater extent than most disciplines do, and this involves both the assessment of evidence in a formal sense *and* a review of the ethical or ideological bases of any conclusions. This makes the study of archaeology a very valuable way of acquiring analytical skills, although this must not be at the expense of accurate information. Archaeology also lends itself to student-based project work, either in the classroom and the school grounds, or in the local countryside, and this kind of approach will encourage teachers towards site- and artefact-based work rather than book-based study, and towards British prehistoric and medieval topics rather than the overworked Ancient Egyptians and Romans.

Equally, archaeology, unlike most of the other areas of the humanities studied in school, has a material base. Its ability to demonstrate how objects can tell stories, and the use of its range of analytical procedures to show how this can be done, is an important educational potential, and one, of course, where museums are crucial. Finally, archaeology offers the broadest perspective of the history of mankind, taking the story back to the earliest days of our species but linking it very firmly to actual places and objects, some of which the student can experience directly in his own neighbourhood, with all the rich enlargement of sympathy and tolerance which this can bring.

Learning and teaching with objects, that is museum-based archaeological education, has been a relatively neglected subject in the past, although Deetz (1981), Henningar-Shuh (1982), Schlereth (1981), Schroeder (1976) and Watson (1983) have all published useful papers. The topic has recently been explored in a valuable publication by Hooper-Greenhill (1988) which sets out to offer a practical, skills-based approach. The learning/teaching sequence begins with the sensory explanation of an object in terms of its materials, colours, size, weight, condition and so on, and then progresses to discussion and analysis oriented towards its production, design, use, materials and association (figure 12.4), and so to the generation of remembering, comparing, and synthesizing processes (figure 12.5). Hooper-Greenhill shows how teachers can draw on the multi-disciplinary, multi-level (for beginners and accomplished learners), concrete/abstract and multi-contexted nature of objects to stimulate discussion and research, and to provoke interaction and emotional response. Organizing a response to objects in the class means organizing concepts about comparison, classification, interpretation, and the evaluation of evidence.

Saying to teachers that archaeology offers all these possibilities is one thing, but bringing the teaching of them about means taking archaeology much further in schools than is usually done at present. At primary level, a museum archaeology programme must be carefully planned, so that re-

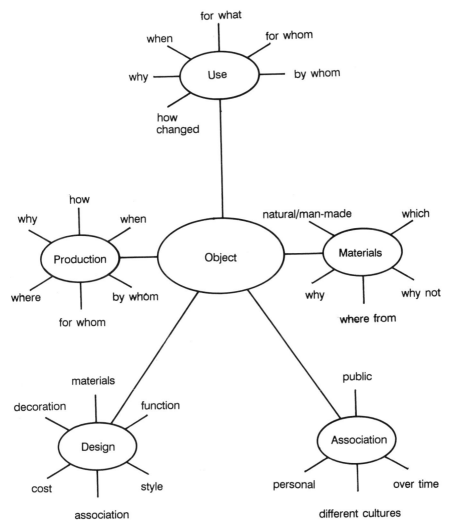

Figure 12.4 Learning with objects: discussion and analysis (Hooper-Greenhill 1988)

sources like handling material (either used in the museum or as part of a Loans service) are integrated with exhibition visits, and backed up by appropriate work and activity sheets, like the *Asterix at the British Museum* Ancient Britons and Gauls Childrens Trail issued by the British Museum Education Service, or the useful activity sheets put out by the Cleveland Archaeology Service on *The Norton Saxons*, with their puzzles and pages on the dig and the cemetery (figures 12.6, 12.7).

These children's resources should be accompanied by a teacher's pack giving further information and ideas for school use, so that the teacher can

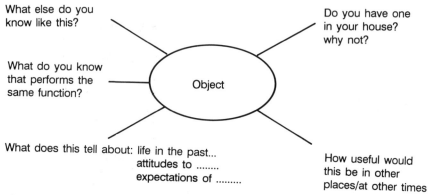

Figure 12.5   Learning with objects: remembering, comparing, synthesizing (Hooper-Greenhill 1988)

integrate the work project into a cross-disciplinary venture which includes stories, art, drama and so on. This may involve direct liaison between archaeologists and teachers in class as Pretty has done (1987) and as the Southampton *Archaeology and Education* team are doing. It means amplifying technical language, so that a 'Drag.28 samian bowl' becomes 'a nice bowl for fruit' (Corbishley 1986). It means imaginative projects which involve genuine archaeological skills like measuring buildings, carrying out a garbage project, constructing sites and excavating them, doing a site survey, learning to draw whole pots from a single sherd and doing a graveyard survey, all of which are within the compass of primary school groups (Pretty 1987: 118), and which can lead on to more senior work at GCSE level. So, as part of a larger project on the archaeology of death, primary children analysed the nature and contents of a hypothetical range of Neolithic and Bronze Age burials and created graphs showing differences over time, place, gender and so on.

Symbolic archaeology can be approached through a study of football colours, and the analysis of dustbin contents can show diet, trading links and status (Hill 1987). The CBA's *Archaeology for Schools* series contains a wealth of work suggestions, on topics ranging from experimenting with ancient food to reconstructing ancient industries, and archaeological computing. Above all, it means a real commitment, so that appropriately qualified education officers become part of the normal personnel of a field unit, a university department and museum (where a good start has been made), and good teaching materials and good archaeologist-teacher training can be generated.

At the secondary level, school archaeology is likely to be directed towards the GCSE, either for the archaeology qualification or for others like history, which may have an archaeological element (Adams 1987). The syllabuses for GCSE are governed by national criteria, and these include the understanding and interpretation of evidence, which must be primary/resource/fieldwork based, rather than textbook based, and which has to be demonstrated by assessed course work as well as by examination. The syllabuses are

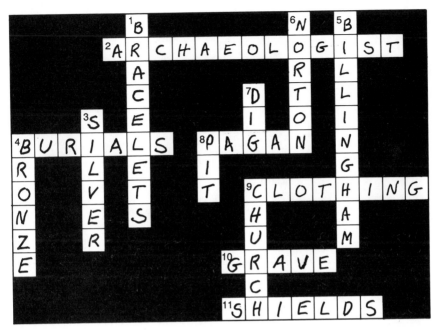

Figure 12.6 The Norton Saxons: Norton Puzzlebox (Cleveland Archaeology)

prepared by five regional examination boards, two of which offer GCSE archaeology (1989), and teachers will choose those most appropriate for their classes. The London and East Anglian Group for GCSE Examinations (LEAG), for example, says that, among other things, its archaeology syllabus aims to introduce students to aspects of man's past through material remains, to provide a sound, general basis of archaeological knowledge through the understanding of primary and secondary evidence and the methods by which it is obtained, and to develop essential skills in extracting information, detecting bias, and constructing a logical argument (LEAG 1987). The qualification involves an examination paper on *The Recognition and Interpretation of Evidence* (Paper I), a paper on the *Archaeology of the British Isles* (Paper II) and an Individual Study, carrying 30 per cent of the marks. Topics suggested for the Study include a Roman town, an Iron Age hill fort, an aspect of 'rescue archaeology' and the experimental construction of a Roman kiln.

A typical object-based question from Paper II shows three Bronze Age axes (figure 12.8) and asks a series of five questions of ascending difficulty, beginning with 'Which metals were used to make bronze?' and ending with 'With the aid of diagrams, explain the different ways in which axes B and C would have been cast'. The mark scheme suggests that a level three (the highest level) answer would give correct diagrams together with a full description of the moulds, and of the casting and finishing techniques, including the use of a clay plug for C (LEAG 1987). Clearly, a substantial

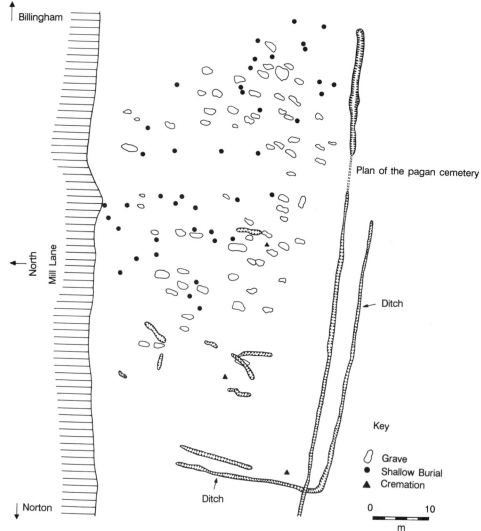

Billingham

North

Mill Lane

Norton

Plan of the pagan cemetery

Ditch

Ditch

Key

⌀ Grave
● Shallow Burial
▲ Cremation

0   10

m

(1) How did the Saxons bury their dead? (2) *What gave* the Norton Cemetery its *boundaries* on the north, south, west and east sides? (3) *Why* do archaeologists think that each grave originally had some kind of marker?

Figure 12.7   The Norton Saxons: The Cemetery, Billingham Bottoms (Cleveland Archaeology)

level of understanding of Bronze Age smithing is required, and obviously this is best learnt by handling bronzes and moulds; but relatively few museums will have the complete range of artefacts and moulds, and, in any case, they are unlikely to be willing to make them freely available, although some examples will probably be on display. Replicas are the best answer, but these

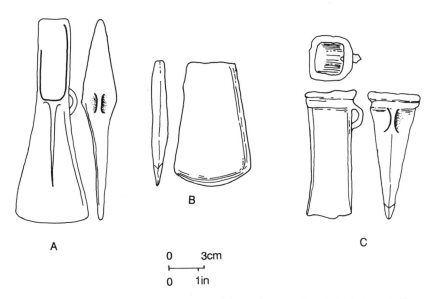

A   B   C

0   3cm

0   1in

Figure 12.8   Drawings used as part of examination question, LEAG Sample Paper,
GCSE, 1987 (after Pearce 1984, figs 2, 8, 19)

are expensive and difficult to obtain. This example points up the problems
which will arise, but these must not be allowed to obscure the very considerable part which museums must play in archaeology GCSE, as in many other
subject areas.

Museum staff are well aware of the opportunities, and several valuable
discussions have appeared in print (Goodhew 1988; Whincop 1987; Ironbridge 1987). As a start curators (and educators) should make contact with
the appropriate LEA adviser/HM Inspector, establish links with local
teachers' centres, and keep in touch with their regional Group for Education
in Museums. Teachers may well approach the museum for resource material, and experience shows that the best results come from joint planning
from the beginning by teachers and museum staff together. Helpful moves on
the part of curators would be the creation of bibliographies giving sources of
information, selective and brief lists of documents, maps and so on which
could be copied, lists of objects available for handling, and a critical look at
existing exhibitions to see what questions they may raise in the visitors'
minds (Whincop 1987).

The potential implications for curatorship are obviously considerable, in
both the primary and secondary spheres. A better understanding of the
nature of archaeology, and of the way in which archaeologists think about
the past, needs to be given to teachers, while archaeologists need to understand more about the aims of contemporary education. A nation-wide forum
to think out the needs and resource implications, perhaps building on the
work of the CBA, may be the answer here. All archaeological institutions,
but perhaps particularly museums, should be involved, and the archaeolog-

ists should recognize that, in the simple sense at least, archaeology has most at stake.

Archaeology, museums and the public

The discussion in the foregoing four chapters suggests several important principles, which are, at present, structuring the relationships between museums, archaeology and the public. Firstly, the ways in which children and most adults view the past, and respond to attempts to interpret it, are not essentially different: the divide lies not in terms of age but in terms of response. Secondly, there exists a very small but very important group of people who visit archaeological displays, attend meetings and so on: these are usually socially middle class, and possess the educational capital which enables them to decipher the academic codes and enjoy what they are offered (Merriman 1989).

Thirdly, there is the large group who have a strong interest in the past, but whose level of appreciation is what an archaeologist would characterize as very poor. Such people do not automatically accept the received wisdom of academic experts at their own valuation but sometimes prefer 'alternative' approaches, they lack the keys to understand traditional museums and similar forms of interpretation, and the archaeology which they receive from the popular media and from formal education tends to be old-fashioned, stereotyped, sexist and racialist.

As Holman and Burtt have said, 'contemporary archaeological thought never reaches the public. By a system of over-simplification, sensationalism, selectivity and dogmatism—presented in museum displays, broadcasting and popular literature—archaeology as presented to the public is reduced to old-fashioned ideas, which, it is presumed, "everyone" can relate to' (1987: 113). As a result, research at Jorvik 'showed misconceptions as fundamental as the belief that the Viking Age came before the Roman Age (because Vikings were "more primitive")' (Addyman 1986). Finally, it is the curators and archaeologists who must bear a substantial share of the responsibility for this situation, and it is they who, in the short term at any rate, have the most to gain or lose. The need is to find ways in which the genuine widespread interest in the past can be transformed into something more worthwhile.

This is clearly an extremely difficult task, and for a whole range of reasons. The curator must be honest, and not betray the fundamental importance which he attaches to the study of the past and the rational principles which this requires, but he must be willing to shed some professional pride, which alienates others. In practice, this means simplifying but not trivializing, offering genuine interpretations without a naive or patronizing tone, trying to appreciate what people want and building on this to broaden and deepen their sympathies, and above all, avoiding the attitude which says that this or that is 'good enough' for those who will be coming to it. All this adds up to nothing less than a genuine shift of sentiment in many traditional curatorial values, and like all such changes it will not come easily.

Recent work has given us a much clearer idea of what people do, and do not, want. The surveys show that interpretative experiences which are visitor-based, that is, which have interactive and self-discovery elements, are preferred, and that people like these to be conveyed through the medium of videos and other audio-visuals, through re-creations either of buildings or of crafts like smithing and cooking, and through a range of activities like trails, quizzes and computer games. All this must be cast in accessible language, and works best if it is tied to a specific, often familiar, place, and if it includes some kind of personal or family link. What people in general do not like are standard 'textbook' approaches, too much raw information, too many broad generalities or concepts, and presentations which are static, and offer no opportunity for visitor involvement. Universally appreciated, however, is the value of seeing 'the actual object', the 'real thing', and if the human interest inherent in the material can be drawn out, it is always exciting. There is much which is positive here, and much which offers food for thought.

A range of enterprises are trying to take these findings into practical effect. Video-making is one obvious field, because as an educational and promotional tool it is second to none, working within generally understood television conventions and conveying a great deal of information very clearly: the techniques of excavation, field-work and the scientific examination of objects respond particularly well to explanation by video. Among others, the Archaeology Department of the University of Sheffield have produced material in this medium and the Glasgow-based firm *Life's Rich Tapestry* uses professional video film makers and archaeologists working to contracts (Grace and Paterson 1987). A similar concern is the Cambridge-based *Archaeologia Musica: Museum and Media Services* who offer cassettes of ancient music played authentically.

Popular magazines are a rather contentious issue, generally agreed to be very desirable in the abstract, but often less successful when produced (Burt 1983; Selkirk 1988a). There are two national popular archaeology publications, *Archaeology Today* (old *Popular Archaeology* renamed) and *British Archaeological Monthly* (apart, of course, from the treasure-hunting magazines which appear to have a considerably wider readership). Linked with these are the popular publications produced locally and intended for the local audience. Crummy's useful survey of such productions by field units (1987) showed that most units do produce these, although the pattern is uneven. The demand for them is considerable, and the quality, judged in terms of colour, graphics and layout, is generally improving. No similar survey has been carried out for archaeology in museums, but the results of such a survey would, probably, be fairly similar. The biggest single problem facing such museum publications is that one booklet often has to do a range of jobs, serving at once as an exhibition guide, a souvenir of the visit, and a general introduction to the archaeology of the area. Sales ventures, both as shops in museums, which are held to 'normalize' the institution, and mail order catalogues like that of *Past Times* ('a unique collection inspired by Britain's heritage—from Celtic jewellery to Victorian toys—over 300 authentic gifts to buy') offer merchandise of varying qualities. All of the materials discussed here can be used inside and outside the museum, as part of display and education programmes. In all of them one message seems clear: they are much more satisfactory if they are produced by several kinds of experts in liaison, if they represent the united skills of curators and communicators.

In-house exhibitions must be geared to the needs of visitors, with greater stress on the production of intelligible knowledge through greater visitor involvement. This might be linked with a much greater access to collections, through, for example, schemes of visible storage, where the displays are the front line in an in-depth exhibition which takes visitors some way, at least, behind the scenes. The practical problems of this kind of approach are considerable, but the potential gains are considerable too, because people are always puzzled by the quantity of apparently very dull material which archaeologists want to keep, and often suspect that exciting things are being 'hidden away'. Visible storage offers the chance to explain something of the detailed work which collections involve, and the information which this can yield, and so help to share the interest and justify the resources which reserve collections demand. Again, it might be possible to link this exhibition approach with a Visitor Enquiries area, where members of the public can themselves compare their object with others of its kind, handling actual material as well as supporting books and information sheets. The preparation of small-scale travelling exhibitions for schools, libraries, and building societies is also helpful.

All these approaches are likely to be more effective if they are pulled together into a well-conceived, co-ordinated programme, targeting areas where public interest can be stimulated, and then developing a carefully-designed package, which at its best, will include the museum building itself, local archaeological sites, local community and school schemes (including multi-cultural ventures), and the local television, radio and press. This kind of programme has been developed in Southampton where the Southampton Archaeology Media Unit was started in 1984, staffed by MSC schemes. The Media Unit has been responsible for the public presentation, explanation, and promotion of the activities of the Museum Archaeology Section, and its staff, with mixed archaeological and media skills, have worked closely with the museum archaeologists and educationalists.

The Unit has prepared information boards and murals for excavation sites, organized display caravans located at major excavations in the city, produced small touring exhibitions and various educational videos, and published popular booklets like *Southampton Castle* (Hodgson 1986). The Unit's total of completed projects is impressive (although its future funding is uncertain). Similar co-ordinated programmes are provided by the Museum of London, and by Leicestershire Museums who made a major communication effort in relation to the Shires excavation in the city centre. Ventures like these surely represent an important area of progress (Plate 13).

The implications of these efforts to involve a wider public are considerable. Such ventures may be called 'the new realism', but they are doomed if they are not taken seriously, and accompanied by a genuine level of time and money. Given the present climate, these needs are unlikely to attract new money and will have to be satisfied from within existing resources and therefore at the expense of other programmes, to a greater or lesser degree. Resource shifts of this kind are often difficult for staff to accept, especially

Plate 13 Information board prepared by Southampton Archaeology Media Unit for the site of the Cook Street excavations, Southampton, April–June 1986. Reproduced by courtesy Southampton City Museums.

when they mean that the staff themselves will be asked to undertake related work of a new kind, and this applies across the board, to curators, designers, administrators and attendants. At the same time, it is unrealistic to expect that staff will command all the new communication skills, and it seems likely that short-term contracts or normal commercial arrangements will be important. What is clear is that museums and their staff must put on a new public face.

13. Futures: AD 2000 and beyond

Several themes have run through this book: the nature of the archaeology museum as a cultural and historical phenomenon, the relationship between the curator and the other kinds of archaeologists, the care and interpretation of the material archive, the principles through which the archive is presented, and the legitimate relationship between the museum archaeologist and his public. The body of theory and practice which has been discussed here in relation to these themes has arisen from our past, the past both of our museums and of our society, of which the museums form a part. Neither are ever static, and in both we are experiencing a phase of radical change which looks likely to run up to the year 2000 and to achieve a substantial reorientation of our working and leisure lives. Past and current events offer some pointers to the shape which this reorientation will take, and how both archaeology and museums will develop.

One important issue revolves around professionalism. It is clear that the more professional an archaeological curator is, that is, the better he is able to support his proposals and practices by a well-marshalled body of information and opinion, backed by reference to a professional organization like the Museums Association or the Society of Museum Archaeologists, the more his views will command respect where it matters when policy issues of all kinds arise. Obviously, the training of archaeological curators is a key issue here, as it is for all museum workers.

Directly linked with this is the undoubted fact that only museums of a certain size are able to support professional curators, together with the training budgets and the complementary expertise in areas like design and information technology, and the broader fields of planning and financial control, which enables professional curatorship to work properly. In Britain today this means in practice that county services and large district services tend to work more effectively, while museums in small districts or boroughs or small private trusts suffer severe problems. Historical reasons have meant that, frequently, archaeological collections have been donated to these larger museums, and, as part of a general rationalization of collections by exchange and gift between museums, the concentration of local or regional material in these larger museums should be encouraged, so that small museums, without professional staff and services, can function sensibly as exhibition centres, rather than as holders of archive.

There are signs that the practice of central government, mediated usually through the Area Museums Councils, is, in a piecemeal fashion, working towards the idea of a network of archaeologically responsible museums, which will be the larger ones just identified. The Frere Report (1975) established the crucial concept of the complete archive which should be 'properly organzied and curated' and held accessibly. The succeeding Dimbleby Report (1978) stated that the archive should be held in a museum, and that appropriate arrangements should be agreed before excavation. This culminated in storage and conservation grant schemes operated by MGC, in which funding for storage is subject to strict conditions which reflect and require professional curation. To this pattern may eventually be added legal requirements relating to the recording, if not the acquisition, of portable antiquities. Resources are inevitably a problem, and the basis of all this appears as administrative arrangement, falling well short of legal requirement, but nevertheless it does begin to come together as a national programme for excavation archive, museum operation and professional archaeological curation.

Improved professionalism, individually and collectively, by no means necessarily supposes that its nature and achievement will be of the traditional kind to which we have been accustomed. The recent British Institute of Management report by Coulson-Thomas (1989) sums up what we all know, that the effectiveness and relevance of standard professional training in all fields is being judged against the new needs to be flexible, to work smoothly with others of different backgrounds, and, simply, to produce high quality work rather than an impressive-sounding qualification. For an archaeological curator this is likely to be best served by a grounding in the practice of research, in the broad sense, and the techniques of collection management, linked with considerable emphasis on personal development, especially in the areas of communication and interpretation skills, and encouraged by experience in team project work.

This brings us to the changing nature of museums themselves, and of the role of archaeological (and other) staff within them. History has meant that virtually all museums are run, in management terms, in the classical style. This means a strong, hierarchical structure in which power is vested in a single Director, and work-place culture is dominated by the identification of individuals and roles, to give us 'curators', 'technicians' or 'attendants', and tasks such as 'art', 'archaeology' and 'design'. What you do is more important than what you are and how well you can perform, and the system is maintained by, precisely, the traditional qualification structure already discussed, expressed in salary scales. Under this kind of regime, museums stand in particular danger of disintegrating into loosely associated groups of individuals, all of whom are doing their own thing, and coherent, large, productive programmes become impossible. We all know museums where this has happened.

Late twentieth-century society expects something different, in a world where no institution escapes the market place yardstick of value for money, and governmental changes, national and local, are unlikely to make to changes here. This will affect museum operation in a number of very significant ways. Successful directors are likely to shift to a behavioural management style in which goals and missions, perceived as relevant by the local community, are defined, and individuals are encouraged to identify with these in terms of their personal development. Work is likely to happen in small, mixed, project groups, which will not be static and in which leaders will come and go, so that opportunities are widely spread. Such directors will strive to maintain contact with as many staff as possible, seeing themselves rather at the hub of the wheel than at the top of the pyramid.

There are signs that this fresh management approach will be linked with some fundamental rethinking of museum structures. Three broad functions are beginning to crystallize, and we may describe these as responsibility for collections, for interpretation, and for field or discipline. People variously called Keeper of Collections, Keeper of Documentation, or Registrar, will be in charge of devising and operating computer documentation systems, and of collection management, including storage and conservation. Keepers of Interpretation will be responsible for the production of exhibition programmes, for the operation of open-air sites, for education and publication programmes, and for the whole theory and practice of clientele targeting, visitor services, and perhaps, also, public relations and publicity. Archaeological (and other) curators will carry out the crucial research into their material, developing all the interpretative insights into the accumulated archive of the past which modern archaeological thinking has revealed, and will integrate this into interpretative ventures of all kinds. They are likely to be operating a whole range of public participation schemes, including rethought enquiry services and programmes of community archaeology. They will provide discipline-based expertise in collection management, and into broad museum objectives like fund-raising. It is clear that this kind of structure marries well with the sort of goal-and-team project style already described.

It is also clear that this will operate within a much sharper climate, in which a diversity of funding sources will be important, and better business management will add a fourth function here. Politicians are, foreseeably, likely to demand that all cultural activities are more self-supporting, and museums will face increasing pressure, which will centre upon the changing relationship between them, central and local government, and the private sector. The concept of 'heritage for profit' involves major changes in traditional attitudes, and may present serious ethical problems about the impact on museum presentations, the nature of the information which museums offer, and the kinds of ways in which people should pay directly for entrance or services. Government is unlikely to accept that museums, or archaeology, are, in any substantial sense, special cases, and museums will have to operate in a climate of plural funding, in which resources are put together in packages which include government grants of various targeted kinds (like the MGC storage grants), sponsorship, serious fund-raising of the kind which the charities understand, co-operative ventures between museums and private firms, and many varieties of museum trading.

Excavation units are now operating in an arena in which market forces for development in both inner cities and the countryside are more important than planning controls, and changes in national government are unlikely to modify much this international trend. Their response has been the British

Archaeologists and Developers Liaison Group Code of Practice, drawn up in 1986 in collaboration with the British Property Federation, with its emphasis on negotiating and management skills, and on co-operation between archaeologists and developers in the provision of time and money for investigation (Hobley 1987a). This co-operation principle is capable of extension into the subsequent museum care of the archive, and into exhibitions of all kinds.

Closely linked with this are the possibilities offered by 'contract archaeology', or 'competitive tendering' through which field units compete for excavation work. The fear here is that this could dislocate the smooth transfer of the archive to the museum, lead to loss of material to local or regionally-based museums, and generally result in poorer standards of recording and archiving. The answer is likely to lie in good housekeeping, flexibility on the part of all concerned, and perhaps an extension of the 1986 Code to direct that adequate safeguards, covering among other things the requirements of the receiving museum, are built into excavation contracts. If this can be well managed, it will have the good result of further clarifying the relationship between excavation units and museums where these are separate. Where excavation is already carried out by museum staff, whether by separate staff or by a curator as part of his job, this may help in the generation of resources.

Competitive tendering has, of course, a much broader application as part of the current process of privatizing public services generally. Carried to its extreme conclusion, this could extend well beyond the opening up of areas like cleaning and maintenance. A museum building and its collections could be seen as a public asset, like a fleet of dust-carts, and their management would go out to tender. The museum would then have to run itself like a private company, and make a bid to continue to operate the service, costing in every facet of its activities, including, for example, the cost of an enquiry or the acquisition and processing of an artefact, and including also administrative charges like the drawing up of salary cheques or official orders. In such circumstances, it would be foolish to suppose that there would be no competition from the public sector, although this competition might be patchy and, of course, the museum services that such firms supplied might bear little relationship to that previously provided. It is obvious that in this kind of climate the cost-effectiveness and customer demand of every element in the museum operation would be under scrutiny, and very cogent cases, linked with new kinds of visitor benefit, would need to be made for the public archaeology service and for the retention of the archive in store.

This takes us to our public, and to questions like, to whom do archaeology and museums really belong, what do people want from them, should this be provided, and if so, how? This brings before us one of the central paradoxes of all serious cultural activity. Those who devote their lives to the humanist tradition of free enquiry, aesthetic analysis, scholarship, and rational science, all of which are expressed in museums and their collections, are unlikely to abandon their principles in favour of demotic alternatives or ideological argument, however difficult all the issues involved may be. Let us not forget that it is precisely the cultivation of this free intellectual play which has enabled us to develop the post-modernist thinking, in archaeology as in other fields, which now provides some of the alternatives. On the other hand, the past is public property, a true inheritance in which (so we believe, directed by the same humanist tradition) everybody has the right to participate. The research carried out by Merriman and Stone shows how powerful people's interest in the past is, a force which has been neglected in many important ways.

Archaeology museums are uniquely placed to grapple with the implications of this, and to develop the enterprise. The ultimate value of archaeological scholarship must not be abandoned as a cardinal principle, in the face of irrational or ill-informed argument; but equally, of course, the definition of what is 'irrational' or 'ill-informed' can only be made by reference to that same body of disciplined study, and argument is therefore self-defeating and unproductive. The way out of the dilemma may be to lift the process away from the combative mode into, firstly, the development of archaeological and curatorial self-awareness, and secondly, the encouragement of a wider consensus. The one means a certain painful shedding of professional pride (as opposed to professional standards) and a willingness to look into our archaeological hearts and be honest about what we find there. The other means the effort to involve as many people as possible in the kinds of past-related activities which we can all regard as fruitful, in the hope of spreading the real appreciation of the past and of the ways in which we can interpret it.

We have solid foundations on which to build. Most people who come to museums are self-motivated. They come because their curiosity and their imagination are genuinely stirred by the prospect of seeing 'the real things', which no amount of film or tape can replace. They do not want to be cheated or misled, and they tend to trust curators with a simplicity which must not be abused or betrayed. The scholarship and connoisseurship which alone enables curators to present their collections in these terms is, therefore, an enormous source of strength. This will not alter, and it provides a necessary perspective to contemporary changes.

Alongside this, it is clear that people want a different kind of museum experience when they come to us. They prefer to be involved in self-discovery, linked to their own families or neighbourhoods, whether this is focused upon an identification service or an archaeology exhibition, an open-air site or a community archaeological programme, which will extend the creation and curation of the archive. People, especially young people, are accustomed to discovery by way of computing and audio-visual equipment, and a substantial investment in information technology is clearly necessary, together with the expertise to create programmes. This can be managed so that it meshes in with the television revolution which will soon be upon us.

The key to all this is access. The archaeological collections themselves, and their data, will need to be opened up, so that they can be seen and used: even flint débitage becomes interesting if you know that it came from the place where your home was built, and that yours is only the last in a long line of human families who have made their living on the spot. Exhibitions might link to and fro with the stored archive, so that the relationship between the two becomes more obvious. Exhibition, in the fullest sense, needs to be much more carefully considered, so that we have a clearer idea of the selection process which determines what is offered, and of the design process which decides how it is received. Visitors will need more staff time for demonstration and discussion, inside and beyond the museum. The new programmes will need mobile units and revised security and opening hours. All this has obvious implications for museum employment, and for the characters and skills of those who hold the jobs.

Within the seamless garment of contemporary life, then, we can identify three powerful forces. There is the enterprise culture which requires the arts and their institutions to justify themselves in the market-place as everybody else must do. For archaeology and museums, this means new management styles, new work practices, new thinking about funding, and more accountability to the public and its wishes. Secondly, there is the nature of people, and of their relationship to the past, which offers a huge potential of interest in antiquity which may work to the enrichment of us all. Finally, there are the professional archaeology curators and their colleagues. These are the crucial link between the first two. Their special understanding and enthusiasm, with all its imperfections, *gives* the past (embodied in its material and intellectual archive, the integrity of which is fundamental) to this and to every succeeding generation. Put at its crudest, this is a marketable skill without which the heritage industry cannot operate, because people instinctively distinguish between genuine expertise and its opposite, to the disparagement of the latter. Put rather higher, there need be no inevitable conflict between new expression and essential curatorial values.

Obviously, all this is not easy to achieve in the day-to-day life of any practising archaeology museum. Change is painful, as many museum workers are discovering. Success in steering through these complicated patterns is likely to be achieved not by formal blue-prints linked to standard procedures, but by detailed person-to-person negotiations which will operate within specific local circumstances. These will take into account particular local assets like sites, collections, buildings and expertise, and link these with local needs in ways which will generate social, financial and political support. Broad objectives must, of course, be formulated, but thinking in the middle ground and at the working edge must be flexible enough to stimulate mixed approaches, matched by an appreciation of opportunities, and a certain determined optimism. Archaeologists spend much time speculating about the nature of social change in those ancient societies which fascinate us so much. In living with change ourselves, we must cherish both our traditional responsibilities and our new endeavours, for, in a very real sense, archaeology museums are the future of the past.

Appendix: Sources

Data surveys

Two data surveys relating to museums in Britain have been drawn on in this book, that entitled *The Museums Database Project* carried out by the Museums Association in 1983–6 (Prince and Higgens-McLoughlin 1987) and that entitled *Survey of Archaeology Departments in British Museums* carried out by the writer in 1986–7.

The Museums Database Project

The Museums Database Project was intended to provide a detailed, analytical survey and an accessible, reliable computer database of information, both generally recognized as urgent priorities by all those concerned with museums. The published report and its associated database place an emphasis on the role and function of contemporary museums, but are not designed to meet distinct objectives drawn from any particular perspectives, whether these might relate to curatorial concerns and collection care, public reaction to museums, or the role of museums in the wider field of leisure and tourism (Prince and Higgens-McLoughlin 1987: 1, 5).

As befits a broadly-based survey, much of the information is not divided into specific discipline areas, and, as is appropriate to a computer database, the intention was to elicit simple 'yes/no' style answers, not expressions of opinion. For the area studied in this book, the material in the database covering those museums listed with archaeological collections and their responses to specific questions was found to be helpful, and the information in figures 1.1–1.8 has been based upon it.

Survey of archaeology departments in British museums

In 1986–7 the writer, who had become acutely aware of the lack of information relating to the history and practice of archaeological curation throughout the country, organized a data survey which was planned to yield this information. The intention of the survey was to elicit both factual detail relating to collection history and management, and qualitative opinions relating to the theory and practice of curation, together with any supporting material which the person making the reply might care to send. Those replying were not asked to give 'single tick' answers, but to write as they chose, in the belief that, although this kind of data cannot be processed statistically in every case, the value of the answers outweighs this difficulty.

Accordingly, the intention was not to question every museum with some archaeological holdings, but to approach those museums with a relatively substantial professional input into archaeology. In practice, this meant that the museums who received the questionnaire were those who employed at least one full-time, paid member of staff, a large part of whose duties concerned the curation of archaeological collections, together with a few museums with large archaeological collections but which, for local and specific reasons, lacked such a person at the time. The criteria were deliberately treated generously rather than strictly, to minimize the risk of omitting a significant institution. In the writer's opinion, these museums comprise the professional heartland where the theory and practice of archaeological curatorship is generated, and which the large additional number of museums listed in the Museums Association Database as holding archaeological material are unlikely to be in a position to develop.

A questionnaire was designed which contained sections on archaeological staffing, history of collections, collections management, exhibitions, relationship to excavation and field work, relationship to local archaeological society and local university/polytechnic/College of Further Education, open-air site management, research and publication, ethics and general comment.

During 1986–7, the questionnaire, entitled *Survey of Archaeology Departments in British Museums* was sent to a final total of 116 museums. In each case where no reply was received after several weeks, a follow-up letter was sent, and in a number of cases the matter was further pursued on the telephone. A final total of 83 replies were received, representing 72 per cent of the whole.

The bar charts shown in the figures in this book (other than figures 1.1–1.8) are derived from the answers to the *Questionnaire*. Where appropriate, the total number of museums represented in the charts adds up to 83. Elsewhere, the total number represented may be less than 83, and in these cases, the difference between the number shown and 83 represents those museums who did not reply to a particular question. Equally, in some cases the number may be more than 83; in figure 2.3, for example, many museums are represented more than once.

Different tones are used in the figures to represent local authority, national, university and private museums. Where the same total of replies was received for two or three museum categories, the relevant section of the bar chart is shown divided between the two or three tones.

In order to fulfil the obligation of confidentiality, it is not possible to publish the names of the museums against their returns, or, in many cases, to attribute comments to named individuals.

Books

In 1986 the World Archaeological Congress met in Southampton. Very soon after the event, most of the papers given at the Congress were issued in three paper-bound volumes containing copies of the typescripts as they were received by the organizers. The volumes were published by Allen and Unwin and appeared as *Archaeological 'Objectivity' in Interpretation*, Vols 1, 2 and 3, 1986.

Subsequently, the Congress papers have been organized into a series of standard production volumes entitled *One World Archaeology*, under the general editorship of Peter Ucko, published by Unwin Hyman. There will be 22 volumes in the series, of which the first appeared in 1988 and the rest are planned for the coming years.

Many of the papers given at the Congress are important to the themes explored in this book, and so it was decided to quote and cite them from the 1986 publication. They appear in the text under their authors' names, and in the Bibliography under the abbreviation *Arch Obj Interp*, followed by the volume number. In the volumes, individual papers have their own pagination, but the volumes do not have page numbers.

A series of useful volumes are produced by the Department of Museum Studies, University of Leicester. These include the *General Bibliography* of Museum Studies literature and the *Bibliography: Archaeology*. Both *Bibliographies* are regularly updated.

Journals

A number of journals publish articles which consider the theory and practice of archaeology, especially in the areas of ethics, politics, documentation, history of the discipline, and public interpretation. The most significant are:

Archaeological Revue from Cambridge	*(Arch Rev Cantab)*
Archaeological Computing Newsletter	*(Arch Comp News)*
Rescue News	*(Res News)*
Current Archaeology	*(Cur Arch)*
Antiquity	*(Antiq)*
Museums Journal ⎫ now linked and published	*(Mus J)*
Museums Bulletin ⎭ as *Museums Journal*	*(Mus Bull)*
The Museum Archaeologist	*(Mus Arch)*

Conferences and meetings

Many important presentations and discussions take place at meetings of all kinds, and although some find their way into print, others remain in the oral tradition.

Significant material arises from meetings of, or arranged by:

Theoretical Archaeology Group (TAG)
Young Archaeologists Conference
Rescue
Institute of Field Archaeologists (IFA)

Society of Museum Archaeologists (SMA)
Museum Professionals Group
Regional Museum Federation Meetings
Council for British Archaeology (CBA)
Museum Documentation Association (MDA)
Area Museum Councils (AMCs)
English Heritage and equivalents in Wales, Scotland and Northern Ireland
Group for Education in Museums (GEM)
United Kingdom Institute for Conservation (UKIC)
International Centre for the Study of the Preservation and Restoration of
    Cultural Property (ICCROM)

Bibliography

Abell-Seddon, B., 1987. *Museum Catalogues: A Foundation for Computer Processing.* Library Association Publishing.

Abercromby, J., 1912. *Bronze Age Pottery of Great Britain and Ireland.* 2 vols. Oxford, Clarendon Press.

Adams, B., 1983. 'Museums', in Corbishley, 1983: 65–77.

Adams, B., 1986. 'Museums as education: the past in action', in *Arch 'Obj' in Interp*, Vol. 3.

Adams, B., 1987. 'Archaeology', *Mus J, 1*: 14–15.

Adams, E.C., 1984. 'Archaeology and the native American: a case at Hopi', in Green, 1984: 236–42.

Addyman, P., 1986. 'Reconstruction as interpretation', in *Arch 'Obj' in Interp*, Vol. 3.

Addyman, P. and Gaynor, A., 1984. 'The Jorvik Viking Centre: an experiment in archaeological site interpretation', *International Journal of Museum Management and Curatorship, 3:* 9–18.

Allason-Jones, L., 1987. 'Metal detecting: a view from the Museums North Archaeology Panel', *North East Museum Service News, 15,* 8: 1.

Ames, M., 1977. 'Visible storage and public documentation', *Curator,* 20: 65–79.

Ancient Monuments and Archaeological Areas Act, 1979. HMSO.

Archaeology Object Card Instructions, 1980. Cambridge, MDA.

Ardener, E., 1972. 'Belief and the problem of women', in Lafontaine, 1972: 135–58. 58.

Ashley-Smith, J., 1982. 'The ethics of conservation', *The Conservator, 6:* 1–5.

Baker, D., 1983. *Living with the Past: the Historic Environment.* Bedford, David Baker.

Barker, G. (ed.), 1981. *Prehistoric Communities in Northern England.* University of Sheffield.

Barker, P. 1987. 'Rescue: antenatal, birth and early years' in Mytum and Waugh, 1987: 7–10.

Barrett, J., 1987. 'contextual Archaeology' *Antiq, 61:* 468–73.

Bell, A. S., 1981. *The Scottish Antiquarian Tradition: Essays to mark the bicentenary of the Society of Antiquaries of Scotland, 1780–1980.* Edinburgh, John Donald.

Benson, D., 1972. 'A sites and monuments record for the Oxford Region', *Oxoniensia, 37,* 226–37.

Binford, L., 1983. *Working at Archaeology.* Academic Press, New York.

Binks, G., Dyke, J. and Dagnall, P., 1988. *Visitors Welcome,* English Heritage, HMSO.

Black, J. (ed.), 1987. *Recent Advances in the Conservation and Analysis of Artifacts.* Institute of Archaeology Publications.

Booth, B., 1986. 'Integrating fieldwork and museum records—a case study', in *Dust to Dust:* 39–41.

Bourdieu, P., 1984. *Distinction.* Routledge, London.

British Museum: Selection and Retention of Environmental and Artefactual Material from Excavations, 1982. Report by a Working Party of the British Museum.

British Museum, 1986. *Archaeology in Britain: New Views of the Past.* British Museum.

Broughton, H., 1986. 'The storage of paper archives', in *Dust to Dust:* 64–6.

Brown, D., 1980. 'Conservation and the study of finds', in Keene, 1980: 10–12.

Burrow, I., 1985. *County Archaeological Records: Progress and Potential*. Association of County Archaeological Officers.

Burt, J., 1983. 'Archaeology and public values, with reference to the magazine *Popular Archaeology*', *Arch Rev Cantab*, 2, 1: 33–40.

Cambridge Research Co-operative, 1983. 'The national survey of public opinion towards archaeology', *Arch Rev Cantab*, 2, 1: 24–6.

Cameron, D.F., 1968. 'The museum as a communications system and implications for museum education', *Curator*, *11*, 1: 33–40.

Carr, E.H., 1961. *What is History? The G.M. Trevelyan Lectures Delivered in the University of Cambridge*. Macmillan.

Carrington, P., 1981. 'The Grosvenor Museum, Chester', in Partington-Omar and White, 1981: 27–8.

Carruthers, A. (ed.), 1987. *Bias in Museums*. Transactions No. 22, Museum Professionals Group.

Carson, R.A.G., 1978–1982. *A Guide to the Principle Coins of the Romans*. British Museum.

Chabot, N., 1988. 'The women of Jorvik', *Arch Rev Cantab*, 7, 1: 67–75.

Champe, J.L., 1961. 'Four statements for archaeology', *American Antiquity*, *27*: 137–8.

Chapman, W.R., 1985. 'Arranging ethnology: A.H.L.F. Pitt Rivers and the typological tradition', in Stocking, 1985: 15–48.

Cheek, A. and Keel, B., 1984. 'Value conflicts in osteo-archaeology', in Green, 1984: 194–207.

Cheetham, L., 1987. *The Innocent Researcher and the Museum*. Museum Ethnographers' Group Occasional Paper No. 3.

Clarke, D., 1984. 'Enquiries', in Thompson, *et al.* 1984: 476–81.

Clarke, D.V., Cowie, T.G. and Foxon, F., 1985. *Symbols of Power at the Time of Stonehenge*. HMSO.

Cleere, H. (ed.), 1984. *Approaches to the Archaeological Heritage*. Cambridge University Press.

Cleere, H., 1986. 'Amateurs and professionals in British archaeology today', in Dobinson and Gilchrist, 1986: 22–4.

Collins, Z., 1981. *Museums, Adults and the Humanities*. Association of American Museums.

Conkey, M. and Spector, J., 1984. 'Archaeology and the study of gender', in Schiffer, 1984: 1–38.

Conservation in Museums and Galleries: A Survey of Facilities in the United Kingdom, 1974. United Kingdom Group of the International Institute for Conservation of Historic and Artistic Works.

Consultation Paper on Portable Antiquities, 1988. DoE/Welsh Office.

Convention on the means of prohibiting and preventing the illicit import, export and transfer of ownership of cultural property, 1970. UNESCO.

Cooper, H., 1986. 'Young children's thinking about the distant past', in *Arch 'Obj' in Interp*, Vol. 3.

Cooper, M.A. and Richards, J.D., 1985. *Current Issues in Archaeological Computing*, British Archaeological Reports International Series: 271. Oxford.

Corbishley, M. (ed.), 1983. *Archaeological Resources Handbook for Teachers*. CBA.

Corbishley, M., 1986. 'Archaeology, monuments and education', in Cracknell and Corbishley: 3–8.

Corfield, M., 1988. 'The reshaping of metal objects'. *Antiq*, *235*, 62: 261–5.

Corti, G., 1988. 'A voluntary contribution', *Cur Arch*, *108*: 12–13.

Coulson-Thomas, C., 1989. *The New Professionals*. Aston Centre/British Institute of Management Report.

Council of Europe, 1981. *Metal Detectors and Archaeology*. Report of the Committee on Culture and Education, Doc. 4741-E, Strasbourg.

Countryside Commission, 1980. *Countryside Conservation Handbook*. Cheltenham.

Countryside Commission, 1983. *Country Parks*. Cheltenham.

Countryside Commission, 1984. *A Better Future for the Uplands*. Cheltenham.

Countryside Commission, 1986. *Heritage Landscapes Management Plans*. Cheltenham.

Cracknell, S. and Corbishley, M. (eds), 1986. *Presenting Archaeology to Young People*. CBA Research Report No. 64.

Cronyn, J., 1980. 'The potential of conservation', in Keene, 1980: 8–9.

Crowther, D., 1983. 'Swords to ploughshares: a nationwide survey of archaeologists and treasure hunting clubs', *Arch Rev Cantab*, 2, 1: 9–20.

Cruickshank, G., 1972. 'Jewry Wall Museum, Leicester: trial by questionnaire', *Mus J*, 72, 2: 65–7.

Crummy, P., 1987. 'Presentation of the results: the popular publication', in Mytum and Waugh, 1987: 59–72.

Crump, T., 1987. 'The role of MSC funding in British Archaeology', in Mytum and Waugh, 1987: 41–6.

Cunliffe, B. (ed.), 1983. *The Publication of Archaeological Excavations (Cunliffe Report)*. DoE and CBA.

Daniel, G., 1950. *One Hundred Years of Archaeology*. Duckworth, London.

Darville, T., 1987. *Ancient Monuments in the Countryside*. English Heritage.

Davies, G.D., 1984. 'Research: archaeological collections', in Thompson *et al.*, 1984: 164–9.

Davies, H., 1984. 'Approaches to ethical problems by archaeological organizations', in Green, 1984: 13–25.

Davies, M., 1986. 'Setting the scene', in *Dust to Dust*: 1–8.

Deetz, J., 1981. 'The link from object to person to concept', in Collins, 1981: 24–34.

Dimbleby Report, 1978. *The Scientific Treatment of Material from Rescue Excavations*. DoE.

Dobinson, C. and Gilchrist, R. (eds), 1986. *Archaeology, Politics and the Public*. York University Archaeological Publications.

Drake, J. and Fahy, A., 1987. *Guide to Archaeology on Community Programme*. IFA Occasional Paper No. 2.

Drury, P.J., 1982. *Structural Reconstruction: Approaches to the interpretation of the excavated remains of buildings*. British Archaeological Reports British Series 110. Oxford.

Duckworth, D., 1984. 'The Smithsonian's new museum support center', *Museum News*, 62: 32–5.

Durbin, G., 1983. *Women's Work and Leisure: A Guide to the Stranger's Hall and Bridewell Museum*. Open University.

Durrans, B., 1986. 'Capitalism as an archaeological problem', in *Arch 'Obj' in Interp*, Vol. 3.

Dust to Dust: Field Archaeology and Museums, 1986. Society of Museum Archaeologists, Conference Proceedings, Vol. 11.

Dyer, J., 1983. *Teaching Archaeology in Schools*. Shire Archaeology, Princes Risborough.

Eligibility Criteria for the Grant Aided Storage of Excavation Archives, 1986. MGC.

Emery, A., 1987. 'The presentation of monuments to the public' in Mytum and Waugh 1987: 53–8.

Emmott, K., 1987. 'A child's eye view of the past', *Arch Rev Cantab*, 6, 2: 129–42.

English Heritage, 1985. *Users of Metal Detectors: Advice about Scheduled Ancient Monuments and Protected Archaeological Areas*. London.

Environmental Standards for the Permanent Storage of Excavated Material from Archaeological Sites, 1984. Archaeological Section, United Kingdom Institute for Conservation.

European Convention on the Protection of the Archaeological Heritage, 1973. Council of Europe.

Evans, J.D., Cunliffe, B. and Renfrew, C. (eds), 1981. *Antiquity and Man: Essays in Honour of Glyn Daniel*. Thames and Hudson, London.

Eyre, K., *Collecting Policies in the London Borough Museums*, 1988. London Museums Service, AMSEE.

Fahnestock, P., 1984. 'History and theoretical development: the importance of a critical historiography of archaeology', *Arch Rev Cantab*, 3, 1: 7–18.

Ferguson, T.J., 1984. 'Archaeological ethics and values in a tribal cultural resource management program at the Peublo of Zuni', in Green 1984: 224–35.

Ford, R.I., 1980. 'A three-part system for storage of archaeological collections', *Curator*, 23: 55–61.

Fowler, P., 1970a. 'The crisis in field archaeology', *Cur Arch*, 23: 343–5.

Fowler, P., 1979b. 'Archaeology and museums, AD 1970–2000, *Mus J*, 70, 3: 120–1.

Fowler, P., 1986. 'Rescue: by which route to what end', in *Dust to Dust*: 9–15.

Francis, Sir F. (ed.), 1971. *Treasures of the British Museum*. Thames and Hudson, London.

Frere, S., 1975. *Principles of Publication in Rescue Archaeology*. DoE.

Fritz, J. and Plog, F., 1970. 'The nature of archaeological explanation', *American Antiquity*, 35, 405–12.

Gathercole, P., 1989. 'The fetishism of artefacts', in Pearce, 1989a: 73–81.

Gibson, M. and Wright, S. (eds), 1988. *Joseph Mayer of Liverpool 1803–1886*. Society of Antiquaries and National Museum and Galleries on Merseyside.

Gimbutas, M., 1982. 'Old Europe in the fifth millenium BC: the European situation on the arrival of the Indo-Europeans', in Polome 1982: 1–60.

Goodhew, E. (ed.), 1988. *Museums and the New Exams*. AMSEE.

Goody, J., 1983. *The Development of the Family and Marriage in Europe*. Cambridge.

Grace, T. and Paterson, L., 1987. 'Fast forwarding into the past: an assessment of the potential applications of video in archaeology', *Theoretical Archaeology Group, Programme and Abstracts*, Bradford.

Graslund, B., 1987. *The Birth of Prehistoric Chronology*. Cambridge.

Green, B. and Gregory, T., 1978. 'An initiative on the use of metal-detectors in Norfolk', *Mus J*, 77, 4: 161–2.

Green, E. (ed.), 1984. *Ethics and Values in Archaeology*. New York, Macmillan Inc.

Green, H.S. and Brewer, R.J., 1987. 'A viewpoint from the National Museum of Wales', *Mus J*, 87, 2: 94–6.

Gregory, T., 1983. 'The impact of metal detecting on archaeology and the public', *Arch Rev Cantab*, 2, 1: 5–8.

Gregory, T., 1986. 'Whose fault is treasure-hunting?' in Dobson and Gilchrist, 1986: 25–25.

Griggs, S.A., 1984. 'Evaluating exhibitions', in Thompson *et al.*, 1984: 412–22.

Guidelines for a Registration Scheme for Museums in the United Kingdom, 1988. MGC.

Hall, Margaret, 1987. *On Display*. Lund, London.

Hartley, E., 1981. 'Stonework', in Partington-Omar and White, 1981: 18–19.

Hartley, E., 1985. *Anglo-Saxon and Viking Life at the Yorkshire Museum*. Yorkshire Museum.

Hassall, T.G., 1979. 'Museums and field archaeology: the view of an independent unit director', *Mus Arch*, 2: 2–9.

Hawkes, T., 1977. *Structuralism and Semiotics*. Methuen, London.

HBMC(E), 1984a. *England's Archaeological Resource: A Rapid Quantification of the Native Archaeological Resource and a Comparison with the Schedule of Ancient Monuments*.

HBMC(E) 1984b. *Introduction: The Historic Buildings and Monuments Commission for England*.

Hebditch, M., 1981. 'Opening address', in Partington-Omar and White,, 1981: 3–5.

Hebditch, M., 1985. *The Museum of London*. Thames and Hudson, London.

Henig, M., 1987. 'The pirates and their treasure from field to Bond Street', in Mytum and Waugh, 1987: 11–16.

Henningar-Shuh, J.H., 1982. 'Teaching yourself to teach with objects', *Journal of Education*, 7, 4: Halifax, Nova Scotia.

Hewison, R., 1986. *The Heritage Industry*. Methuen.

Hill, C., 1987. 'Archaeology and the media', in Mytum and Waugh, 1987: 73–8.

Hill, J.D., 1987. 'Confessions of an archaeologist who dug in school: or, is archaeology in schools a good or desirable thing?', *Arch Rev Cantab*, 6, 2: 143–56.

Hill, J.D. and Mays, S., 1987. *Dead men Don't Tell Tales: A Graveyard Project for Schools*. Archaeology and Education Project 5, University of Southampton.

Hobley, B., 1982. 'Roman military structures at "The Lunt" Roman Fort', in Drury, 1982: 223–73.

Hobley, B., 1987a. 'The archaeologists' and developers' Code of Practice—a great leap forward', in Mytum and Waugh, 1986: 35–40.

Hobley, B., 1987b. 'City archaeology: archaeological investigations in the City of London—before and after Big-Bang', *History and Archaeology Review*, Spring 1987.

Hodder, I., 1982. *Symbols in Action: Ethnoarchaeological Studies of Material Culture*. Cambridge University Press.

Hodder, I., 1986. *Reading the Past*, Cambridge University Press.

Hodder, I. (ed.), 1987. *The Archaeology of Contextual Meanings*, Cambridge University Press.

Hodder, I., 1988. Material culture texts and social change: a theoretical discussion and some archaeological examples', *Procs Prehistoric Society*, 54: 67–76.

Hodges, R. and Smith, K., 1987. 'A secure future for Roystone Grange Archaeological Trail', *Antiq*, 62: 473–4.

Hodgson, J., 1986. *Southampton Castle*. Southampton City Museums Archaeology Series.

Holman, N. and Burtt, F., 1987. 'Archaeology as education: theme editorial', *Arch Rev Cantab*, 6, 2: 110–14.

Hooper-Greenhill, E. (ed.), 1988. *Learning and Teaching with Objects*. Department of Museum Studies, University of Leicester.

Hooper-Greenhill, E., 1989. 'The museum in the disciplinary society', in Pearce 1989a: 61–72.

Horie, V., 1981. 'Conserved metals', in Partington-Omar and White 1981: 21–2.

Horne, D., 1984. *The Great Museum*. Pluto Press.

Hunter, M., 1971. 'The Royal Society and the origins of British archaeology', *Antiquity*, 45: 113–21, 187–92.

Hunter, M., 1983. *Elias Ashmole 1617–1692*. Oxford, Ashmolean Museum.

Impey, O. and MacGregor, A. (eds), 1985. *The Origins of Museums: The Cabinet of Curiosities in Sixteenth and Seventeenth Century Europe*. Oxford University Press.

Ironbridge, 1987. *The GCSE and Museums: A Handbook for Teachers*. Ironbridge Gorge Museum.

Jenkins, I., 1986. 'Greek and Roman Life at the BM', *Mus J*, 82, 2: 67–9.

Jones, A., 1981. 'Organic samples' in Partington-Omar and White 1981: 16–17.

Jones, B., 1984. *Past Imperfect. The Story of Rescue Archaeology*. Heinemann, London.

Jones, S. and Pay, S., 1986. 'The legacy of Eve: towards a discussion of the interpretation of women's past experience with reference to current research practice and the presentation of the past to the public', in *Arch 'Obj' in Interp*, Vol. 2.

Jordan, P., 1981. 'Archaeology and television', in Evans, Cunliffe and Renfrew 1981: 207–17.

Keene, S. (ed.), 1980. *Conservation, Archaeology and Museums*. Occasional Papers Number 1, United Kingdom Institute for Conservation.

Kent, J., 1981. 'Coins', in Partington-Omar and White 1981: 20.

Kidd, D., 1977. 'Charles Roach Smith and his Museum of London antiquities', *British Museum Yearbook*, *2*: 105–35.

Kinnes, I. A., Longworth, I.H., McIntyre, I.M., Needham, S.P. and Oddy, W.A., 1988. 'Bush Barrow gold', *Antiq*, *62*, 234: 24–39.

Knez, E.I. and Wright, A.G., 1970. 'The museum as a communications system: an assessment of Cameron's viewpoint, *Curator*, *13*, 3: 204–12.

Kristiansen, K., 1984. 'Denmark', in Cleere 1984: 21–36.

Kuhn, T.S., 1970. *The Structure of Scientific Revolutions* (2nd edn). Chicago University Press.

LaFontaine, J.S. (ed.), 1972. *The Interpretation of Ritual*. Tavistock Publications, London.

Lambrick, G. (ed.), 1985. *Archaeology and Nature Conservation*. Oxford.

Lavell, C., 1986. 'Putting the key in keyword: some thoughts on data retrieval', in *Dust to Dust*: 85–7.

Lavell, C., 1987. 'Getting it back: some desiderata for information retrieval in archaeological computer archives', in Richards 1987: 75–9.

Lawson, A.J., 1987. 'Symbols of power: an exhibition and catalogue', *Scottish Archaeological Review*, *4*, 2: 127–33.

Lawson, G., 1980. 'Stringed musical instruments', in Keene 1980; 12–14.

Lazarowicz, M., 1987. 'Museums and Politics', in Carruthers 1987: 16–17.

LEAG, 1987. *Archaeology Syllabus ... with Specimen Question Paper and Marking Scheme*. London and East Anglian Group for GCSE Examinations.

Leahy, K., 1988. *The Lost Kingdom: The Search for Anglo-Saxon Lindsey*. Scunthorpe Borough Museum and Art Gallery.

Leigh, D., 1982. 'The selection, conservation and storage of archaeological finds', *Mus J*, *82*, 2: 115–16.

Lewis, E., 1981. 'Winchester city museums', in Partington-Omar and White 1981: 34.

Lewis, G., 1979. 'The restitution and return of cultural property', *Mus Arch*, *2*: 17–20.

Lewis, G., 1988. *Legislation relating to the Acquisition and Disposal of Museum Collections in the United Kingdom*. Museum Studies Notes 2, Department of Museum Studies, University of Leicester.

Lewis, R.H., 1976. *Manual for Museums*. Washington DC, National Park Services.

Liddle, P., 1983. *Guide to Twenty Archaeological Sites in Leicestershire*. Leicestershire Museums Service.

Liddle, P., 1985. *Community Archaeology: A Fieldworker's Handbook of Organization and Techniques*. Leicestershire Museums Service.

Light, R.B. and Roberts, D.A., 1984. *Microcomputers in Museums*. Cambridge, MDA Occasional Paper 7.

Lipe, W., 1984. 'Value and meaning in cultural resources', in Cleere 1984: 1–11.

Lock, G. and Wilcock, J., 1987. *Computer Archaeology*. Shire Books, Princes Risborough.

Longworth, I., 1980. 'The British Museum and British archaeology: an acquisitions policy', *Mus Arch*, *5*: 3–5.

Longworth, I., 1986. 'To preserve the past is to safeguard the future', in *Dust to Dust*: 72–5.

Longworth, I., 1987. 'The British Museum: a case study', *Mus J*, *87*, 2: 92–3.

Loynd, M., 1981. 'Storage buildings' in Partington-Omar and White 1981: 7–9.

Loynd, M., 1987. 'The disposal of museum collections: the law', *Mus J*, *83*, 3: 122–3.

McKinley, J., 1981. 'Textiles', in Partington-Omar and White 1981: 13–15.

Marsden, B., 1984. *Pioneers of Prehistory*. Ormskirk.

Martlew, R., 1984. *Information Systems in Archaeology*. Gloucester, Alan Sutton.

Matthews, P., 1988. 'Coroners' courts and treasure trove', *Mus Bull*, *27*, 11: 211–12.

Mattingley, J., 1984. *Volunteers in Museums and Galleries*. The Volunteer Centre.

Megaw, J.V.S., 1976. *To Illustrate the Monuments*. Thames and Hudson, London.

Merriman, N., 1987. 'Value and motivation in prehistory: the evidence for "Celtic Spirit"', in Hodder 1987: 111–16.

Merriman, N., 1989. 'The social basis of museum and heritage visiting', in Pearce 1989a: 153–71.

Michelmore, D., 1981. 'Archaeological records', in Partington-Omar and White 1981: 25–6.

Miles, R.S., Alt, M.D., Gosling, D.C., Lewis, B.N. and Tout, A.F. (eds), 1988. *The Design of Educational Exhibits*. Unwin Hyman, London.

Miller, G., 1973. *That Noble Cabinet: A History of the British Museum*. Deutsch, London.

Mitchell, S. and Reeds, P.J., 1985. *Coins of England and the United Kingdom* (21st edn). Seaby, London.

Moffett, J., 1989. 'Report on the Museum Computer Network Conference, Santa Monica, California, Oct. 1988', *Archaeological Computing Newsletter*, 17: 16–20.

Moore, H., 1986. *Space, Text and Gender*. Cambridge University Press.

Museums and Galleries Commission, 1986. *Eligibility Criteria for the Grant Aided Storage of Excavation Archives*.

Myerscough, J. *et al.*, 1988. *The Economic Importance of the Arts in Britain*. Policy Studies Institute.

Mytum, H., 1985. 'Excavation, reconstruction and display: some issues in the presentation of archaeology to the public', *CBA Group 4 Forum*, 1984–5: 17–24.

Mytum, H., 1986a. 'Microfiche and archaeological publication: a positive view', *Scottish Archaeological Review*, 4, 1: 46–8.

Mytum, H., 1986b. 'The reconstruction of an Iron Age roundhouse at Castell Henllys, Dyfed', *Bulletin Board of Celtic Studies*, 23: 283–90.

Mytum, H. and Waugh, K., 1987. *Rescue Archaeology—What's Next?* Department of Archaeology, University of York Monograph 6.

National Audit Office; Management of the Collections of the English National Museums and Galleries, 1988. HMSO.

National Heritage Act, 1983. HMSO.

Nicholson, S. and Warhurst, M., 1984. *Joseph Mayer 1803–1886*. Merseyside County Museums Occasional Papers 2.

Norman, B., 1983. 'Archaeology and television', *Arch Rev Cantab*, 2, 1: 27–32.

Norman, M., 1981. 'Storage Study Group, U.K.I.C.', in Partington-Omar and White 1981: 12.

O'Keefe, P.J. and Prott, L.V., 1984. *Law and the Cultural Heritage. Vol. 1: Discovery and Excavation*. Abingdon Professional Books.

Orna, E., 1983. *Build Yourself a Thesaurus*. Norwich.

Orna, E., 1987. *Information Policies for Museums*. Cambridge, MDA.

Ovenell, R.F., 1986. *The Ashmolean Museum 1683–1894*. Oxford, OUP.

Packaging and Storage of Freshly-Excavated Artefacts from Archaeological Sites, 1983. Conservation Guidelines No. 2, Archaeology Section, United Kingdom Institute for Conservation.

Partington-Omar, A. and White, A.J., 1981. *Archaeological Storage*. Society of Museum Archaeologists and Yorkshire and Humberside Federation of Museums and Art Galleries.

Pearce, S.M., 1970–1. 'A Late Bronze Age hoard from Glentanar, Aberdeenshire', *Procs of the Society of Antiquaries of Scotland, 103*: 57–64.

Pearce, S.M., 1974. 'The role of the archaeological curator in the wider pattern of archaeological research: some suggestions', *Mus J*, 73, 4: 149–52.

Pearce, S.M., 1984. *Bronze Age metalwork in Southern Britain*. Shire Books, Princes Risborough.

Pearce, S.M., 1986a. 'Objects, high and low', *Mus J, 86,* 2: 79–82.

Pearce, S.M., 1986b. 'Objects as Signs and Symbols', *Mus J, 86,* 3: 131–5.

Pearce, S.M., 1987a. 'Exhibiting material culture: some thoughts on interpretation and legitimacy', *International Journal of Museum Management and Curatorship, 6:* 181–6.

Pearce, S.M., 1987b. 'Objects in structures', *Mus J, 86,* 4: 178–81.

Pearce, S.M., 1988. 'Information services', *Museum Studies Notes, 4,* Department of Museum Studies, University of Leicester.

Pearce, S.M. (ed.), 1989a. *Museum Studies in Material Culture.* Leicester University Press.

Pearce, S.M., 1989b. 'Objects in structures' in Pearce 1989a: 47–60.

Peponis, J. and Hedin, J., 1982. 'The lay-out of theories in the Natural History Museum', *9H 2,* 3: 21–5.

Petrie, F.W.M., 1904. *Methods and Aims in Archaeology.* New York.

Pierpoint, S.J., 1981. 'Land settlement and society in the Yorkshire Bronze Age', in Barker 1981: 41–55.

Piggott, S., 1976. *Ruins in a Landscape: Essays in Antiquarianism.* Edinburgh University Press.

Pinsky, V. and Wylie, A. (eds) 1986. *Critical Traditions in Contemporary Archaeology.* Cambridge University Press.

Planel, P., 1986. 'New archaeology, new history: when will they meet', in *Arch 'Obj' in Interp,* Vol. 3.

Polome, E.C. (ed.), 1982. *The Indo-Europeans in the Fourth and Third Millennia.* Ann Arbor.

Porges, J., 1987. 'Congress of Independent Archaeologists: some impressions', *Cur Arch, 107:* 372–4.

Portsmouth, O., 1979. 'The real enemies of archaeology', *Popular Archaeology, 1,* 4: 15.

Practical Museum Documentation, 1981. Cambridge MDA.

Prag, A.J.N.W., 1983. 'Archaeology alive at the Manchester Museum', *Mus J, 83,* 1: 79.

Pratap, A. and Rao, N., 1986. 'Theme editorial', *Arch Rev Cantab, 5,* 1: 2–4.

Pretty, K., 1987. 'Archaeological education for everybody', *Arch Rev Cantab, 6,* 2: 115–18.

Price, N. (ed.), 1984. *Conservation of Archaeological Excavations.* Rome, ICCROM.

Price, N., 1986. 'Conservation and information in the display of prehistoric sites', in *Arch 'Obj' in Interp,* Vol. 3.

Prince, D.R. and Higgens-McLoughlin, B., 1987. *Museums UK: The Findings of the Museums Data-Base Project.* Museums Association.

Proposal for Legislation on Marine Wrecks, 1984. Department of Transport.

Protection of Wrecks Act, 1973. HMSO.

Pye, E., 1984. 'Conservation and storage: archaeological material', in Thompson *et al.* 1984: 203–38.

Rahtz, P., 1974. *Rescue Archaeology.* Penguin.

Ramer, B., 1989. *A Conservation Survey of Museum Collections in Scotland.* Scottish Museums Council, HMSO.

Rance, A., 1973. *The Cataloguing of Archaeological Collections in Museums.* Unpublished typescript.

Rance, A., 1976. *Thesaurus for use with Sites and Monuments Records in the Wessex Region* (second report). Unpublished typescript.

Rance, A., 1978, *Archaeology and Provincial Museums.* Lecture presented to the AGM of CBA Group 12 at Southampton University (amended in 1979).

Rayner Report, 1982. *Scrutiny of the Departmental Museums: Science Museum and Victoria and Albert Museum.*

Reiter, R. (ed.), 1975. *Toward an Anthropology of Women*. New York, Monthly Review Press.

Report of the Committee of Enquiry into the Sale of Works of Art by Public Bodies, 1964. HMSO.

Renfrew, C., 1967. 'The requirements of the research worker in archaeology', *Mus J*, 67, 20: 111–34.

Renfrew, C. (ed.), 1972. *The Explanation of Culture Change: Models in Prehistory*. Duckworth, London.

Renfrew, C., 1987. *Archaeology and Language*. Jonathan Cape, London.

Reynolds, P., 1978. *Iron Age Farm: The Butser Experiment*. British Museum Publications Ltd.

Reynolds, P.J., 1982. 'Substructure to superstructure', in Drury 1982: 173–98.

Rhodes, M., 1986. 'Preparation of the Post-Excavation archive in London, with special reference to the finds', in *Dust to Dust*: 25–36.

Richards, J.D., 1987. *Computer Usage in British Archaeology*. IFA Occasional Paper No. 1.

Richards, J.D. and Ryan, N.S., 1985. *Data Processing in Archaeology*. Cambridge.

Richardson, B., 1988. *Archaeological Collections in London*. London Museums Service (AMSEE).

Roberts, D.A., 1985. *Planning the Documentation of Museum Collections*. Cambridge, MDA.

Roberts, D.A., 1986. *The State of Documentation in Non-National Museums in South East England*. Cambridge, MDA Occasional Paper 9.

Roberts, D.A. (ed.), 1988. *Collections Management for Museums*. Cambridge, MDA.

Robertson, I., 1987a. 'Law commission and treasure trove', *Mus Bull*, 27, 8: 142–3.

Robertson, I., 1987b. 'Archaeological collections', *Mus J*, 87, 3: 127–30.

Rodwell, W., 1981. *The Archaeology of the English Church*. Batsford, London.

Royal Ontario Museum, 1976. *Communicating with the museum visitor: guidelines for planning*. Toronto, Canada, Communications Design Team of Royal Ontario Museum.

Ruggles, C.N.L. and Rahtz, S.P.Q. (eds), 1988. *Computer and Quantitative Methods in Archaeology, 1987*. British Archaeological Reports International Series: 393, Oxford.

Rumsby, J.H., 1981. 'The Mortimer Collection, Hull City Museums', *Mus Arch*, 7: 13–19.

Rutland, R.A., 1984–5. 'Frank Cottrill: an appreciation', *Leicestershire Archaeological and Historical Society Transactions*, LIX: 93–7.

Schadla-Hall, T., 1981. 'Hampshire County Museum Service', in Partington-Omar and White 1981; 29–30.

Schadla-Hall, T., 1984. 'Slightly looted: a review of the Jorvik Viking Centre', *Mus J*, 84, 2: 62–4.

Schadla-Hall, T., 1987a. 'Regional and national collections of archaeology', *Mus J*, 82, 2: 89–91.

Schadla-Hall, T., 1987b. 'Museums; how to redeem their role in archaeology', in Mytum and Waugh 1987: 47–52.

Schadla-Hall, T. and Davidson, J., 1982. 'It's very grand but who's it for? Designing archaeology galleries', *Mus J*, 82, 3: 171–5.

Schiffer, M., 1976. *Behavioural Archaeology*. Academic Press, New York.

Schiffer, M. (ed.), 1984. *Advances in Archaeological Method and Theory*, Vol. 7. New York, Academic Press, New York.

Schlereth, T., 1981. 'Seven teaching strategies', *History News*, 33, 4: 1–5.

Schofield, J., 1986. 'Excavation archives in London', in *Dust to Dust*: 20–4.

Schroeder, F., 1976. 'Designing your exhibits. Seven ways to look at an artefact', *History News*, 31, 11: 7–12.

Selkirk, A., 1985. 'Congress of Independent Archaeologists', *Cur Arch, 96*: 3.
Selkirk, A., 1988a. 'Magazines', *Cur Arch*, 107: 356–7.
Selkirk, A., 1988b. 'Portable antiquities', *Cur Arch, 107: 39*.
Serrell, B., 1983. *Making Exhibit Labels*. Nashville, USA, American Association for State and Local History.
Shanks, M. and Tilley, C., 1987a. *Re-Constructing Archaeology*. Cambridge, CUP.
Shanks, M. and Tilley, C., 1987b. *Social Theory and Archaeology*. Oxford, polity Press.
Sheldon, H., 1986. 'Rescue: a near-death—towards a renaissance', in Mytum and Waugh: 123–8.
Shell, C. and Robinson, P., 1988. 'The recent reconstruction of the Bush Barrow lozenge plate', *Antiq, 235*, 62: 248–60.
Shennan, S., 1975. 'The social organization of Branc', *Antiq, 49*: 279–88.
Shennan, S., 1986. 'Towards a critical archaeology?', *Procs Prehistoric Soc, 52*: 327–56.
Shoard, M., 1980. *The Theft of the Countryside*. Bath.
Signposts for Archaeological Publication, 1976. CBA.
Simcock, A.V. (ed.), 1985. *Robert T. Gunther and the Old Ashmolean*. Oxford, Museum of the History of Science.
Slocum, S., 1975. 'Woman the gatherer: male bias in anthropology', in Reiter 1975, 36–50.
Smith, P., 1977. 'Some aspects of commercial restoration and conservation', *The Conservator, 1*: 14–21.
Sorsby, B.D. and Horne, S.D., 1980. 'The readability of museum labels', *Mus J, 80*, 3: 157–9.
Southworth, E. (ed.) 1988. *The Interpretation of Archaeological Sites and Monuments*. SMA.
Spriggs, J., 1981. 'Unconserved ironwork', in Partington-Omar and White 1981: 23–4.
Stansfield, G., 1981. *Effective Interpretative Exhibitions*. Cheltenham, Countryside Commission.
Stansfield, G., 1988. 'Documentation of collections', *Museum Studies Notes 2*. Department of Museum Studies, University of Leicester.
Stewart, J. (ed.), 1980a. *Micro-computers in Archaeology*. Cambridge, MDA Occasional Paper 4.
Stewart, J., 1980b. 'Integrated excavation and museum recording systems: methods, theories and problems', *Mus Arch, 5*: 11–27.
Stewart, S., 1984. *On Longing: Narratives of the Miniature, the Gigantic, the Souvenir, the Collection*. Baltimore, Johns Hopkins University Press.
Stocking, G.W. (ed.), 1985. *Objects and Others: Essays on Museums and Material Culture*. History of Anthropology Vol. 3. University of Wisconsin Press.
Stone, P., 1986a. 'Interpretations and uses of the past in modern Britain and Europe: Why are people interested in the past? Do the experts know or care? A plea for further study', in *Arch 'Obj' in Interp*, Vol. 3.
Stone, P., 1986b. 'Are the public really interested?', in Robinson and Gilchrist 1986: 14–21.
Stone, S., 1978. 'St. Albans Museums Documentation Project', *Mus J, 77*, 3: 117–19.
Stone, S., 1979. 'Excavation recording at St. Albans', *Mus Arch, 2*: 10–15.
Strong, R., 1983. 'The museum as communicator', *Museum, 138*: 75–81.
Stubbs, J., 1984. 'Protection and presentation of excavated structures', in Price 1984: 79–96.
Suddards, R.W., 1988. *Listed Buildings*. Sweet and Maxwell.
Suffield, F., 1986. 'Multi-cultural perceptions of the past by children and their parents in relation to teaching within schools', in *Arch 'Obj' in Interp*, Vol. 3.
Suler, P., 1988. *Museum Expositions as Translation*. University of Brno, Czechoslovakia.

Sutcliffe, R. (ed.), 1978. *Chronicle: Essays from Ten Years of Television Archaeology*. BBC Publications.

Sutton, A., 1987. 'The use of computers in publishing archaeology', in Richards 1987: 69–75.

Sutton Hoo, 1986. 'Proposals for site management and presentation', *Bulletin of the Sutton Hoo Research Committee*, 4: 65–89.

Swann, V., 1984. *The Pottery Kilns of Roman Britain*. RCHM(E).

Swiecimski, J., 1987. 'Museum exhibitions as an object of theoretical investigation', *Museological News*, 10, 211–17.

Tawney, R.H., 1938. *Religion and the Rise of Capitalism*. Pelican Books.

The MDA Museum Documentation System, 1976–87. Cambridge, MDA.

Thesaurus of Archaeological Terms, 1986. RCHM(E).

Thomas, J., 1986. 'J.E. Pritchard and the Archaeology of Bristol', *Transactions of the Bristol and Gloucestershire Archaeological Society*, 104: 7–25.

Thomas, N., 1986. 'Chairman review', in *Dust to Dust*: 89–91.

Thompson, G., 1978. *The Museum Environment*. Butterworths, London.

Thompson, J., Bassett, D., Davies, O., Duggan, A., Lewis, G. and Prince, D. (eds), 1984. *Manual of Curatorship*. Butterworths, London.

Town and Country Planning Act, 1971. HMSO.

Tremain, B., 1986. 'Housing the photographic archive', in *Dust to Dust*: 60–3.

Trigger, B. and Glover, I., 1981. 'Editorial', *World Archaeology*, 13, 2: 133–7.

Trustram, M., 1987. *More than just an Enquiry Service? A discussion of history museum enquiries based on an attachment at the Museum of London, Modern Department*. Department of Museum Studies, University of Leicester. Unpublished.

Ucko, P., 1986. 'Political uses of archaeology' in Dobinson and Gilchrist 1986: 45–9.

Ucko, P., 1987. *Academic Freedom and Apartheid*. Duckworth.

Wainwright, G., 1986. 'The policy of English Heritage in respect of Grants for the Storage of Archaeological Archives', in *Dust to Dust*: 52–3.

Walsh, Sir D., 1969. *Report of the Committee of Enquiry into the arrangements for the Protection of Field Monuments, 1966–68 (Walsh Report)*. HMSO.

Ware, E., 1988. *Museum Collecting Policies and Loan Agreements*. Association of Independent Museums Guideline No. 14 (2nd edn).

Watkins, M., 1986. 'Order or chaos?', in *Dust to Dust*: 54–9.

Watkinson, D. (ed.), 1987. *First Aid for Finds*. Rescue/United Kingdom Institute for Conservation.

Watson, M.L., 1983. 'Assessing the interpretive value of historic structures: an artefact approach', *Journal of Interpretation 8*, 1: 8–12.

West, S., 1985. *West Stow Anglo-Saxon Village*. Bury St. Edmunds.

Whincop, A., 1987. 'GCSE for Curators', *Mus J*, 2: 3.

White, A., 1979. 'Towards a collecting area policy for the East Midlands', *Mus Arch*, 4: 13–14.

White, A., 1981. 'Lincolnshire museums' in Partington-Omar and White 1981: 31–2.

White, A. (ed.), 1985. *Archaeology Display*. Society of Museum Archaeologists.

Williamson, T. and Bellamy, L., 1983. 'Ley-lines: sense and nonsense of the fringe', *Arch Rev Cantab*, 2, 1: 51–8.

Wilson, V. and Planel, P., 1987. *Porchester Castle*. Archaeology and Education Project 3, University of Southampton.

Winter, J.C., 1984. 'The way to somewhere: ethics in American archaeology', in Green 1984: 36–50.

Worsaae, J.J., 1849. *The Primeval Antiquities of Denmark* (trans. Thoms, W.J.).

Wright, C.W., 1973. *Provincial Museums and Galleries (Wright Report)*. Department of Education and Science, HMSO.

Young, C.J., 1980. *Guidelines for the Processing and Publication of Roman Pottery from Excavations*. Directorate of Ancient Monuments and Historic Buildings, Occasional Papers No. 4, Department of the Environment.

Young, R.M.R., 1972. *Museum Enquiries*. Information Sheet No. 11, Museums Association.

Zimmerman, L., 1986. 'Human bones as symbols of power: aboriginal American belief systems towards bones and "grave robbing" archaeologists', in *Arch 'Obj' in Interp*, 3.

Index